WORLD RELIGIONS

AT YOUR FINGERTIPS

Michael McDowell, Ph.D., and Nathan Robert Brown

ALPHA

A member of Penguin Group (USA) Inc.

ALPHA BOOKS

Published by the Penguin Group

Penguin Group (USA) Inc., 375 Hudson Street, New York, New York 10014, USA

Penguin Group (Canada), 90 Eglinton Avenue East, Suite 700, Toronto, Ontario M4P 2Y3, Canada (a division of Pearson Penguin Canada Inc.)

Penguin Books Ltd., 80 Strand, London WC2R 0RL, England

Penguin Ireland, 25 St. Stephen's Green, Dublin 2, Ireland (a division of Penguin Books Ltd.)

Penguin Group (Australia), 250 Camberwell Road, Camberwell, Victoria 3124, Australia (a division of Pearson Australia Group Pty. Ltd.)

Penguin Books India Pvt. Ltd., 11 Community Centre, Panchsheel Park, New Delhi—110 017, India

Penguin Group (NZ), 67 Apollo Drive, Rosedale, North Shore, Auckland 1311, New Zealand (a division of Pearson New Zealand Ltd.)

Penguin Books (South Africa) (Pty.) Ltd., 24 Sturdee Avenue, Rosebank, Johannesburg 2196, South Africa

Penguin Books Ltd., Registered Offices: 80 Strand, London WC2R 0RL, England

International Standard Book Number: 978-1-59257-846-7
Library of Congress Catalog Card Number: 2008935068

11   10   09   8   7   6   5   4   3   2   1

Interpretation of the printing code: The rightmost number of the first series of numbers is the year of the book's printing; the rightmost number of the second series of numbers is the number of the book's printing. For example, a printing code of 09-1 shows that the first printing occurred in 2009.

Printed in the United States of America

Note: This publication contains the opinions and ideas of its authors. It is intended to provide helpful and informative material on the subject matter covered. It is sold with the understanding that the authors and publisher are not engaged in rendering professional services in the book. If the reader requires personal assistance or advice, a competent professional should be consulted.

The authors and publisher specifically disclaim any responsibility for any liability, loss, or risk, personal or otherwise, which is incurred as a consequence, directly or indirectly, of the use and application of any of the contents of this book.

Most Alpha books are available at special quantity discounts for bulk purchases for sales promotions, premiums, fund-raising, or educational use. Special books, or book excerpts, can also be created to fit specific needs.

For details, write: Special Markets, Alpha Books, 375 Hudson Street, New York, NY 10014.

     Publisher: **Marie Butler-Knight**

     Editorial Director: **Mike Sanders**

     Senior Managing Editor: **Billy Fields**

     Executive Editor: **Randy Ladenheim-Gil**

     Development Editor: **Nancy D. Lewis**

     Production Editor: **Megan Douglass**

     Copy Editor: **Krista Hansing Editorial Services, Inc.**

     Cover/Book Designer: **Kurt Owens**

     Indexer: **Celia McCoy**

     Layout: **Brian Massey**

     Proofreader: **John Etchison**

CONTENTS

INTRODUCTION

Every day the world is getting smaller. I do not mean by this that the world is losing mass. I mean that people are becoming intricately connected around the world through ease of mobility, education, immigration, and globalization. People from Afghanistan to Zimbabwe and every place in between are interacting with one another like never before in world history. Because of this, the likelihood that you and I will engage individuals from other religious perspectives is nearly 100 percent! This is why a book like *World Religions At Your Fingertips* has real potential for assistance.

People may leave their countries—sometimes for a short visit, sometimes for a season, and sometimes for a lifetime—but they rarely leave their religion. As everyone knows, Buddhists from China do not immediately convert to Christianity after immigrating to America. Hindus from India do not travel to Israel and convert to Judaism, and so forth. Therefore, this text is designed to give you a basic understanding of the various religions that you might encounter in dialogue with neighbors, co-workers, fellow students, and acquaintances. In this book you will find out why it's not a good idea to invite your new Muslim neighbor over for beer and pork chops (Islam forbids adherents to partake of alcohol or eat pork). Social faux pas aside, there are also significant worldview differences that may produce a great deal of misunderstanding. This book offers insight into those differences and explains why they matter to the religious believer.

Each chapter is organized systematically, presenting a description and explanation of different religions from around the world. Each chapter includes sections on fundamental tenets, sacred texts, rituals and holidays, origins and founder, historical developments within the religion, and present-day facts. The *At Your Fingertips* series includes in each chapter a "Words to Go" feature that, in this book, serves as a quick and easy reference guide to the key terms and doctrines of each religion. This feature helps you access and assimilate vital information for understanding the core commitments of that religion. Since world religions are often interrelated, another important feature is the "See Also" section, which cross-references relevant materials in other chapters. This is particularly helpful in demonstrating the many relationships of various religious perspectives.

It is my hope that this book will be a helpful reference guide that brings increased understanding and allows fruitful and constructive dialogue between people about what is, for many, the most important thing in their lives.

Dr. Michael McDowell

Acknowledgments

Dr. McDowell: I dedicate this book to Jim and Arlene McEachern, for their enormous investment of time, treasure, and love; Lynda (McEachern) McDowell, for *always* believing in me; Bobby and Jeanette McDowell, for a lifetime of love and support; and Dr. Craig Mitchell, for being a mentor and, more important, a friend. I would also like to give special thanks to the University of Texas at Arlington Philosophy and Humanities Department for providing the avenue for me to participate in this project.

Nathan Brown: First and foremost, I wish to extend my most sincere thanks to Randy Ladenheim-Gil, the most wonderful acquisitions editor in the world. Your confidence, encouragement, guidance, and patience throughout this project have been much appreciated. I would also like to thank Nancy Lewis, for her hard work as development editor, and Megan Douglass, for her awesome work as production editor. I dedicate this book to Christina Walker, who has taught me more about life and love than she may ever realize.

Trademarks

All terms mentioned in this book that are known to be or are suspected of being trademarks or service marks have been appropriately capitalized. Alpha Books and Penguin Group (USA) Inc. cannot attest to the accuracy of this information. Use of a term in this book should not be regarded as affecting the validity of any trademark or service mark.

1

THE UNIVERSALITY OF RELIGION

1.1 DEFINING RELIGION

The Universality of Religion

Adherents of Faith

The Universality of Religion

Throughout world history, religion has been an almost universal phenomenon. Its pervasiveness is as undeniable as its influence. It has been a vital force found in all places and at all times. Religion has inspired more passion, creativity, and vision than any other sociological phenomenon. Religion also is responsible for promoting important societal virtues such as justice, love, and hope. In fact, morality is so intricately tied to religion that today some mistakenly equate religion with morality. However, religion may have a dark side as well. As critics are quick to point out, religion has at times spawned violence, prejudice, persecution, and destruction. Human rights have been violated in the name of religion. However, religion over the centuries is responsible for far more good than evil in the world by any objective measurable standard.

Adherents of Faith

Of the roughly six billion people in the world, well over five billion describe themselves as adherents to a particular faith tradition. To put it another way, 84 people out of 100 are committed to a religion or religions. This points to the reality that human beings are inherently religious. Although some thoughtful and wonderful people are not religious, most of the people in the world are committed to a faith tradition that matters a great deal to them.

The universality of religion might be undeniable, but defining the notion of "religion" presents a perennial difficulty for philosophers of religion. Even as I write this, I realize that this may sound a bit contradictory. I just told you that religion is the most pervasive human phenomenon on the face of the earth, and now I'm telling you that the big problem lies in defining it. Let me explain. You might be able to identify a red, somewhat round, sweet thing with a stem as an "apple" fairly easily, but some notions are not as easily and specifically defined. The word *religion* is a mental abstraction that can be defined broadly or narrowly and with much less specificity. For example, I have met Christians who deny that the Christian faith is a religion. This is an example of someone having a very narrow understanding of this abstraction. Thus, whether one thinks Christianity is a religion depends on how that person defines religion (that is, in a broad or narrow sense).

On an entirely different front and for different reasons, a long-standing debate circulates among philosophers of religion about whether Confucianism is a religion or a philosophical system. As should become clearer, debate swirls over precisely what components must be included for a belief system to be identified as a religion. For example, is a belief in God necessary? If it is, then some forms of Buddhism, Jainism, and Confucianism are excluded. Or is a sacred text necessary to be considered a religion? If that is the case, then Wicca, Shinto, and Deism are excluded, and so forth.

Religion Defined

Perhaps another approach would be helpful. From an etymological standpoint, the English word *religion* is derived from the Latin word *religio,* which means "respect for what is sacred, religious scruple, awe." This definition would seem to provide broad parameters for a number of belief systems to be included as religions. William James, in his *The Variety of Religious Experiences* (New York: Barnes & Noble Classics, 2004), defines religion as "the feelings, acts, and experiences of individual men in their solitude, so far as they apprehend themselves to stand in relation to whatever they may consider divine." These definitions lend themselves to the inclusion of a number of human philosophies, rites, and practices from around the world. This includes, perhaps surprisingly for Westerners, religions that consider belief in God as unimportant and religions that do not have sacred texts.

Given this broad definition of religion, we could identify hundreds of perspectives. Naturally, this required some narrowing—unfortunately, we could not include some perspectives in our treatment of world religions. In this text, we have attempted to present all the major religions and some more recent additions to the religious catalogue. We offer our apologies in advance if your religious perspective is not included.

1.2 PERCEPTIONS OF THE DIVINE

Before one can begin studying world religions, it is important to have a basic understanding of the different ways in which human beings view the divine, or God. For many, the divine is viewed as a single entity, as one Supreme Being. For others, the divine is separated into a specific number of separate but interactive entities, and so forth. Some emphasize that divinity is personal; others argue that the divine is unknowable. Throughout this book, you will see the terms used to identify these differing perceptions of the divine.

Throughout time, humans have viewed the divine from a number of different perspectives ...

By relation to the world:

▶ **Theism:** Belief that God is immanent in the world yet transcend(s) the world. In this view, God is not identical with the creation, but independent of it. The divine is, however, personal and actively involved in the created order. This view includes Judaism, Christianity, Islam, and some sects within Hinduism.

▶ **Pantheism:** Belief that God and the physical universe as a whole are one. Basically, that God is everything, and everything is God. This was commonly seen in primal religions, especially those that involved nature or animal worship. In this view, God or the experience of the divine is a kind of all-inclusive entity that either is a mode of that entity or is identical with it. The divine being is unknowable, but all existence is connected to this being. Today the main pantheistic religions being practiced in the world are Taoism, Wicca, and some sects within Hinduism.

▶ **Nontheism:** Belief that whether God exists does not matter; however, this term doesn't necessarily refer to a religion that doesn't believe there is a God. Religions such as these simply address spirituality, while leaving the subject of the divine out of the equation. The main nontheistic religion currently being practiced is Buddhism.

By number of deities:

▶ **Polytheism:** Belief in an often unspecified number of gods, demigods, and/or other deities. In the ancient world, this was the most common form of religion. Today it is mainly found in Hindu Dharma and Wiccan practice.

▶ **Ditheism:** Belief in two equal Gods. Few religions still adhere to this view. However, some religions that view the universe as a dichotomy of good and evil (such as Zoroastrianism) still do.

▶ **Monotheism:** The belief in only one God. Judaism, Christianity, and Islam are all monotheistic religions.

▶ **Atheism:** Belief that there is no God, divine entity, or Supreme Being in the cosmos. Technically, this is not a religion, but simply a statement of nonbelief in a divine entity of any kind. Therefore, it is never used to describe religious practices.

One caveat regarding our classifications of the divine as defined here: Due to the personal nature of religion, we are bound to run into someone who says, "You have my religion wrong." Of course, we acknowledge that any religious perspective and its practices are fluid and pliable. A book that sought to treat the various expressions of, for example, Buddhism, would be a very large book indeed. In this text, we attempt to present generally accepted categories for each religion.

1.3 PRIMAL RELIGIONS

Animism

Magic/Divination

Religious Taboos

Other Common Elements of Primal Religions

Almost all religions that have descended from ancient or prehistoric traditions began as what are called "primal religions." The word *primal* is often misunderstood to be synonymous with words like *primitive* or *savage*, likely because the word is often used to describe our prehistoric ancestors. In truth, the word *primal* is defined as "being first in time" or "the original member of a group."

Primal religions were far simpler, as they sought to answer the first "big questions" that humans of even the most ancient and primitive civilizations contemplated. How did we get here? Where did we come from? How is life created? Has life always existed? Where did the world/existence come from? What existed *before* existence? What happens to us after we die? The only answers that could be provided to questions such as these were found in religious cosmologies, or "primal myths."

Our knowledge of primal religions is limited. The beliefs and practices of preliterate humanity are shrouded in mystery, but archaeologists and anthropologists continue to gain insight into the religious practices of these people through research and study. Two well-documented examples of surviving primal religions are Native American religions and traditional African religions. These are but two representations of primal religions found throughout the world. The sections that follow cover some of the basic components of primal religions.

Animism

The term *animism* is frequently misunderstood to mean "animal worship." However, while animal worship can be a part of animism, this is not what the term means. The term *animism* comes from the Greek word *anima*, which can mean "spirit," "breath," "air," or "life." Animism, in reference to ancient religions, is the belief that every single thing, whether animate or inanimate, is endowed with a soul—animals, insects, plants, rocks, air, water, and so on.

When one considers that prehistoric humans lived in direct contact with the natural world, perhaps it should not be surprising that they came to view themselves as related to that world. Many of the early animist cultures believed themselves to be brothers of the animals, and therefore attributed the idea that each animal had its own divine spirit, just as humans have their own god. Other animist views included the belief that everything in nature had both a soul and intelligence of its own. If a man spoke out loud in the woods, even if he was alone, the trees were believed to be able to listen and understand his words.

Also, during this age of hunting and gathering, prehistoric humans were dependent upon the environment, upon its animals and vegetation, for their survival. This gave them a very strict awareness of their environment and encouraged the animistic belief that all things in nature deserved respect. One surviving example of this is illustrated by a practice of certain Native American tribes in which a prayer or offering of thanks is given up to the spirit of an animal after it has been killed in a hunt. Even though the animal will be eaten, it has died so that the tribe may survive; therefore, the hunter's respect is demanded.

Magic/Divination

Magic in a primal religion refers not to a sleight of hand by a professional magician, but to an attempt by a priest or **shaman** to control nature or do evil to enemies of a tribe or people group.

Shamans trained to read and interpret the signs commonly used divination to predict the future. Ancient practices included, among other things, examining the entrails of sacrificed animals, studying bird flights, and interpreting the pattern of cracks in a tortoise shell.

Religious leaders in these first religions were thought to provide protection and leadership to the tribe.

Religious Taboos

Primal religions almost always have taboos, certain actions that are to be avoided. For example, touching the dead is often considered taboo. There is usually a period of ritual uncleanness for those who handle the dead. Menstruating women also are taboo during their monthly cycle. In some of these ancient cultures, concern about this is so great that women are required to live separately from men during this period. Taboos are still common features of many religious perspectives.

Other Common Elements of Primal Religions

▶ **Myth:** Almost every religion in the world has its own primal myth, often referred to today as "creation stories." To say that these creation stories are "myths" is not to claim that they are false, but instead to acknowledge universal expressions of early man's relationship to both the divine and the world around him.

▶ **Rituals:** A wide variety of rituals are practiced in primal religions. One of the most common is sacrifice. This ritual is associated with placating spirits, including gods, dead ancestors, demons, and other spirits within an animistic worldview.

▶ **Ancestor veneration:** Common to primal religions is a pattern of honoring the dead or practicing ancestor worship. This is more than a simple memorial. Many cultures believed the dead lived on in some form and could bring either good or harm to those alive in this world. In some cultures, offering sacrifices of food, drink, and even blankets to deceased relatives was thought to create positive energy between the world of the living and the world of the dead. There also seems to have been great fear concerning the harm that a deceased relative could bring upon his family.

Ultimately, however, while the study of primal religions offers many insights into the origin of religions, this is beyond the scope of this book. Our approach is to present information on religions that are currently practiced by a large number of adherents.

WORDS TO GO . . . WORDS TO GO . . . WORDS TO GO

A **shaman** is one who is thought to be possessed by the spirits. The shaman serves multiple functions in primal religions, including predicting the future and communicating with the spirits on behalf of the tribe.

1.4 GEOGRAPHY OF MAJOR RELIGIONS 1.4

While primal religions can be found on every continent, the major religions of the world seem to have developed in three primary geographic areas.

A number of religions originated on the Indian subcontinent. These include Hinduism, Jainism, Buddhism, and Sikhism. Buddhism, though no longer prominent on the Indian continent, is very strong in other Asian nations. These religions share a common goal of gaining release from the cycle of life, death, and rebirth, also known as reincarnation.

Taoism and Confucianism originated in China, while the nature-centered religion of Shinto arose in Japan. These religions emphasize worshipping nature, practicing ancestor veneration, and living harmoniously with one another.

The largest combined groups of religious adherents found in the world today are from religions originating in the Middle East. These include Zoroastrianism, Judaism, Christianity, Islam, and Baha'i. While Christianity and Islam are currently the two largest religions in the world, it is important to note their ancient connection to Zoroastrianism and Judaism. These religions share a belief in one Supreme God and a coming day of judgment for all. Their common goal is to enjoy an afterlife with God.

1.5 RELIGION IN TODAY'S WORLD

The Dialogue of Religion and Science
Religion's Personal Role

Religion plays a key role in modern society. Even today, religious views can influence people in their choices of social activities, political affiliations, and even family relationships. From primal civilizations to our modern world, religions has followed humanity every step of the way.

The Dialogue of Religion and Science

Religion continues to play an important role in the advance of human civilization. With the advent of the modern and postmodern age, scientific methodology and technology have ascended to prominence. As a result, religion now carries on a dialogue with these gifts of modernity. The dialogue between faith and reason has resulted in many important advances and discoveries regarding the universe. It has also provided a moral compass as our science and technology have sped ahead of our ethical development.

While some view science as adversarial to religion, the truth is that religion is a partner and aid to science, and science is a partner and aid to religion. This being said, it should also be stated that religion answers many questions that science cannot and will not ever be able to answer. This plays a large role in understanding the religiosity of the world and the longevity of religion in time.

Religion's Personal Role

What motivates people to accept certain religions over others? Why does one person choose to become a Buddhist while another chooses to become a Christian? Even more, why does a person feel the need to practice a religion at all? In today's world, humans practice their particular religions for a number of possible reasons:

▶ **Social:** The need to belong or "fit in" is a part of human nature. Many people view religion as a part of their social network. For example, in certain communities, the church is a means by which to view and (sometimes) judge one's neighbors. In certain situations, other members of a community may view a person as "abnormal" if that person is not seen at church.

▶ **Cultural:** Sometimes one's cultural or ethnic background has a great influence on the choice of religion. For example, a Caucasian born in the United States with a middle- to upper-class background likely practices some form of Christianity. The cultural dynamic of a person can have a big impact on religious choice. For example, many of the cultural traditions of Mexico have close ties to Roman Catholicism. So perhaps it is no surprise that Catholicism is the dominant religion of Mexico. The same can be said of the Japanese religion of Shinto, which was long the official state religion of that country.

▶ **Familial:** Simply put, a person may practice a religion because his or her parents did so. In the United States, it is not uncommon to inquire about a person's religion and hear an answer along the lines of, "Well, I was raised a Southern Baptist, but now I am nondenominational." Such answers are strong evidence that one's familial background is often directly connected to one's choice of religion. In Judaism, this is very prevalent: people born into a Jewish family are considered Jews whether or not they actively practice the religion. When this occurs, such adherents are often referred to as "ethnic Jews."

▶ **Spiritual:** Everyone acknowledges that the practice of religion is spiritual, but that's not what we mean here. In this case, a person with no social, cultural, or familial influence chooses a religion because it fulfills some spiritual need or personal void. Religious adherents in this category are usually converts, although that's not always the case. This is because, at times, when people are "raised" to practice a religion, they later find that they don't truly understand why they do so. Such revelations often lead them to search for a spiritual home.

This list does not seek to prove or invalidate any of the reasons why a person chooses to practice a religion. It only seeks to present some sociological reasons.

2

JUDAISM

2.1 FUNDAMENTAL TENETS

Basic Information on Judaism
The Core Beliefs of Judaism
The Thirteen Articles of Faith

Judaism is a religion that is centered on the notion of one God who is actively working in history to bring about his eternal purposes in a group of His "chosen people" also known as the Hebrews or *Jews*. While defining **Jewishness** is complicated, the focus of the chapter will be on explaining the basics of religious Judaism.

Basic Information on Judaism

▶ Origin Date: Second millennium B.C.E.

▶ Founder/Originator: Moses.

▶ View of God: Monotheistic; the one God of Judaism is often referred to as YHVH through a transliteration of Hebrew consonants. His name is pronounced Yahweh, Yahovah, or Jehovah. In Judaism, however, the proper name of God is rarely used out of reverence to His Holy Name.

▶ Dietary Restrictions: **Kosher;** no carnivores, carrion feeders, or shellfish. Fish must have both fins and scales. In order to be permissible, four-legged beasts must both chew cud and have cloven hoof. No eggs, milk, or other products if they come from prohibited animals. No blood may remain in meat. Some parts of permitted animals are also forbidden. The fat surrounding internal organs is not permissible, but the fat under the skin and around muscles is. Meat and dairy are not to be mixed. Fruits, vegetables, and grains may be eaten with either meat or dairy. Animals must be slaughtered according to **kashrut** procedure. Grape products made by non-Jews may not be eaten.

▶ View of Life/Death: There is very little commentary on death in the Jewish scripture, since it is a religion of life, so there are many opinions on what happens in the afterlife. There is discussion of a place called "*Sheol*" in some Hebrew texts but little is explained about it. It seems to be a place that one shouldn't be all that anxious to go to. It is the "place of the dead" and its inhabitants are waiting for a future judgment. It is for this reason that some Jews believe they will "rest with their fathers" until the end of time and final judgment. Still others reading **Jewish mystical texts** believe in various forms of reincarnation.

▶ Lifestyle Foci: The focus of a practicing Jew is the "*Shema*" found in Deuteronomy 6:4-5. It states "Hear, O Israel: The Lord Our God, the Lord is one. Love the Lord your God with all your heart, with all your soul and with all your strength." In the Hebrew view, the human soul has a capacity to move toward good, that is, loving God and enjoying His creation and blessing, or to move toward evil, that is, loving the things of the world (pleasures, property, and security) and neglecting God. Judaism, like Islam, believes in orthopraxy, correct action as evidence of faith. Correct action is defined by the **Torah** (Law), the *N'vi-im* (Prophets), and the *K'tuvim* (Writings) and the Talmud.

▶ Worship Restrictions: Judaism has a broad range of beliefs regarding who can practice Judaism. Some religious Jews argue that to be Jewish is to be born Jewish and thus are very restrictive. Others teach that to be truly Jewish is to practice the faith of Judaism. It seems that most are of the latter.

The Core Beliefs of Judaism

The core beliefs of Judaism are as follows:

▶ Belief that YHVH exists and is the one and only true God

▶ Belief that YHVH is eternal and incorporeal, transcending both time and material reality

▶ Belief that YHVH, while far beyond human understanding, is worthy of prayer and worship

▶ Belief in the validity and truth of the words of the ancient Prophets (such as Moses)

▶ Belief that Moses was the greatest of all YHVH's Prophets

▶ Belief that YHVH knows the hearts and deeds of humans, and that the good are rewarded and the wicked are punished

▶ Belief in the Messiah, but that he has not yet come

The Thirteen Articles of Faith

During the twelfth century C.E., Moses Maimonides set down the *Thirteen Articles of Faith*. In his lifetime, Maimonides lived in North Africa and Egypt and became a well-versed **rabbi,** talented physician, and Jewish philosopher. His ideas, the majority of which met with extreme opposition during his lifetime, later proved extremely influential, not only on the ideas of Judaism, but also on the development of Christianity, especially Catholicism (St. Thomas Aquinas is said to have been an enthusiastic admirer of Maimonides' work).

◀ *SEE ALSO 4.5, "Historical Development of Catholicism"* ▶

Maimonides' philosophy proclaims that the human intellect is incapable of discovering truths that contradict God's revelations to humankind. Maimonides also stated that God could be described only in "nonstatements," or negative statements. For example, Maimonides claimed that a statement such as "There is only One God" would be incorrect and should instead be worded as "God is not more than one." Though his writings regarding Judaic law were often strongly opposed during his lifetime, after his death he came to be recognized by Jewish rabbinical authorities as a talented Jewish scholar, or **Posek.**

Maimonides compiled and authored the *Thirteen Articles of Faith,* also referred to as the *Thirteen Foundations of Judaism,* which he based solely upon writings found in the canon of Jewish scripture (see 2.2, "Sacred Texts"). The *Thirteen Articles of Faith* outline the truths of existence that an individual must accept, or at least acknowledge, for him/her to be considered a member of the Jewish faith:

1. To believe in the existence of God the Creator.

2. To believe in the Unity of God, that God is One.

3. To deny the misconception of God's physicality, and to accept that God cannot be depicted by images, identified by gender, or described with shapes. God does not partake in the physical activities performed by humans.

4. To believe that God existed before the creation of the physical realm, or cosmos, and will continue to exist after the cosmos ceases to.

5. To acknowledge and practice the belief that God is worthy of praise, worship, glorification, and obedience.

6. To believe in the Prophets and the truth of their prophecies.

7. To believe that Moses was the first and greatest Prophet, the predecessor and father to all later Prophets. Four statements in this article outline why this is so: I. God spoke to Moses directly, not through an angelic intermediary; II. Whereas most Prophets had not the ability to receive their knowledge except through dreams or visions (often unexpected ones), Moses could receive them at any time he wished by only standing in a particular spot near the **Ark of the Covenant;** III. Moses did not suffer from panic during his prophetic communications, as did many other Prophets (such as when the archangel Gabriel came to Daniel); IV. Moses

was the only Prophet who could receive his prophecies at any time he needed them, having the ability to come into the presence of God whenever he willed.

8. To believe that the teachings of the *Torah* (see the next section) come from God and were given by God to Moses.

9. To believe that the teachings of the *Torah* are not lacking, but complete.

10. To believe that God witnesses and/or is aware of the actions of humans, and that no action escapes God's awareness.

11. To believe that a person who lives righteously (mainly through adherence to the Ten Commandments) will be rewarded, while one who refuses to acknowledge the truth of scripture, or is sinful or wicked, will be punished (either in life or after death).

12. To believe in the coming of the Messiah, and that it has not yet occurred, but to refrain from attempting to calculate the date of His arrival (as this is not possible and a waste of energy).

13. To believe in the Resurrection of the Dead (of all 13 articles, this one is almost never directly addressed or explained, even by Maimonides).

WORDS TO GO . . .WORDS TO GO . . .WORDS TO GO

Defining what it means to be **Jewish** is complicated because of several different categories of Jew that can be identified. All Jews are not religious, thus there is a distinction between cultural/ethnic Jews and religious Jews. For example, one can be a cultural/ethnic Jew and be an atheist. This simply means one remains within the Jewish way of life without religion. One can also be a cultural/ethnic Jew and a religious Jew. Finally, one can convert and become a religious Jew regardless of cultural or ethnic background.

Kosher refers to the dietary restrictions of the Jewish religion.

Kashrut refers to the proper method by which animals must be slaughtered before they can be considered kosher.

There are a number of **Jewish mystical texts** accepted by some within the Jewish religious community. The classic texts that acknowledge the possibility of reincarnation for Jews are the *Zohar*.

YHVH is the Hebrew personal name for God that is ineffable. In order to protect this name from "being taken in vain," the Hebrews have only given the consonants without the vowels. It is considered so holy that the Hebrews will always substitute another name for God (*Adonai* or Lord) rather than utter it when reading their sacred text. In traditional Judaism, YHVH is the source of all being and expresses the mercy and condescension of Almighty God.

Rabbi is the Hebrew word for "teacher" and is commonly used to refer to the spiritual leaders/advisors of Judaism.

Posek is a title used to refer to a Jewish scholar who is not necessarily considered a *rabbi*.

The **Ark of the Covenant** was a container in which the ancient Jews kept the writings God gave to Moses, such as the Ten Commandments. The Ark is considered one of the most sacred objects in the history of Judaism, before or since.

The *Torah* is the first text, consisting of five books (sometimes called the *Pentateuch,* or "five texts") of the Jewish canon of sacred law, which is called the *Tanakh.*

2.2 SACRED TEXTS

Tanakh

Talmud

Zohar

The Sacred Texts of Judaism play a definitive part in the lives of adherents. The *Tanakh* is the foundation of Judaism with the *Talmud* as a supplement to interpret, explain, and apply the *Tanakh*. The *Zohar* is a text of the mystical branch of Judaism and has recently become an important sacred text within some sects of Judaism.

Tanakh

The traditional Jewish canon of scripture, called the *Tanakh*, consists of 24 books. The TaNaKh is an acronym for the three divisions of the Hebrew Scriptures. Traditionally, the *Tanakh* is arranged into three main sets of books:

1. *Torah:* The collection of the books of Hebrew law. The Torah consists of the first five books of the *Tanakh,* and is therefore sometimes called the *Pentateuch,* or "five texts." These first five books are *Bre'shith* (Genesis), *Shemoth* (Exodus), *Vayikra* (Leviticus), *Bemidbar* (Numbers), and *Devarim* (Deuteronomy).

2. *Nevi'im:* A collection of the books of the Prophets. It is often divided into two periods, the Early Prophets and the Latter Prophets. The first section, the Early Prophets, consists of *Yo'heshua* (Joshua), *Shoptim* (Judges), *Sh'mael* (Samuel), and *M'lakhim* (Kings). The second section, the Latter Prophets, consists of *Y'shayahu* (Isaiah), *Yir'mi'yahu* (Jeremiah), *Y'khez'qel* (Ezekiel), and The Twelve Prophets (sometimes called the "Minor Prophets").

3. *Kethuvim:* (Also spelled *Kethubim.*) A collection of the books of Hebrew writings. In Greek, it is commonly referred to as the *Hagiographa,* which means "holy writings." This book is traditionally thought of in three distinct sections:

   ▶ *Sefrei Emit:* The Book of Truth, meaning *T'hilim* (Psalms), *Mishlei* (Proverbs), and *Lyob* (Job)

   ▶ *Megilot:* The Five Scrolls, which are the *Shir Hashirim* (Song of Songs), Ruth, *Eik'hah* (Lamentations), *Qohelet* (Ecclesiastes), and Esther

   ▶ Other Writings: Daniel, Ezra, and *Divrey Hayamim* (Chronicles)

The 24 books that are found in the Jewish Tanakh are the same books differently arranged and divided that make up the 39 books found in the Catholic and Protestant Canon (excluding the apocrypha).

Talmud

For an untold number of centuries, the teachings of the *Talmud* were kept alive among the Jews by way of oral tradition called the *Mishnah*. However, a number of failed attempts by the Palestinian Jews to revolt against the Roman Empire between 66 C.E. and 123 C.E. resulted in the destruction of that Jewish commonwealth and caused them to suffer extreme losses. As a result, the number of Palestinian Jews who were well versed in the oral tradition became fewer and fewer.

To secure the Talmudic teachings, a Jewish leader named Rabbi Yehudah HaNasi (meaning "Judah the Prince" or "Judah the Patriarch"), also known by the name Judah ben Simeon, arranged for the Talmud to be written down in 200 C.E. A successful and well-educated man (even the Romans admired him, and his family was on very good terms with Roman Emperor Marcus Aurelius), Rabbi Yehudah edited and personally oversaw the composition of the *Mishnah* section of the *Talmud* text. He is referred to multiple times in the *Talmud* by the name *Rabbenu Ha-Qadosh*, meaning "Our Holy Teacher." As it was such an immense undertaking, the compilation took decades. Also, it is widely believed that the work on the initial *Talmud* begun by the Palestinian Jews was never actually finished.

The Hebrew word *Talmud* roughly translates as "teachings," yet the term can also mean "learning." There are two extant versions of the *Talmud*, commonly referred to as the "Palestinian *Talmud*" and the "Babylonian *Talmud*." These versions are named for the cities in which they were composed, both centers of rabbinical study at the time. The Palestinian version is referred to as the *Mishnah*, meaning "Oral Law."

The Babylonian version of the *Talmud*, written down by the Jewish community of Babylon between the third and fifth centuries C.E., is referred to as *Gemara*. The word *Gemara* comes from the Babylonian dialect of Aramaic and (same as the Hebrew word *Talmud*) translates as "to study or learn." However, the Babylonian version of the *Talmud* was still written in Hebrew, not Aramaic. Often the term *Gemara* is used interchangeably with *Talmud*, as it is now the most commonly used version of the text. The *Mishnah* came first, and the *Gemara* is very similar to it in both structure and content. However, the *Gemara* text includes many parts that are absent from the *Mishnah*. Both the *Gemara* and *Mishnah* are included in the currently used Babylonian *Talmud*, primarily for comparative purposes.

To give a detailed explanation of the differences between the Palestinian and Babylonian versions of the *Talmud* would take a book in itself. In addition, the differences between the two versions of the text are an issue that the rabbinical authorities of Judaism are still studying and debating.

The *Talmud* contains the statements, teachings, and studies of the most talented Jewish Rabbis. Though many of the writings within are commentaries on the *Tanakh*, the *Talmud* is revered not as divine revelations, but as religious study. The writings within are considered very insightful and valuable, but not necessarily sacred.

The *Talmud* consists of two specific types of writings—*Halakha* and *Aggadah*. The *Helakha* writings are commentaries on the laws contained in the five books of the *Torah* (contained within the *Tanakh*). *Aggadah* writings are more flexible in content and subject matter. The *Aggadah* writings of the *Talmud* are nonlegalistic and are often more contemplative and/or philosophical in nature.

Zohar

The Hebrew word *Zohar* translates as "splendor," and the text is often referred to as the Book of Splendor. The *Zohar* is most easily described as a series of mystical commentaries on the writings of the *Tanakh*. Probably the most controversial Jewish text, the *Zohar* is the primary book of the mystical Judaic sect of *Qabalah* (also often spelled Kabbalah), which means "to receive."

The writings of the *Zohar* text are mostly in dialectic form, told through conversations between rabbinical scholars, friends, or members of a family. The *Zohar*, like the *Talmud*, is believed to have first been conveyed via an oral tradition. The teachings of the *Zohar* are believed to have been composed sometime near the turn of the age, roughly 2,000 years ago, from between the first century B.C.E. and the first century C.E. It is quite possible that it was actually composed earlier. This dating is based on the fact that, during this time period a high-ranking Qabalah Rabbi known as Shimon bar Yochai revealed its mystical teachings to one of his most talented students, a younger Qabalah Rabbi by the name of Abba.

Rabbi Abba, a Babylonian Jew, transcribed the *Zohar* from Hebrew into Aramaic. For hundreds of years, the *Zohar* became a matter of hostility in the world of Judaism. The more traditional rabbinical schools viewed it as sorcery, at worst, and blasphemy, at best. So for hundreds of years, the practice of Qabalah was restricted to small, secretive groups. However, in recent years, the practitioners of Qabalah have found it safe enough to step out of the shadows and practice openly. A number of Hollywood celebrities, such as Demi Moore and Madonna, even claim Qabalah as their religion.

One of the main symbols found in the Qabalah texts is known as the Tree of Life, or the Qabalah Tree.

2.3 RITUALS AND HOLIDAYS

The Judaic Calendar

Jewish Holidays

Understanding Hanukkah

Bar Mitzvah

Jews observe their own calendar, from which the holidays they celebrate are dated. A year on the Jewish calendar is 354 days long. Therefore, Jewish holidays fall on a different date each year on the Gregorian calendar. Judaic calendar years are counted from a hypothetical "year two," the estimated date of God's completion of the Creation (as written in Genesis), which was calculated by rabbinical scholars to have occurred on August 22 in the year 3760 B.C.E. on the Gregorian calendar. The year 2009 on the Gregorian calendar corresponds to the year 5769 and part of 5770 on the Judaic calendar.

The Judaic Calendar

The Jewish calendar also has its own set of months, most between 29 and 30 days long, in accordance with the lunar cycle. The calendar commonly has 12 months, except during leap years when it has an additional thirteenth month. The months of the Jewish annual calendar, along with their lengths and most common Gregorian equivalents, are as follows:

1. *Nisan:* 30 days long—March/April

2. *Iyar:* 29 days long—April/May

3. *Sivan:* 30 days long—May/June

4. *Tammuz:* 29 days long—June/July

5. *Av:* 30 days long—July/August

6. *Elul:* 29 days long—August/September

7. *Tishri:* 30 days long—September/October

8. *Chesvan:* (referred to in the Tanakh as the month of *Bul*); usually 29, but can be 30 days long, depending on lunar position—October/November

9. *Kislev:* Usually 30 days long, but can be 29 days long, depending on lunar position—November/December

10. *Tevet:* 29 days long—December/January

11. *Shevat:* 30 days long—January/February

12. *Adar* I: 30 days long (but occurs only during Jewish leap years)—February/March

13. *Adar* II: 29 days long (commonly, this is the twelfth month and is called just *Adar;* it becomes the thirteenth month and is given the numerical distinction of *Adar* II only during leap years); 29 days long—February/March

Jewish Holidays

While some sects of Judaism celebrate more holidays than others, the majority still observe certain ones universally. The most universal sacred days in the Jewish religion, along with their descriptions and Gregorian calendar dates from 2009 to 2011, when applicable, are as follows (please note that all Jewish holidays begin on sunset of the previous day):

▶ *Shabbat:* The most important of all Jewish holidays is the *Shabbat* or Sabbath. It is a reminder to Jews of God's creation of the world and his deliverance of their people through the Exodus. Jews are to guard the day of *Shabbat* and the world can thank Judaism for the idea of a six-day work week. Jews are not to labor during this day but to treat it as holy and rest. The definition of labor is defined in the twenty-first century by the sect of Judaism that an individual belongs to. It is to be a time of spiritual rejuvenation after a hard week of work. *Shabbat* begins at sundown on Friday night and continues until sundown on Saturday night. Most Conservative and Orthodox Jews attend **synagogue** during the day on Saturday.

▶ *Rosh Hashanah:* Often called Jewish New Year, this date marks the first day of the annual Judaic calendar year. Dates for the next three years are September 19, 2009; September 9, 2010; and September 29, 2011.

▶ *Yom Kippur:* The Jewish Day of Atonement, this tenth day in the seventh Jewish month of *Tishri* is meant for prayer and repentance for one's **sins** over the past year, whether committed against God or fellow human beings. Jews commonly believe that any sins not atoned for by the passing of this date will become permanent in the Book of Judgment, in which the sins of every human are recorded. Dates for the next three years are September 28, 2009; September 18, 2010; and October 8, 2011.

▶ *Sukkot:* The word *sukkot* means a "booth" or "temporary dwelling." This is a very joyous seven-day-long festival that commemorates the 40-year period during which God ordered the Jews to live in the desert before they could enter the Promised Land. During this festival, Jews often reside in temporary dwellings, called *sukkahs,* that they must construct from natural materials in remembrance of what their ancestors endured (wood dowels and cotton canvas tarps are frequently used). Dates for the next three years are October 2–9, 2009; September 22–29, 2010; and October 12–29, 2011. On the second and third days of *Sukkot,* two smaller holidays also occur (though they are considered by many modern Jews as encompassed by the *Sukkot* holiday)—*Shemini Atzeret* and *Simchat Torah.*

▶ *Purim:* This holiday is observed on the fourteenth day of *Adar* in the Judaic calendar, and *Adar* II on leap years. During leap years, the fourteenth day of *Adar* I is called *Purim Katan,* or "Little Purim," but the actual holiday is not celebrated. The origins of this holiday come from the story of *Esther* in the *Kethuvim* section of the *Tanakh.* In the tale of *Esther,* an evil advisor to the King of Persia, named Haman, chose the thirteenth day of *Adar* to execute a plan to kill a very large number of Jews in the region by way of a macabre sort of lottery (the word *Purim* actually means "lots"). The Jews fought a terrible battle for their lives, and on the fourteenth day of *Adar,* they celebrated their victory. Dates for the next three years are March 10, 2009; February 28, 2010; and March 20, 2011.

▶ *Pesach/Passover:* Passover is a very special day on the Judaic calendar, falling on the fifteenth day of *Nisan,* and is considered perhaps one of the most sacred. This date commemorates the story of God's judgment of Egypt, written of in the book of *Shemoth* in the *Torah* (Exodus in the Old Testament of the Christian Bible). The story states that after a series of plagues God sent an angel of death upon the firstborn sons of Egypt, but that the angel "passed over" the homes and children of the Jews if they placed the blood of an unblemished sacrificial lamb on the top and sides of the doorframes of their homes. During the Passover meal participants are reminded of God's deliverance out of bondage through this plague. Participants reenact this event as they share a meal that include foods eaten the evening before the plague. These include lamb, unleavened bread, bitter herbs, and so forth. Dates for Passover for the next three years are April 9, 2009; March 30, 2010; and April 19, 2011.

▶ *Lag B'Omer:* This 49-day period occurs between the second day of Passover and *Shavu'ot.* On every evening of this period, Jews recite a blessing prayer in which they count the number of days that have passed. This is called the period of *omer* (meaning "measurement"), at the end of which Jews once collected a measurement of their barley crops and brought them to the temple as offerings.

▶ *Shavu'ot:* This two-day long festival is also called the Festival of Weeks. This holiday commemorates God's revelation to Moses of the *Torah* atop Mount Sinai. Work is not permitted during *Shavu'ot.* Many Orthodox Jews stay up the entire first night and study the *Torah,* ending with a prayer early the next morning. The dates of *Shavu'ot* for the next three years are May 29–30, 2009; May 19–20, 2010; and June 8–9, 2011.

> ▶ *Tisha B'Av:* Meaning "The Ninth Day of *Av*," this date is observed as a universal day of mourning for the many terrible occurrences that have befallen the Jewish people. However, it originally began as a commemoration of the first and second Jewish temples in Jerusalem being destroyed. The dates of *Tisha B'Av* for the next three years are July 30, 2009; July 20, 2010; and August 9, 2011.

Understanding Hanukkah

The eight-day-long festival of Hanukkah (also spelled Chanukah) occurs on the twenty-fifth day of *Kislev* on the Judaic calendar. Christians and other non-Jews often misunderstand Hanukkah, thinking it to be the Jewish equivalent of Christmas. However, this is absolutely not the case, and many Jews take issue with this misperception.

It should be mentioned that Hanukkah isn't mentioned in any of the canonized Jewish scriptures but has its origin from within the Talmud. The origins of this day commemorate the revolt of the Jewish **Maccabean** against the persecution of the Seleucid Emperor Antiochus IV Epiphanes, one of the successors of Alexander the Great, during the latter half of the second century B.C.E.

According to tradition, after defeating the Syrians, regaining control of Jerusalem, and more importantly their temple the Hebrews found that there was only one jar of undefiled "ritual olive oil" remaining to burn the menorah. The jar should have only been enough to burn for one day but instead burned for eight days, which is exactly the amount of time necessary for fresh olives to be pressed, extracted, and made ready as ritual oil. In remembrance of the event, Jews light a candle for each day.

The only religious activity that Jews perform during Hanukkah is the lighting of candles on a *menorah*. A *menorah* consists of nine candle placements, a line of four on both sides with a single candle in the center that is slightly higher and is called a *shammus*, which means "servant." On the first night of Hanukkah, a candle is placed and lit in the far-right space. The center *shammus* candle is also placed and lit on the first night, followed by the recitation of three *berakhot* (blessing) prayers—*l'hadikh neir* (the candle prayer), *sheh-asah nisim* (an offering of thanks to God for the miracles performed for the Jews), and *sheh-hekhianuh* (a prayer of thanks to God for the time of Hanukkah).

The dates for Hanukkah over the next three years are December 11–19, 2009; December 1–9, 2010; and December 20–28, 2011.

Bar Mitzvah

Though not a holiday on the Jewish calendar, the Bar Mitzvah is an important event in the life of the Jewish community. It identifies a young man as having reached the age of an adult male (usually when he reaches his thirteenth birthday). This achievement brings with it privilege and responsibility within the Jewish community and is celebrated with a *"Seudah"* or festive meal to commemorate the event. A later innovation practiced by some sects of Judaism is the Bat Mitzvah, the celebration of young woman reaching the age of adulthood (in Jewish tradition, twelve years old).

2.3

WORDS TO GO . . .WORDS TO GO . . .WORDS TO GO

A **synagogue** is a place of prayer, a place of study and education, and a place that does social and charity work. Jewish believers gather at the synagogue on Sabbath for weekly worship.

A person's **sins** must be atoned for according to the Torah. Sin is a straying away from what God has declared as good and right. It is a term used in archery to indicate that the arrow has missed its target. According to Hebrew Scripture sins could be atoned for in the ancient conception by animal sacrifice. Sacrifice was thought to gain the pardon of God. This was not the only means of atonement, however. It was later determined that "repentance," "prayer," and "good deeds" were sufficient means to gain God's forgiveness. On many of the high holy days within Judaism, these means have been substituted for animal sacrifice.

The **Macabees** were a band of Hebrew warrior rebels who rose up against the Seleucid Emperor Antiochus IV Epiphanes for his persecution of the Jewish people.

2.4 ORIGINS AND FOUNDER

Abraham

Isaac

Jacob

Moses

Jewish history and its origins are tied to many narratives that teach worship, faith, and obedience. The following are only examples of a few of these stories.

Abraham

Abraham (or Avraham) is credited with first spreading the Judaic faith, is the first patriarch of Judaism, and is commonly referred to as the Father of the Hebrew Nation. Abraham is said to have been born with the name Abram, which can mean either "exalted father" or "exalted is my father." He was born the son of a merchant family in the city of Ur, Babylon, in the year 1948 of the Judaic calendar (1800 B.C.E. on the Gregorian calendar). However, God later ordered Abram to change his name to Abraham, which means "father of many" (sometimes the broader, implied translation of "father of many nations" is used).

The book of *Bre'shith* in the *Torah* (Genesis 12 in the Christian Bible) tells the story of how the one true God of the Jews came to Abraham with the offer of a **covenant.** Abraham was told to depart from the city of Ur and travel to Canaan, leaving behind the only life he'd ever known. He left Ur with his wife, Sarai, his father Terah, and his nephew Lot, and all his material possessions. In return, God promised to bless him and make him and his descendents into a great nation. Abraham agreed to this covenant with God, which is expanded in at least three other places in the Genesis narrative (chapters 15, 17, and 22). Central to the story is a promised son that is critical to fulfilling God's promise of becoming a great nation. He and Sarah would later bear a son, despite the fact that both were *extremely* old (in fact, Abraham is written to have been nearly 100 years old). The son of Abraham and Sarah was named Isaac, and he would become the second patriarch of the Hebrew Nation.

Isaac

Abraham's unwavering "faith" in God keeping His covenant (promise) is the quality that is most emphasized about him in Hebrew history. Isaac was involved in Abraham's most difficult trial of faith. YHVH (meaning God) told Abraham to bind his son Isaac to an altar, and to kill him as a sacrifice. This test is called **Akeidah,** meaning "the binding," in Hebrew. God does eventually stop Abraham from carrying out His order. In Judaism, the point of this story is often debated. Some say that it was a test of loyalty, which Abraham passed. However, some schools of thought argue that Abraham failed, that God despises human sacrifice, and that this story should be seen as evidence to this.

According to Judaic tradition, Isaac was well aware that his father had been ordered to offer him up as a sacrifice. Despite this terrifying knowledge, Isaac did not run. Nor did he resist. Isaac's submission to the will of YHVH, even in the face of death, is seen as an early indication of his future as a leader of God's nation. The obedience of both father and son in this event led God to bless both Abraham and Isaac.

Isaac later married *Riv'kah*, commonly transliterated as "Rebecca," and the two bore twin sons—*Ya'kov*, more commonly seen in the transliterated form of Jacob, and Esau.

Jacob

Jewish lore states that the fraternal twin sons of Isaac, Jacob and Esau, quarreled with one another in the womb of their mother, Rebecca. The two brothers were constantly at odds with each other for much of their lives. Esau grew up to be a talented hunter and was therefore a good provider; because of this, he was greatly favored by his elderly and increasingly frail father, to be the next leader of the people. However, Rebecca favored Jacob, who was a man of the spirit and not a hunter like his brother.

Esau cared mainly for material satisfaction and wanted little to do with the spiritual path of his father, Isaac, and grandfather, Abraham. One day, Esau was hungry and saw Jacob cooking a pot of lentil stew. He asked for a bowl, which Jacob offered to give in exchange for Esau's birthright as spiritual leader of the Hebrew Nation. Esau hastily agreed, selling his birthright to Jacob for a bowl of stew.

As Isaac continued to age, his eyesight began to fail him. Rebecca took advantage of this and arranged for Jacob to enter his father's tent with food, something that Esau had traditionally done. She had Jacob do this so that he might receive his father's blessing, one which he had meant to bestow upon Esau. When Esau learned of this, he was furious, having already given up birthright. Jacob fled his brother's wrath and went to live with his uncle.

While living with his uncle, Jacob fell deeply in love with a woman named Rachel. Unfortunately, he was tricked into agreeing to marry Rachel's older sister, Leah. However, he was eventually given God's permission to marry Rachel as a second wife. Later, he also married two other women, named Bilhah and Zilphah, who were both his wives' servants at the time. Jacob sired 12 sons and a daughter between his four wives.

After a long period of time, Jacob returned home, with the intention of making peace with Esau. He began by sending many gifts to his brother before traveling to see him. The night before he was to meet with Esau, Jacob had his wives, children, and property taken across the river ahead of him so that he might be alone to speak with God. That night, a muscular figure approached Jacob and engaged him in a fierce wrestling match. The pair wrestled all night long. As the sun broke the horizon the next morning, Jacob demanded a blessing from the wrestler, who then revealed himself as an angel of God. He bestowed a blessing upon Jacob and gave him a new name *Yisrael* (Israel), meaning "he who wrestled God" or "Champion of God." This name is the reason the Jews came to refer to themselves as the "Children of Israel." After this experience, Jacob went to meet his brother. Esau welcomed him into his home, and the rift between them was mended.

Moses

Moses is the single most important character in the history of Judaism. Moses was born during the period of time when Israel was in captivity to the Egyptians. It is Moses who interacts with God at the burning bush (that was not consumed). God reveals His name "YHVH" to Moses. Moses receives his mission from YHVH to lead the people out of Egyptian captivity at the burning bush. With God's direction he warns the Egyptian Pharaoh to release the Hebrews. The 10 plagues sent by God upon the Egyptians are each halted by Moses with a call for the release of the Hebrews. It is Moses who leads the Israelites out of Egypt and through the Red Sea on dry land. It is Moses that begins the journey with the Israelites to the "promise land." According to the book of *Genesis*, this is a land that was promised to Abraham and his descendents in a covenant made with God 400 years earlier. It is Moses who receives from God and writes the most sacred holy text of Judaism: the Torah. Moses speaks to God directly and at any time of his choosing. It is Moses who establishes a covenant with God on behalf of the people of Israel. This covenant made provisions for God's protection and blessing as long as the people remained faithful to Him. Through this covenant Moses provides the Torah ("The Law") for national Israel. Within "The Law" is found one of the most famous moral codes in history, sometimes called "The Ten Commandments." Moses, however, does not enter the promised land. According to the Torah, he sinned against God and was denied entrance. In spite of this, however, Moses is considered the greatest Prophet in Israel's history.

WORDS TO GO . . .WORDS TO GO . . .WORDS TO GO

A **covenant** *(berit)* is a relationship between human partners or between God and humans. A covenant is a legally binding agreement between two parties with duties and responsibilities to be fulfilled by both. In Hebrew history, God commits himself in covenant relationship to Abraham and his descendents through the Abrahamic covenant. He also later commits himself to the people of Israel in the Mosaic covenant.

The Hebrew term **Akeidah,** which means "the binding," is used in reference to the trial of Abraham, in which he was ordered to bind his son Isaac to an altar so that he might be sacrificed. However, God stopped Abraham at the last moment.

2.5 HISTORICAL DEVELOPMENT

Modern Orthodox Judaism

Haredim and Hasidim

Reform Judaism

Conservative Judaism

The whole of Jewish history covers more than 4,000 years. In no way could it ever be summed up in a single section, chapter, or book. Therefore, this section covers the different sects of Judaism that have evolved over the centuries. Jews are often seen in two main views—practicing Jews, who actively practice a form of the Judaic faith, and "ethnic" Jews, who are less strict in their observance of the faith but still embrace their Jewish ethnicity, history, and culture. Please keep in mind that the sects in this chapter are those of practicing Jews.

Modern Orthodox Judaism

Modern Orthodox Judaism (sometimes simply called Orthodox Judaism) strictly adheres to the traditions and ancient beliefs of the Jewish religion. This sect upholds both the written and oral tradition of Judaic laws, believing these writings to be divinely inspired and therefore the direct word of God. Orthodox Jews follow established ritual practices, daily prayer rites, and fasting, including the observance of the Sabbath and kosher dietary restrictions. Simply put, Orthodox Judaism is the most traditional sect of the Jewish faith.

More than any other sect of Judaism, Orthodox Jews follow the guidelines of Maimonides' *Thirteen Articles of Faith*. Orthodox Judaism arose sharply in the nineteenth century in response to many new, nontraditional schools of Jewish thought. Orthodox Jews are critical of the modern world and ways of life, and therefore often take steps to live away from modern society.

Haredim and Hasidim

Haredim and Hasidim Jews fall into a category of Judaism commonly referred to as "Ultra-Orthodox." However, it is important to note that Haredim and Hasidim Jews commonly take offense at the term *Ultra-Orthodox*. They refer to themselves as simply "Jews," as they view all liberal forms of Judaic practice as "non-Jewish." Hasidim, which comes from the word *Hasid*, or "joy," Judaism is sometimes seen as separate from Haredim. However, it is simply a secondary movement within the Haredim.

There exist a number of Ultra-Orthodox Jewish communes, similar to those created by the Amish, in which self-sufficient communities of Haredim Jews are able to live without allowing themselves to be influenced by a world that they have come to view as morally bankrupt and corrupt. Television, films, secular publications, and the Internet are not allowed in Haredim or Hasidim communes. In the sovereign Jewish state of Israel, Haredim Jews are granted exemption from military service (normally required of Israeli citizens).

Haredim Jews are easily identifiable by their mode of dress. The dress of the Haredim is meant to maintain a sense of traditional and encourage nonmaterialism. Today's Haredim Jews dress in the same manner that their ancestors did in Europe during the eighteenth and nineteenth centuries. Haredim males wear dark suits and white shirts. They keep their heads covered at all times, usually with wide-brimmed black hats. Most Haredim males also grow long beards and *peyot,* which are curled side-locks that descend in front of the ears. Haredim women wear long skirts, along with long-sleeved tops with high necklines. Married Haredim women are required to cover their heads at all times, usually with scarves. However, they sometimes also use hats. On rare occasion, some use wigs.

Reform Judaism

Reform Judaism arose in the middle of the nineteenth century and strongly contrasts with Orthodox and Ultra-Orthodox Judaism. As the name suggests, Reform Judaism sought to update the religion by discarding practices that they deemed as outdated, superstitious, or barbaric. The movement made a number of very controversial reforms, some of which were later rescinded.

Some of the practices and updates that reformed Jews have integrated into their communities are the following: men and women are allowed to sit together in synagogue with uncovered heads; the vernacular is used throughout most of the worship service with Hebrew only occasionally interspersed; restrictions have been relaxed on the Sabbath and keeping Kosher. Reformed Jews have also ordained women as Rabbis and allowed interfaith marriages.

Conservative Judaism

Conservative Judaism is often seen as having a stance that is between the strict theology of the Orthodox/Ultra-Orthodox and the extreme liberal views of Reform Judaism. Conservative Judaism recognizes the authority of the Hebrew Scriptures, while allowing that certain ideas and/or practices may need to be changed with the times.

Conservative Judaism is governed by the Committee on Jewish Laws and Standards (CJLS). For the most part, this organization acts as a guide for individual community-based rabbis. However, on very rare occasion, the committee votes on what is referred to as a "standard change." A minimum 80 percent vote of the CJLS membership (which means all members, including those not present) is required for any standard change to pass. In addition, the Rabbinical Assembly, which represents the rabbinical community of Conservative Judaism, must also concur with at least a majority vote.

2.6 PRESENT-DAY FACTS

In today's world, the two countries with the largest Jewish populations are the United States and Israel. The United States currently has the world's largest Jewish population, with more than 5.4 million adherents. In Israel, the sovereign Jewish state, there are more than 5.3 million adherents.

Worldwide, most estimates put the global number of Jews at between 12 million and 18 million. There are no exact global estimates on the number of Jewish adherents by the schools of Judaism they practice. However, most global estimates of Jewish adherents, separated by the main practices/types, are within the ballpark of the following numbers:

▶ Orthodox Judaism: Between 2 million and 3 million adherents

▶ Reform Judaism: Between 3 million and 4.5 million adherents

▶ Conservative Judaism: Between 1.5 million and 4.5 million adherents

▶ **Ethnic Jews:** Between 5 million and 6 million

WORDS TO GO . . .WORDS TO GO . . .WORDS TO GO

Ethnic Jew is a term used to identify a person of Jewish parentage or background who is not practicing religious Judaism but who is Jewish by birth.

3

CHRISTIANITY

3.1 FUNDAMENTAL TENETS

Basic Information on Christianity
The Core Beliefs of Christianity

As the largest religion in the world with over 2 billion adherents, Christianity is both a unified and diverse religious perspective. On the one hand, it is unified about its story or narrative. It is on the basic elements of the story that most Christians around the world agree. On the other hand, there is a great deal of diversity on what those elements mean and how the faith should be practiced. Fairness to all expressions of Christianity will not be possible in this book. We have attempted in this chapter to provide the story during the formative years of the Christian faith. In Chapters 4 and 5 we will discuss the beliefs, history, and makeup of the two largest sects in the Christian faith, Catholicism and Protestantism. In order to gain a more accurate understanding of Christianity, this chapter should be read in conjunction with both of the next two chapters.

Basic Information on Christianity

▶ Origin Date: Marked by the turn of the Common Era, C.E., originally referred to as A.D., an abbreviation of the Latin *Anno Domini*, meaning "Year of our God/Lord." This was a shortening of *Anno Domini Nostri Jesu Christi*, meaning "Year of our God/Lord Jesus Christ."

▶ Founder/Originator: Jesus of Nazareth, or Jesus **Christ.**

▶ View of God: Monotheistic.

▶ Dietary restrictions: None.

▶ View of Life/Death: Belief in judgment in the afterlife in which one goes either to Heaven or Hell.

▶ Lifestyle Foci: **Repentance** and obedience to Christ's commands; for example, a Christian is commanded to love all people as brothers/sisters, and to forgive others as Christ forgave humanity's sins.

▶ Worship Restrictions: None; anyone may practice Christianity.

The Core Beliefs of Christianity

During the first century of Christianity, most of their core beliefs were nearly identical to those of the Jews. The main difference was that the Christians believed that Jesus was the Messiah/Christ, whereas traditional Jews did not.

The Core Beliefs of Christianity are as follows:

- ▶ Belief that Jesus Christ is the Messiah and the Son of God
- ▶ Belief that Jesus Christ was born of a virgin
- ▶ Belief that Jesus Christ provided redemption for mankind through his death on the cross
- ▶ Belief that Jesus Christ resurrected from the dead three days after his death
- ▶ Belief that salvation comes through Jesus Christ alone
- ▶ Belief that Jesus Christ is returning again

WORDS TO GO . . . WORDS TO GO . . . WORDS TO GO

Christ is not indicative of a last name. It is derived from the Greek term *christos* meaning the "anointed one." There have been, in fact, many who have claimed to be the Christ or Hebrew equivalent meaning "messiah" throughout the ages.

The New Testament term **repentance** simply means a change of mind about living in disobedience to God (sin) and a turning to obedience and living according to God's will.

3.2 SACRED TEXTS

The early church universally recognized the Hebrew Bible as sacred. Christian writings contained many quotations and confirmations from the Law and the Prophets. These were thought to predict and verify the authenticity of Jesus and his ministry as messiah.

Probably the earliest Christian writings were the letters of Paul. These letters were written to congregations established by the church's first missionary, the apostle Paul. It is likely Paul who first attempts to explain and present the meaning of the life, death, and resurrection of Jesus.

The teachings of Christ, in early Christianity, survived by way of an oral tradition since Jesus wrote no texts himself. These were likely written down in the mid to late first century. These uniquely Christian works were called Gospels, which is Old English for "good news." These books would become the initial sections of the New Testament **canon** of Scripture. Two gospels, Matthew and John, according to tradition, were written firsthand by apostles of Jesus. Two gospels, Mark and Luke, were written by associates of apostles (Peter and Paul).

WORDS TO GO . . .WORDS TO GO . . .WORDS TO GO

Canon literally means "measuring rod" and "standard." It is a group of sacred writings that a religious group accepts as authoritative in the life of that community.

3.3 RITUALS AND HOLIDAYS

Early Christianity had the same sets of holidays and rituals as Judaism. Baptism and communion were important rituals for the group.

Baptism was an identifying mark indicative of full membership in the community. It identified one as having repented and begun a new way of life. This new way of life was encouraged through gathering together weekly with other Christians for worship and celebration of God's salvation.

Christians also practiced a rite that is unique to their perspective. This ritual consists of the communal sharing of wine from the same cup and bread broken from the same loaf.

Shortly before Jesus' crucifixion, he assembled his disciples for a modest meal referred to as the Last Supper. At this gathering he shared bread and wine with them, explaining that the elements of the meal—the bread of his flesh and the wine of his blood—represented the sacrifice that he was about to make for them. He then told his disciples "Do this in remembrance of me."

Over the centuries, the significance and/or meaning of the baptism and the communion ritual have been debated among Christians. These disagreements have resulted in numerous sects and denominations.

3.4 ORIGINS AND FOUNDER

The Birth and Early Life of Jesus

John the Baptist

The Three Temptations

Jesus' Mission

The Crucifixion

The originating figure of Christianity was Jesus, or *Yeshua* in Aramaic. *Jesus* is the Greek pronunciation of the name. Christ, as he is often referred to in the West, means "holy/anointed one" and is actually the Greek equivalent of the name *Yeshua Messiah*. Jesus was born a Galilean Jew.

The Birth and Early Life of Jesus

There are two primary accounts of the Christ's birth narrative found in the gospels. According to the Gospel of Matthew, an angel came to Jesus' mother, Mary, and told her that she would conceive a child by the power of God and that this child would be the Messiah. At the time, Mary was betrothed to a carpenter named Joseph. When Joseph learned that Mary was pregnant, he at first wished to abandon her. However, Scripture states that an angel then appeared to Joseph and explained that his fiancée was carrying the Messiah. This caused Joseph to reconsider, and the two were soon married.

According to the Gospel of Luke, around the time when Mary was about to give birth, Joseph received an order to report to the house of his clan, the House of David, for a census of the Jews that was being conducted by the Roman governor Quirinius. Unable to refuse, Joseph brought Mary along with him. Mary went into labor while they were in Bethlehem. There were a large number of travelers due to the census, and all of the inns were full. As a result, they were forced to take shelter in a nearby stable, where Mary gave birth.

Exact dates have never been determined for Jesus' birth; however, the story of his miraculous birth is well known. Some have asserted that the two accounts present contradictory accounts. Christians have asserted that the birth narratives only contain two different accounts and that they can be harmonized.

Jesus lived as the son of Mary and Joseph during the early years of his life. However, it is interesting to note that, after the story of his birth, the Gospel of Matthew goes immediately to Jesus as an adult, when he is in his early 30s. There are almost no stories about Jesus' childhood, aside from one in the Gospel of Luke that tells of how Mary and Joseph once lost track of Jesus when the family had come to Jerusalem for the celebration of Passover. Believing he had gone ahead with relatives, they left the city. That evening, however, they realized that he was not with the caravan. They immediately turned back to the city.

For three days, Mary and Joseph frantically searched the crowded streets of Jerusalem for their son. On the third day, Mary found Jesus in the temple speaking and debating with a group of very impressed doctors, scholars, rabbis, and other learned men on a number of matters that surpassed his young age. According to Scripture, after being chastised by his worried-sick mother, Jesus replied, "How is it that you needed to look for me? Wouldn't you know that I should be attending to my father's business?" Though they knew their son was to be the Messiah, Mary and Joseph did not understand what Jesus meant by these words.

John the Baptist

Before Jesus began teaching, the arrival of the Messiah was being loudly announced by a prophet named John. John had begun symbolically purifying people by baptizing them in the Jordan River. This is why he came to be called John "the Baptist." According to Matthew, John was an interesting figure, to say the least. He wore rough clothing made from camel hair, held together by a simple leather belt at his waist. He lived solely off the land, eating locusts and wild honey for nourishment.

When Jesus heard of this, he traveled to the Jordan to be baptized. According to Scripture, this occurred just before Jesus set out to fulfill his destiny as the Messiah. When he arrived at the Jordan River, John the Baptist immediately recognized Jesus as the son of God. At first he tried to dissuade Jesus, saying, "It is I who need to be baptized by you. And yet you come to me?" Jesus replied "Let it be so; for in this way it is fitting that we fulfill all that which is righteousness."

According to the Gospel of Matthew, upon Jesus' baptism, a voice called down from the heavens, saying, "This is my beloved son, with whom I am well pleased."

The Three Temptations

After his baptism, God led Jesus into the desert for a 40-day/40-night period of fasting. During this time of ritualistic purification, the tempting spirit of evil (*Satan*, or "the adversary") approached him with temptations on three occasions. When Jesus was in the throes of hunger pangs, the devil tempted him by saying that the son of God could easily turn the nearby stones into loaves of bread.

The second time, he took Jesus to the top of the high temple in Jerusalem and said that he should throw himself off because, if he was truly the son of God, angels would fly in to save him. Again Jesus refused, and replied with a quotation from *Deuteronomy*, "You shall not test the Lord God." Finally, he took Jesus to the top of a high mountain and told him that he would give to Jesus all that could be seen from there if he would only bow in worship to him. For the third and final time, Jesus refused the temptation. This time, he ordered the adversary away and again quoted *Deuteronomy*, saying, "Be gone! For it is written, 'You will serve the Lord your God, and serve him only.'"

Jesus' Mission

Having completed his baptism and 40 days in the desert, both of which are viewed as rituals of purification meant to prepare his body and spirit for the trials and tasks with which he would soon be faced, Jesus learned that John the Baptist had been arrested. He then headed for the Sea of Galilee and began to assemble his disciples.

First he approached Simon, "who was called Peter," and his brother Andrew, who were casting fishing nets. He told them, "Follow me and I will make you fishers of men." So they put down their nets and followed him. Next he approached James and John, the sons of Zebedee, who were mending nets with their father. Jesus simply called their names, and it is written that they immediately left the boat and followed him.

At this time, Jesus began his ministry in the region of Galilee. He preached the "gospel" and performed miracles by healing the sick and exorcising demons. Soon he began to travel away from Galilee, and the crowd that followed him became larger and larger the farther he walked. When Jesus realized just how vast the crowd had become, he stopped on a mountainside and delivered one of his most famous sermons, now called the "Sermon on the Mount," which is described in the Gospel of Matthew. In this sermon, Jesus said the following:

> Blessed are the poor in spirit, for they will inherit the kingdom of Heaven. Blessed are the mournful, for they shall be comforted. Blessed are the meek, for they shall inherit the earth. Blessed are those who hunger and thirst for righteousness, for they shall be satisfied. Blessed are the merciful, for they shall receive mercy. Blessed are the pure of heart, for they will surely see God. Blessed are the peacemakers, for they shall be called sons of God.

The Crucifixion

After what most believe to have been around three years of preaching his message to the people, Jesus was handed over to Jewish authorities by Judas, one of his own disciples. Some scholars date the crucifixion in the year 30 C.E., but the truth is that no one knows for certain.

After the temple guards arrested him, the Jewish authorities handed Jesus over to the Roman governor, Pontius Pilate, claiming that he was a criminal and requesting that he be executed. It is written that, when Jesus refused to speak in his own defense, Pilate determined to do the politically expedient thing and let the people choose. Since it was customary for the Roman governor to offer amnesty and freedom to one prisoner during the time of Passover, he brought Jesus before the crowd, along with a local hero and rebel leader named Barabbas. The people, persuaded by the chief priests and elders, asked for Barabbas to be released. This condemned Jesus to death, even though he had committed no crime. Pontius Pilate refused to address the matter any further. Pilate dipped his hands in a basin in a well-known gesture meant to show that Jesus' blood would not be on his hands.

Jesus was taken into Roman custody and, according to the biblical text, beaten, flogged, mocked, and spat upon. A crown of thorns was shoved strongly down onto his head as an insult. The next day, he was nailed to a cross and raised up on the hill of Calvary, which was also called *Golgotha*. Upon his death, according to the Gospels, Jesus said, "It is finished."

According to the Gospel of Matthew, at the moment of Christ's passing, a great earthquake shook the ground and a number of tombs broke upon as a result. Many holy people who were recently deceased arose from the tombs, brought back to life. Also according to Matthew, a rich Judean by the name of Joseph of Arimathea went to Pontius Pilate to request the body of Jesus. He wrapped Jesus' body in clean linen and placed him in the sealed tomb.

Pilate later sent guards to Jesus' tomb, so as to make sure that no one tried to remove the body and claim that Jesus had returned to life as he'd promised. The Roman guards reinforced the tomb's large stone with a heavy sealant, likely a type of mortar. They also posted a constant guard. On Sunday, the first day of the week, however, some of his disciples found the tomb had somehow been opened and that the body of Jesus was missing.

Jesus first appeared to Mary Magdalene, one of his followers, and later to his disciples (all but Judas, of course, who Scripture states hanged himself out of remorse for betraying Jesus).

In all four gospels, the passion narrative (the narrative that describes the arrest, trial, death, and resurrection of the Christ) is consistently given preeminence in the stories. The crucifixion is connected to Christ's sacrifice for sin. The resurrection, however, is the single most important event for the Christian believer. It authenticates Jesus' claims about himself as savior and verifies his promises of future resurrection to those who believe in his person and message.

3.5 HISTORICAL DEVELOPMENT

For the first few centuries after the death of Jesus, Christianity was a religion that had to be practiced in secret. Rewards were offered for turning in Christians, and many of the religion's early martyrs were killed during this period. Their religion outlawed by the Roman Empire, Christians often lived under the constant threat of being discovered and executed.

A number of Roman emperors developed creative and horrific ways in which to punish or execute Christian adherents. For example, the sentence for being a Christian included such things as being fed to lions, being burned alive, being forced to fight or die in the gladiatorial arena (or just being publicly executed as entertainment between events), and, of course, being crucified.

Christians would not be able to openly, or even safely, practice their religion until about 313 C.E., when the Roman Emperor Constantine announced the toleration of Christianity in the Edict of Milan. Constantine would declare himself a Christian and become known as the first Christian emperor of the Roman Empire.

3.6 PRESENT-DAY FACTS

Over the last 2,000 years, Christianity has evolved into a countless number of sects and denominations; it is still the world's most widely practiced religion. Christians make up about one third of the Earth's current population, with over 2.1 billion adherents worldwide.

The United States currently has the largest population of Christians in a single nation. Christians make up about 85 percent of the country's population, with roughly 225 million adherents. The United States is followed by Brazil, which has about 140 million Christian adherents, making up about 95 percent of the population.

4

CATHOLICISM

4.1 FUNDAMENTAL TENETS

Basic Information on Catholicism

The Core Beliefs of Catholicism

The Nicene Creed

The Sacramental Economy Within Catholicism

The Veneration of Saints

The title "catholic" means "universal" and has an ancient tradition within Christian history. It has been used to identify the churches from the east and west that affirmed, at the least, the Nicene Creed (325). This creed confirmed by an ecumenical council of bishops defined the key teachings of Christianity in conjunction with Scripture. The unity of the "universal church" was short-lived, however, as a dispute over papal authority began to strain the relationship between the bishops in the eastern and western portions of the Roman Empire. Catholicism eventually split into two major sects becoming Roman Catholicism and Eastern Orthodox in 1054. While there is still a breach within Catholicism (Eastern and Western) over papal authority, the core doctrinal differences between the two sects are quite small and even these differences seem to be a matter of emphasis more than substance. Due to space limitations, this chapter will attempt to explain the basic belief system of Roman Catholicism interspersing occasional comments on the Eastern belief system. Unfortunately, no attention will be given to the other various sub-sects that identify themselves as Catholic.

Basic Information on Catholicism

- ▶ Origin Date: Catholics date their origins to the time of Christ and the twelve apostles in the first century.

- ▶ Founder/Originator: According to Roman Catholic belief, Jesus Christ through the apostle Peter; in Eastern Orthodox, Jesus Christ through one of the twelve apostles.

- ▶ View of God: Monotheistic.

- ▶ Dietary restrictions: In general, none; however, Catholics do observe certain dietary rules on specific days of the year related to fasting rituals.

- ▶ View of Life/Death: Belief in judgment in the afterlife, and that the soul may travel to one of three primary places after death—Heaven, Hell, or Purgatory (sometimes also called "limbo").

▶ Lifestyle Foci: As stated by the *Catechism of the Catholic Church*, "the whole liturgical life of the church revolves around the **Eucharist** sacrifice and participation in the **sacraments** of the Church."

▶ Worship Restrictions: Anyone can become Catholic but in order to convert to Catholicism, one must be baptized, confirmed, and celebrate the Eucharist.

The Core Beliefs of Catholicism

4.1

The core beliefs of Catholicism are as follows:

▶ Belief in the core beliefs of Christianity (see Chapter 3).

▶ Belief in the divinity of Christ and the Holy Trinity (Father, Son, and the Holy Spirit).

▶ Belief in the magisterium (teaching authority) of the Roman Catholic Church. The magisterial teaching of the church is the combination of **Sacred Tradition** and Sacred Scripture as interpreted and defined either by bishops in union with the pope or by the pope speaking *ex cathedra.* The sacred magisterium is believed to provide infallible teaching to the Catholic Church.

▶ Belief that participation in the sacraments of the church is essential to salvation.

▶ Belief in the veneration of saints.

The Nicene Creed

The Nicene Creed, which states the basic beliefs of the Catholic faith, is used by both the Roman Catholic and Eastern Orthodox Churches. It states:

We believe in one God, the Father Almighty, Maker of heaven and earth, and of all things visible and invisible.

And in one Lord Jesus Christ, the only-begotten Son of God, begotten of the Father before all worlds, God of God, Light of Light, Very God of Very God, begotten, not made, being of one substance with the Father by whom all things were made; who for us men, and for our salvation, came down from heaven, and was incarnate by the Holy Spirit of the Virgin Mary, and was made man, and was crucified also for us under Pontius Pilate. He suffered and was buried, and the third day he rose again according to the Scriptures, and ascended into heaven, and sits on the right hand of the Father.

And he shall come again with glory to judge both the quick and the dead, whose kingdom shall have no end.

And we believe in the Holy Spirit, the Lord and Giver of Life, who proceeds from the Father and the Son, who with the Father and the Son together is worshipped and glorified, who spoke by the prophets. And we believe in one holy Catholic and Apostolic Church. We acknowledge one baptism for the remission of sins. And we look for the resurrection of the dead, and the life of the world to come. Amen.

The Sacramental Economy Within Catholicism

The importance of the sacraments within Catholicism cannot be overemphasized. These are viewed by adherents as means of grace given by Christ through the Holy Spirit that heal and transform the adherent. Within Roman Catholicism there are seven. These are called the seven "principal" mysteries within Eastern Orthodox. They are as follows:

1. The Sacrament of Baptism—Baptism of infants is the norm.

2. The Sacrament of Confirmation—This usually takes place around age thirteen and is viewed as the "perfection of baptism."

3. The Sacrament of Eucharist—This is also called communion or the "Lord's Supper."

4. The Sacrament of Penance and Reconciliation—Catholics confess their sins regularly to priests and receive conditional **absolution.**

5. The Sacrament of Anointing of the Sick—This is commonly known as "last rites" and is given to those who are seriously ill and/or dying.

6. The Sacrament of Holy Orders—Catholics are "set apart" into different groups/orders for the ministry of the church with this sacrament.

7. The Sacrament of Matrimony—Marriage of Christians is the norm.

The Veneration of Saints

The veneration of saints is an often misunderstood part of Catholic life. There are more than 10,000 recognized Roman Catholic saints, and these are considered to be alive and active in Heaven. Saints are venerated for their holy lives and examples of godliness. Catholics do not worship saints but pray to them asking them to intercede and take their specific needs to God. In this view, Christians both alive and deceased are one community interconnected through prayer. Sainthood is reserved for those exceptional Christians who through service to the Church and miracles associated with their lives have shown themselves to have a special relationship with God on earth. If miracles continue after a candidate for sainthood dies, this is thought to be indicative of a special rela-tionship with God that continues after death. In order to be declared a saint within Roman Catholicism, there is a lengthy process of investigation completed when the pope canonizes the saint.

WORDS TO GO . . .WORDS TO GO . . .WORDS TO GO

Eucharist is the centerpiece of one of seven sacraments celebrated by Roman Catholics as an action of thanksgiving to God for the sacrifice of Christ for sin and the promise of resurrection. Catholics also believe that the weekly cele-bration of Eucharist is indicative of the literal presence of Christ in the visible expression of the assembled Church. The transformation of the two Eucharis-tic elements of bread and wine into the body and blood of Christ (transubstan-tiation) has long been a controversial doctrine in Christian history.

Sacraments in general are simply outward signs or rites that convey an unseen reality within the adherent. The two most common throughout all of Christianity are baptism and Eucharist. Within Roman Catholicism there are seven sacraments.

Sacred Tradition is a technical term within Roman Catholicism given to the Christian tradition taught by Jesus to his first followers and passed down to the Church. According to Catholic teaching, this tradition is part of the "deposit of faith" given to Christians, and this combined with Sacred Scrip-ture is the entirety of Jesus Christ's divine revelation. Sacred Tradition includes but is not limited to creedal statements like the "Apostles' Creed" and the "Nicene Creed."

Ex cathedra literally means "from the throne." In Catholicism, the throne sym-bolizes the pope's authority to teach the entire Church. When a pope speaks *ex cathedra,* his teaching is according to church doctrine "infallible."

Absolution or forgiveness is granted by a priest with the condition that an act or acts of contrition are performed by the penitent depending on the serious-ness of the sin.

4.2 SACRED TEXTS

The Canon of the New Testament Scripture was identified and set at 27 books very early in Christian history (officially Synod of Hippo 393, but unofficially the 27 books were identified as early as 200). The entire Hebrew canon was also adopted into the Christian canon. Catholicism of both the Roman Catholic and Eastern Orthodox sects, however, also acknowledge a series of deuterocanonical (literally "belonging to the second canon") texts as authoritative. These are texts that were not included in the Hebrew canon but have a style and similarity to books within that canon. These texts are sometimes called the *apocrypha.*

WORDS TO GO . . . WORDS TO GO . . . WORDS TO GO

Apocrypha is a designation that is sometimes assigned to a group of deuterocanonical texts in the Catholic Bible. These texts were adopted into the Catholic canon from the Greek Septuagint (a Greek translation of the Hebrew Scriptures that included some apocryphal works). The controversy surrounding the apocrypha is that these texts are believed by some to have a questionable origin, thus explaining why they were not accepted into the Hebrew canon as Scripture.

4.3 RITUALS AND HOLIDAYS

Catholicism is a Christian religion, and therefore shares many holidays with other sects within Christianity. This section will present the most important Christian holidays from a Catholic perspective. The emphasis within Catholicism on Easter is visible from the number of holy days in connection with this day.

Christian holidays that are traditionally considered Catholic are as follows:

▶ Feast of the Annunciation: This holiday is observed almost exclusively by the Eastern/Greek Orthodox Church, and falls on March 25 of every year. This day is observed in commemoration of the Virgin Mary's reception of the divine revelation that she been impregnated with the unborn Christ. In the Eastern/Greek Orthodox Church, Mary is referred to by the Greek title of Theotokos, which means "Bearer of God" or "the one who will deliver God." This title was declared for her in 431 C.E. by the third ecumenical council, the Council of Ephesus, which proclaimed that Jesus was both man and God simultaneously.

▶ Advent: This holiday season begins four Sundays before Christmas. It is a time of preparation for the coming of the Christ. It is also sometimes called "little Lent" because it is a time of repentance, prayer, and fasting.

▶ Christmas Eve: This holiday is celebrated December 24 in the west. It is the culmination of the advent season.

▶ Christmas Day: This holiday celebrates the birth date of Jesus Christ on December 25. While the New Testament does not give a date for Christ's birth, there is a Christian tradition from the early third century that sets the date at December 25. Knowing the exact date, however, is not the primary focus, but celebrating the birth of "God in the flesh." This date correlates with the "Feast of the Annunciation" (see above).

▶ Ash Wednesday: This holiday is observed exactly 40 days before Easter. Ash Wednesday is the first day of Lent, a 40-day period of fasting and prayer observed by devout Catholics. Ash Wednesday gets its name from an act by priests in which they rub oil and ashes in crosses onto the foreheads of adherents as a symbol of repentance. The ashes that are used come from burned crosses of palm from the Palm Sunday of the previous year.

▶ Palm Sunday: This holiday is observed on the Sunday before Easter Sunday and commemorates Christ's celebrated arrival into Jerusalem. In the Christian Bible, it is written that people placed palm leaves on the ground in front of Jesus as he entered the city riding a donkey. On this day, priests distribute Palm Crosses, which are (as the name suggests) palm leaves tied into crosses. In locations where palm leaves are hard to come by, the leaves may be substituted with willow branches or boughs of yew.

▶ Holy Thursday: Also called Maundy Thursday, this holiday is celebrated on the Thursday before Easter. This holiday is observed in commemoration of the Last Supper of Christ and his disciples. Four biblical events that are related to the Last Supper are commemorated: Christ's washing of his disciples' feet, the first Eucharist (Communion), Christ's moment of internal struggle in the Garden of Gethsemane, and Judas Iscariot's betrayal of Christ (also in Gethsemane).

▶ Good Friday: On the Friday before Easter, this holiday is observed in commemoration of Christ's crucifixion. Adherents of both Roman and Eastern/Greek Orthodox Catholicism believe that Christ was crucified on a Friday.

▶ Easter: This is the most important day in the Christian calendar. It is the day that commemorates the resurrection of the Christ on the third day after his crucifixion. It is a movable holiday and is celebrated on a designated Sunday during March or April according to the lunar calendar. It is this date that determines many of the other feasts and preparations of the Catholic calendar.

▶ Corpus Christi: Meaning "Body of Christ," this holiday is celebrated on the first Thursday after the Catholic Holy Week (the period from Palm Sunday until Easter). The holiday of Corpus Christi celebrates the Eucharist but does not commemorate any particular biblical event.

▶ The Feast of Divine Mercy: Observed on the Sunday that follows Easter, this is a day that was originally set aside for a special **indulgence,** whereby a person could approach a specific fountain and be absolved of all sins. Jesus is said to have appeared in a revelation to the Catholic Saint Faustina and granted this indulgence at the woman's request. Today this holiday is no longer widely observed. However, Catholics who still observe this holiday often do so by simply going to confession (most Catholics confess frequently during the weeks preceding Easter, which may be why few still observe this holiday).

▶ Ascension Day: Also called Ascension Thursday, this holiday is observed on the fortieth day after Easter Sunday (which, obviously, is always a Thursday). This holiday is celebrated in commemoration of Jesus Christ's bodily ascension into Heaven, an event witnessed by his apostles.

▶ Pentecost: Commonly called "Whitsun" in the United Kingdom, Pentecost is observed 49 days (or on the seventh Sunday) following Easter. This is a feast in honor of the Holy Spirit's descent and appearance to the followers of Jesus. The Eastern/Greek Orthodox church celebrates this holiday 50 days after Easter. In fact, the word Pentecost originates from Greek and means "fiftieth day."

▶ Trinity Sunday: Celebrated on the Sunday after Pentecost by the Roman Catholic Church, and on the Sunday of Pentecost by the Eastern/Greek Orthodox Church. Therefore, adherents of the Eastern/Greek Orthodox Church honor the divinity of the Holy Trinity during Pentecost, while Roman Catholics separate the two.

▶ The Feast of the Sacred Heart: Also referred to as the Solemnity of the Sacred Heart, this holiday is observed on the nineteenth day after Pentecost. On this day, white **vestments** are worn during **Mass.**

4.3

WORDS TO GO . . .WORDS TO GO . . .WORDS TO GO

The word **indulgence** comes from the Latin *indulgeo,* meaning "to be kind or tender." In Roman Catholicism, indulgences are partial remissions of punishment for sins. In the past, indulgences could replace severe penance and the church practiced the sale of indulgences in return for monetary donations.

Vestments are liturgical robes worn by the clergy in the performance of ceremonies, such as Mass, blessings, and sacraments.

Mass was a term originally used to mean "sacrifice," referring to the act of taking Communion. Today, the term is used to refer more broadly to Catholic chapel services.

4.4 ORIGINS AND FOUNDER

According to Christian tradition, the founder of the church is Jesus Christ through his twelve apostles. It is for this reason that "apostolic succession" becomes an important doctrine of the Catholic Church. Apostolic succession is a belief in an unbroken line of bishops that stretch all the way back to the original twelve apostles. This unbroken chain of testimony assures Catholics of the veracity and trustworthiness of their origins. It also provides a context for the magisterial teaching of the Church. Roman Catholicism traces its lineage back to the apostolic testimony of the Apostle Peter. Other sects trace their lineage back to other apostles. Virtually all branches of Christianity claim some form of apostolic succession, with the exception of Protestantism.

4.5 HISTORICAL DEVELOPMENT

The Battle of the Milvian Bridge

The Edict of Milan

The Arian Schism

The East–West Schism

St. Thomas Aquinas's *Summa Theologica*

The Rise of Protestantism

Vatican II

The historical development of Catholicism is a complex combination of politics, theological debate, and cultural shifts. The events listed here are only a few turning-point events of a multitude of events in the history of the Church.

At the turn of the fourth century C.E., the Roman Tetrarchy, or "four-ruler system," that had been established in 293 C.E. by Emperor Diocletian had already begun to unravel. Perhaps the most powerful Tetrarch was the one who ruled the Western Roman Empire. The first *Augustus* of Western Rome (at this time, *Caesar* had actually become a lesser title and *Augustus* the title given to most Tetrarchs) was the former general Maximianus Herculius (often referred to simply as Maximian). Initially, Maximian shared his rule with Diocletian, who forced him to retire in 305 C.E. Shortly thereafter, Diocletian was succeeded as *Augustus* of Western Rome by Constantius Chlorus. Constantius Chlorus, however, died on July 25 in 306 C.E.

The Tetrarchy did not recognize succession by heredity, however. Therefore, Constantius's son, Constantine, would have to appeal to the Roman Senate for the appointment. However, Maxentius, son of Maximian, had already occupied Rome. In 308 C.E., a conference was held in the Roman Senate to settle the matter, and it was decided that the rule of Western Rome would pass to Maxentius.

However, back in Western Rome, the loyal troops of the late Constantius had already (though very unofficially) proclaimed Constantine as *Augustus* of Western Rome. They refused to recognize the decision of the Roman Senate, and soon followed Constantine on a bloody campaign against his rival, Maxentius. By 309 C.E., the forces of Constantine had secured Britain, the Germanic regions, Gaul, and Spain. Maxentius had likewise secured Italy, Sardinia, Sicily, Corsica, and the Roman provinces of Africa.

By 312 C.E., the struggle for power between Constantine and Maxentius came to a head as their armies met for a final battle just outside Rome, north of the Milvian Bridge (now called *Pons Milvius*). No one yet knew the impact that this event would have on the future of the Roman Empire, Western civilization, and the world at large.

The Battle of the Milvian Bridge

In 312 C.E., Constantine had already begun leading his forces south across Italy. His army decimated the defensive forces of Maxentius at both Turin and Verona. As a result, Northern Italy now belonged almost entirely to Constantine. In addition, Constantine showed mercy and compassion to captured soldiers and proclaimed that the people were not to be punished simply because they were ruled by Maxentius. This tactic caused the son of Constantius to gain the favor and support of the people, and many of the captured soldiers of Maxentius swore new allegiances to Constantine. This caused the ranks of the invading force to increase as it continued to march south toward Rome. Most historians estimate Constantine's forces at not quite 100,000 troops, with roughly between 90,000 and 95,000 basic infantrymen and between 7,500 and 8,500 cavalry.

As Constantine's forces approached the outskirts of Rome on October 27 in 312 C.E., most assumed that Maxentius would choose to force his rival into laying siege to the city. This was a tactic that had proven successful a number of times in the past and would have put Constantine at a serious disadvantage. In fact, the necessary siege provisions had already been stored within the city walls. However, Maxentius chose to march his army out of the city to face Constantine's forces head on. It is widely believed that he based this decision on good omens and that his belief in these signs was likely influenced by the fact that the next day marked the one-year anniversary of his rule.

On the evening of October 27, according to most accounts, Constantine had a vision as he watched the setting sun. In the sun he saw a cross, intertwined with the Greek letters X and P, chi and rho, which were the first two letters in the Greek spelling of Christ. Traditionally, it is said that Constantine heard a voice saying, in Latin, *In Hoc Signo Vinces*, meaning "In this sign, conquer (or win)!" According to the accounts of the historian Eusebius of Caesarea, however, Constantine saw this statement not in Latin, but in Greek, and he experienced the vision while his army was still campaigning in Northern Rome. Regardless of the details, what is known is that Constantine took this as a sign that he was favored and protected by the God of the Christians. He ordered all of his soldiers to paint the symbol he'd seen, which later came to be called the *Labarum,* on their shields as a symbol of his conversion.

Maxentius marched his army across the Milvian Bridge, the only route to the city, and ordered his men to destroy it. Then he had a makeshift bridge constructed by tying together pontoon boats. When Constantine first arrived, he found that Maxentius had brought far more troops than he'd anticipated. However, the high morale, better training, and Constantine's efficient command of the battlefield began to steadily drive Maxentius's troops back toward the river. Soon the forces of Maxentius were in full retreat, scrambling for their lives across the pontoon bridge. Maxentius's decision to destroy the Milvian Bridge would turn out to be a fatal mistake.

Panicked, the troops of Maxentius made an en masse rush to safety. This proved too much for the pontoon bridge, which collapsed under the extreme weight and divided Maxentius's army. Those trapped on the north side of the river were either captured or killed. Many of them drowned in the river. Only a small number of them ever made it back to Rome. The body of Maxentius was later found in the river. He had drowned in a desperate attempt to swim across the river. Constantine had now destroyed his only rival and soon continued his march on Rome. He was now *Augustus* of the Western Roman Empire, as there was no longer anyone to oppose his hold on the region. By 324 C.E., Constantine had expanded his territories to include the entire Roman Empire. He was now the Roman Emperor.

The Edict of Milan

In 313 C.E., Constantine established the Edict of Milan, which stated that all religions were now legal within his Western Roman Empire. Primarily, he created this edict to legalize Christianity. This is rather interesting, since his father, Constantius, had been notorious for persecuting Christians. This edict also decreed that all lands and property that had been seized from Christians be immediately returned.

However, the Edict of Milan did not end the Christian persecution taking place in the rest of the Roman Empire. Soon the Tetrarch of the Eastern Roman Empire, Licinius, marched his forces against Constantine. The Edict of Milan and fear of Constantine's growing popularity were likely the main catalysts to Licinius's uprising. By protesting against Constantine's Edict of Milan, Licinius gained the support of non-Christian rulers (most of whom still observed the ancient polytheistic religion of Rome). Constantine quickly defeated Licinius and had him executed, and the Edict of Milan stood.

Though the Edict of Milan did not bring an ultimate end to Christian persecution in the Roman Empire, the religion was given a chance to spread for many years. Later, Emperor Julian, often called The Apostate, tried to diminish the presence of Christianity in the Roman Empire. However, the roots put down by Constantine appear to have become too strong for him to bring the religion down.

The Arian Schism

Not long after the Edict of Milan, during the first half of the fourth century, the first major schism took place within the Christian Church. This is commonly referred to as the Arian Schism (not to be confused with the word *Aryan*), which is named after an Alexandrian priest of Libyan descent named Arius.

Most Christians of the period believed that Christ was not only the Son of God, but God incarnate. Arius, however, was preaching that Christ was indeed the Son of God, but not himself God in human form. Arius claimed that Christ was a being, created by God. He argued that, therefore, Christ was not infinite but had a specific time at which he was created. This did not sit well with the majority of the newly established Roman Church. Arius's most controversial statement regarding Christ was "there was when he was not," by which he meant that Christ had a beginning, unlike God.

In 321 C.E., the Bishop of Alexandria, Alexander, became concerned with the increasing number of followers to Arius's teachings (most of whom were of Syrian descent). After having debated the issue with Arius personally, Bishop Alexander's concern only worsened. He assembled a committee of approximately 100 bishops to address the issue. The committee declared Arius a heretic and had him excommunicated from the church. Arius is believed to have gone to Palestine, where he continued to write many works about his beliefs.

Nearly all of Arius' writings no longer exist, since the church had them destroyed after deeming all Arian beliefs as heretical. At the First Council of Nicaea in 325 C.E., the issue of the Arian teachings was officially debated by the leading scholars of the Catholic Church. In the end, the teachings of the Arian sect were officially declared heresy and the Nicene Creed was established in an attempt to prevent similar occurrences in the future.

The East–West Schism

In 484 C.E., the Bishop of Constantinople, Acacias, authorized a compromise with Eastern Roman Emperor Zeno, one that was not approved by the pope (who was supposed to have absolute authority). Pope Felix III, enraged perhaps not as much by the compromise as he was at the fact that his authority had been super-seded, excommunicated Acacias and all the bishops who signed his compromise, as well as the bishops of Antioch and Alexandria. Simply put, he excommuni-cated the entire Eastern Roman Church. This is often referred to as the First Schism.

Later, the two sides made amends and the church was unified once more, if but for a short time, when Pope John the First met with Eastern Emperor Justin I, who gave the Bishop of the Western Roman Church a proclamation of his faith to Orthodox Christianity. After this, the pope crowned Justin and thus validated his claim to the throne. Also around this time, the Eastern Roman Church began to increase its use of Greek, while the Western Roman Church increased its use of Latin.

4.5

Over the next five centuries, the church experienced four more schisms. The second, third, and fourth schisms were mended. However, the fifth schism, which is often referred to as the Great Schism, held firm. As the roles of both the Western and Eastern churches became more political in nature, the bishops constantly found themselves at irreconcilable odds. This final schism, like the first, was the result of a papal decree of excommunication.

In 1050, the Patriarch Cerularius (Patriarch was now the title for the Imperial Bishop) of Constantinople closed all churches still using the Latin language and began to speak out openly against the papacy for its recent modifications and additions to the Nicene Creed. Patriarch Cerularius proclaimed that the papacy did not have the authority to do such things. This disagreement became increas-ingly heated until, in 1054, Pope Leo IX died. Before a new Pope could be appointed, Cardinal Humbertus, Pope Leo's Papal Legate, had Patriarch Cerular-ius and nearly all of the Eastern Church excommunicated. To make the situation more hostile, Humbertus did this without any papal authority, as a successor to Pope Leo had not yet been appointed. Unfortunately, this action proved to be the final cut that permanently split the Roman Orthodox Church into two indi-vidually controlled churches:

- ▶ The Roman Catholic Church
- ▶ The Eastern Orthodox Church (sometimes called the Greek Orthodox Church)

St. Thomas Aquinas's *Summa Theologica*

St. Thomas Aquinas, or more accurately Thomas of Aquino, is considered by most to be the greatest Roman Catholic theologian and philosopher. He is sometimes called the "angelic doctor" and is one of only 33 recognized doctors within the Catholic tradition. His greatest contribution would be his authorship of the *Summa Theologica*, which would become the basis of all Catholic theology.

He lived during the mid-thirteenth century C.E., from 1225 to 1274, at a time when the manuscript of Aristotelian *Corpus* (meaning "Body") had been translated into Latin, which was now the official language of the Roman Catholic Church. The Aristotelian *Corpus* consisted of the compiled works of the famous Greek philosopher and scholar Aristotle, who had been the personal tutor to Alexander the Great. The ideas in this text debated the relationship between reason and religion, and its sudden availability steadily sent increasing shockwaves through the ranks of the Catholic clergy, which had until now enjoyed a period of relative stability following the "Great Schism" of the Roman Catholic Church with the Eastern/Greek Orthodox Church.

In 1265 C.E., at the age of 40, Aquinas began writing the text for which he would be most remembered—*Summa Theologica* (which translates as "A Summary of Theology" or "The Sum of Theology"). From the first page of the text, Aquinas states it clearly that he intended the work to be used as an introductory manual for students of theology. The text offers a fairly comprehensive compilation of the primary theological teachings of the time period. The introductory paragraph of Aquinas's *Summa Theologica* states (please note that by "we," he is referring to the church):

> Because the doctor of Catholic truth ought not only to teach the proficient, but also to instruct beginners [...], we purpose in this book to treat of whatever belongs to the Christian religion in such a way as may tend to the instruction of beginners. We have considered that students in this doctrine have not seldom been hampered by what they have found written by other authors, partly on account of the multiplication of useless questions, articles, and arguments, partly also because those things that are needful for them to know are not taught according to the order of the subject matter, but according as the plan of the book might require, or the occasion of the argument offer, partly, too, because frequent repetition brought weariness and confusion to the minds of readers. Endeavoring to avoid these and other faults, we shall try, by God's help, to set forth whatever is included in this sacred doctrine as briefly and clearly as the matter itself may allow.

Most important, the *Summa Theologica* was Aquinas's attempt to bridge the perceived gaps between faith and reason. In the text, Aquinas attempted to illustrate the ways in which the main elements of faith could be supported firmly by reason. He divided the text into three main parts, the second of which is divided into two pieces. There is a final section of the existing text that was not written by Aquinas, but compiled and composed shortly after his death. The extant version of *Summa Theologica* is arranged in the following order:

1. *Prima Pars*, "The First Part," which addresses the subjects of Sacred Doctrine, the Unity of God, the Holy Trinity, Creation, Angels, the First Six Days (in the book of *Genesis*), and the Government of Creatures.

2. Since the second part addresses the broader subject of human behavior, Aquinas divided it between negative behavior and positive behavior.

4.5

2.1 *Prima Secundæ Partis*, "The First of the Second Part," which deals with the Final End of Man, Human Actions, Passion, Habitual Behavior, Vice, Law, and Grace.

2.2 *Secunda Secundæ Partis*, "The Second of the Second Part," which deals with Faith, Hope, Charity, Forethought, Justice, Fortitude, Moderation, and a final section on "Acts That Pertain to Certain Men."

3. *Tertiæ Pars*, "The Third Part," dealing with Christ as God Incarnate, Christ's Life, the Sacraments, Baptism, Confirmation, the Eucharist, and Penance (please note that Aquinas died before completing his section on Penance).

4. *Supplementum Tertiæ Partis*, "The Supplement to the Third Part," which is the section of *Summa Theologica* written by Reginald of Piperno after Aquinas's death. This section first completes the incomplete section on Penance, then goes on to address the issues of Extreme Unction (Last Rites), the Three Holy Orders of the Church, Holy Matrimony (Marriage), and the Resurrection. Lastly, Reginald of Piperno offers a section of appendixes to aid in the ease of the text's use.

In 1270 C.E., the Bishop of Paris declared as heresy all teachings of the Greek and Arab philosophers (mainly Aristotle and Averroes), including any and all teachings that were inspired or supported by them. Of course, Aquinas's works immediately came under heavy attack. The Dominican Monastic Order, fearing what might happen to Aquinas, had him relocated to Italy.

In January of 1274 C.E., Aquinas was sent to the Second Council of Lyons by Pope Gregory X with an important task. He was to determine if there existed any plausible way in which the differences between the Roman Catholic and Greek Orthodox churches could be settled. Though he'd fallen ill, Aquinas accepted the task. During the journey, however, his condition soon drastically worsened. He died seven weeks later on March 7, 1274, at the age of 49. He had not yet completed his *Summa Theologica*. The last part of the text was compiled and written by his close friend and fellow Dominican monk Reginald of Piperno, based primarily on Aquinas's notes.

In a rather odd turn of events in 1277 C.E., three years after his death, the Bishop of Paris condemned Thomas Aquinas's writings as heretical texts. He also issued an order for Aquinas's posthumous excommunication from the church. These declarations caused the majority of Aquinas's writings, including his *Summa Theologica* (now considered one of the greatest theological works of the period), to be disregarded for some time. However, within the passage of less than a decade, Aquinas's reputation as a heretic sharply faded and his works ceased to be prohibited. Fifty years after his death Aquinas was pronounced a saint of the Roman Catholic Church, and in 1879 Pope Leo XIII declared that Aquinas's theology was to be the basis of all Catholic teaching on Christian doctrine.

The Rise of Protestantism

In the sixteenth century, a group of reformers sought to change the Roman Church from within. These sought to correct a tradition that they believed had departed from its "true" Christian origins and emphasis. After being condemned and in some cases excommunicated, these reformers left Roman Catholicism and began forming new communities.

Vatican II

The history of conflict and strife between Protestants, Eastern Orthodox, and Roman Catholics goes back to the Middle Ages. Pope John XXIII convened the Second Vatican Council (meeting at intervals from 1962 to 1965) in an attempt to heal some of those wounds. This Council, which invited representatives from Eastern Orthodox and Protestant Christian groups to act as observers, took several steps toward reconciliation with those groups. It was during these proceedings that non-Catholics were recognized as true Christians by the Roman Catholic Church. The Church also began an outreach toward dialogue with other non-Christian religions.

◀ SEE ALSO *Chapter 5, "Protestantism"* ▶

◀ SEE ALSO *Chapter 3, "Christianity"* ▶

WORDS TO GO . . . WORDS TO GO . . . WORDS TO GO

Heresy is a term used to designate adopted beliefs that contradict or alter the orthodox (literally, right belief) position of a given community. The measurement of what is orthodox is determined by a given community (Roman Catholic, Eastern Orthodox, Prostestants, etc.). Heresy occurs when adherents step outside the boundaries of acceptable belief as defined by that community.

4.6 PRESENT-DAY FACTS

Today Roman Catholicism is the world's largest religion, with an estimated total of more than one billion adherents worldwide.

Eastern Orthodox follows just behind Roman Catholicism and is the world's second-largest religion, with an estimated total of more than 350 million adherents worldwide.

The estimated number of total practicing Catholic adherents worldwide (from the Eastern and Western sects, as well as the scattered subsects) is approximately 1.5 billion.

Presently, the Roman Catholic Church is under the leadership of Pope Benedict XVI. According to the official list of all recognized popes of the Roman Catholic Church, called the *Annuario Pontifico,* Pope Benedict is the 265th.

5

PROTESTANTISM

5.1 FUNDAMENTAL TENETS

Basic Information on Protestantism

The Core Beliefs of Protestantism

Salvation by Faith Alone

Protestant Denominations

Protestantism, currently the most widely practiced form of the Christian religion in the United States, has a large number of groups and denominations. Therefore, it would be nearly impossible to include the entirety of Protestantism and the beliefs of all its denominations in a single chapter. The information in this section includes the basic or most commonly shared tenets of the majority of Protestant denominations. Please keep in mind that some denominations may or may not have the same beliefs and/or restrictions included here.

Basic Information on Protestantism

▶ Origin Date: 1517 but believed by adherents to be a restoration of the first century **"faith and practice"** of Christians.

▶ Founder/Originator: Martin Luther and a host of other reformers.

▶ View of God: Monotheistic.

▶ Dietary restrictions: None.

▶ View of Life/Death: Belief in judgment in the afterlife in which one goes either to Heaven or Hell.

▶ Lifestyle Foci: Salvation by faith alone; obedience to the teachings of Jesus Christ; other foci vary depending on the denomination.

▶ Worship Restrictions: None. However, some denominations consider baptism to be a requirement.

The Core Beliefs of Protestantism

The core beliefs of Protestantism can change somewhat from one denomination to another. However, nearly all denominations agree upon a number of common beliefs. The most commonly shared core beliefs of Protestant Christianity are as follows:

▶ Belief in the core beliefs of original Christianity (see Chapter 3).

▶ Belief in the divinity of Christ and the Holy Trinity (Father, Son, and Holy Spirit).

▶ Belief that the Bible/Scripture is **inspired** by God.

▶ Belief that "Scripture alone" is the guide for "faith and practice." The Bible is the final authority for the Christian. Thus there is a rejection of the "magisterium" of Catholicism and the importance of apostolic succession.

▶ Belief that "salvation is by faith alone" in Jesus Christ. Thus there is a rejection of the "sacramental economy" of Catholicism. Protestants largely view the **sacraments** as symbolic and without salvific value.

▶ Belief in the "priesthood of all believers" through Christ alone. The only mediator between God and man is Christ. All believers have direct access to Christ. Thus there is a rejection of the papacy, a priestly order, and the intersession of deceased saints on behalf of Christians.

As becomes obvious from this list, it is for good reason that Christians of this persuasion are called Protestants. Protestants, however, share much Christian heritage with their Catholic brethren. Roman Catholic, Eastern Orthodox, and Protestants accept the basic biblical teaching set forth in the Nicene Creed. It is for this reason that many Protestants identify themselves as a "restorationist movement." They view themselves as remaining true to the Christian faith as it was originally taught.

Salvation by Faith Alone

Protestants teach that salvation is a gift of God given by grace through faith in Jesus Christ's atoning death for sin. There is no good work that earns salvation; there is no church that grants salvation; thus salvation is not based on "faith plus anything." Salvation is based on belief/acknowledgment by the adherent that he or she is a sinner in need of God's forgiveness and that Christ (that is, God) took their sin upon himself. Upon personal acknowledgement of this truth, that is, faith, the adherent is said to be reconciled with God and ready to start a new life as a believer in Jesus Christ.

Protestant Denominations

A few of the main denominations of Protestantism are as follows, in no particular order:

- ▶ Lutheran

- ▶ Methodist

- ▶ Baptist

- ▶ Assemblies of God

- ▶ The Reformed Church

- ▶ Presbyterian

- ▶ Anabaptists

- ▶ The Holiness Churches

- ▶ Pentecostal

- ▶ Churches of Christ

- ▶ Evangelical

◀ *SEE ALSO Chapter 3, "Christianity"* ▶

◀ *SEE ALSO Chapter 4, "Catholicism"* ▶

WORDS TO GO . . . WORDS TO GO . . . WORDS TO GO

Christian **faith and practice** is the beliefs, doctrines, and practices that are supported by a given Christian community. Protestants claim to be restoring the original first-century doctrines and practices of Christianity that have been corrupted over time.

The idea of the Bible as **inspired** is a difficult notion to grasp in the modern world. The biblical notion as presented in 2 Timothy 3:16 is that all Scripture is "God-breathed." This still needs clarification. "Inspiration" or "God-breathed" Scripture simply means that God the Holy Spirit worked together with the minds and hearts of the authors (apostles, prophets, etc.) to produce a trustworthy and reliable revelation of God's salvation story in the world. This is done through a complementary interworking between God and the human writer so that Scripture can truly be said to have dual authorship: Divine Author/human author.

The two commonly acknowledged **sacraments** in Protestantism are water baptism and communion, sometimes called "the Lord's Supper." These rites are important to the life of these Christian communities and are considered by some within Protestantism as a means of sanctifying but not salvific grace. Others view these rites as symbolic only and not as a means of grace. Some denominations reject the label of "sacraments" altogether, renaming baptism and communion to "ordinances" or "rites" in order to distinguish their views from Catholicism.

5.2 SACRED TEXTS

The Holy Bible

The Ninety-Five Theses on the Power of Indulgences

The Holy Bible

While Protestants don't believe the tradition of the Church to be on an equal plane with Scripture, they do recognize their linkage to the ancient Church, for example, most Protestants will affirm the content of the Nicene Creed (325 C.E.). The Catholic Church officially recognized the canon of the New Testament as containing 27 books in 393 C.E. at the Synod of Hippo. Unofficially, however, a number of the early **Church Fathers** had already identified all 27 of the canonical texts as early as 200 C.E. Protestants and virtually all sects of Christianity affirm the same 27 books of the New Testament as Scripture. These books include four gospels, one historical record of the spread of the early church, thirteen letters (to churches and/or individual church leaders) by the apostle Paul, eight letters by other apostles, and one apocalyptic book.

Protestants accept as well the 39 books accepted by the Hebrews into their canon as inspired of God. These Old Testament books play an important role in understanding God's plan through history. Protestants, however, reject the deutero-canonical books or apocrypha as Scripture. This exactly demonstrates the Protestant tendency to abandon "tradition" if it deems tradition was wrong in its original assessment. Catholicism accepted the apocrypha or deuterocanonical texts into their canon; Protestants deny these canonical status.

The Ninety-Five Theses on the Power of Indulgences

While not a sacred text, *The Ninety-Five Theses on the Power of Indulgences* by Martin Luther was the written work that sparked the beginnings of the Protestant Reformation. Traditionally, it is said that Martin Luther posted this work as a challenge on the door of the Castle Church in Wittenberg on October 31, 1517. While some have argued the truth of this claim, most spiritual leaders of the Protestant movement agree that where the work was first posted is of no consequence.

This work protests against the Catholic Church's practice of selling indulgences. This practice allowed the sale and purchase of absolutions for sins, thereby reducing the amount of time a person might have to spend in **purgatory.** Over time, as would be expected, this practice came to be a great source of revenue for the Roman Catholic Church. The church even began to hire nonclergy to travel around and sell indulgences, and many of these men were corrupt and abused the position for their own personal gains.

In his work, Luther argued that salvation was granted by the grace of God alone, not through the purchase of indulgences. In this work, he went on to argue that physical acts such as going to confession, taking pilgrimages, and viewing sacred relics also had no value when it came to salvation. In Luther's view, God's gift of salvation was free, so it was ludicrous for the church to claim that it could sell something that already belonged to humans by divine right.

To give a better perspective of how this work challenged the well-established Roman Catholic Church, listed below are the first five theses of Martin Luther's *Ninety-Five Theses*:

1. Our Lord and Master Jesus Christ, when he said *Poenitentiam agite* (meaning "You must repent") willed that the whole life of believers should be repentance.

2. This word cannot be understood to mean sacramental penance, i.e., confession and satisfaction, which is administered by priests.

3. Yet it means not inner repentance only; nay, there is no inward repentance which does not outwardly work divers mortifications of the flesh.

4. The penalty, therefore, continues so long as hatred of self continues; for this is the true inward repentance, and continues until our entrance in the Kingdom of Heaven.

5. The pope does not intend to remit, and cannot remit any penalties other than those which he has imposed either by his own authority or by that of the Canons.

◀ SEE ALSO Chapter 3, "Christianity" ▶

◀ SEE ALSO Chapter 4, "Catholicism" ▶

The **Church Fathers** are bishops of the early Church who write and teach the content of the apostolic message in the successive generations after the apostles have died. There are a number of early Fathers who identify apostolic writings as "inspired" that would later be included in the New Testament canon. These include, but are not limited to: St. Clement of Rome, Polycarp, Irenaeus of Lyons, Origen, Tertullian, Ambrose, Augustine, and so forth.

Purgatory, Heaven, and Hell are the three possible destinations for a soul upon death, according to Roman Catholic doctrine. Purgatory is a third place for those who are not ready for Heaven but not condemned to Hell. It is a place of purification, often associated with fire, and includes painful punishment for a period of time. Protestants reject purgatory as unbiblical and argue that the only two destinations presented in the Bible are Heaven and Hell.

5.2

5.3 RITUALS AND HOLIDAYS

Protestant Christianity has limited the number of holidays that it celebrates. It is from two major holy days that almost all Protestant denominations build their holidays around. Most but not necessarily all of the following holidays are celebrated by Protestants:

▶ **Advent:** This holiday season begins four Sundays before Christmas. It is a time of spiritual preparation recalling the coming of the Christ.

▶ **Christmas Eve:** This holiday is celebrated December 24 in the West. It is the culmination of the advent season.

▶ **Christmas:** While the New Testament does not give a date for Christ's birth, there is a Christian tradition from the early third century that sets the date at December 25. Knowing the exact date, however, is not the primary focus, but rather celebrating the birth of "God in the flesh."

▶ **Palm Sunday:** This holiday is observed on the Sunday before Easter Sunday and commemorates Christ's celebrated arrival into Jerusalem. In the Christian Bible, it is written that people placed palm leaves on the ground in front of Jesus as he entered the city riding a donkey.

▶ **Good Friday:** On the Friday before Easter, this holiday is observed in commemoration of Christ's crucifixion. It is called "good" because Christ died for the sins of the world.

▶ **Easter:** This is the most important day in the Christian calendar. It is the day that commemorates the resurrection of the Christ on the third day after his crucifixion. This holiday's date can change depending on denomination. Commonly, it's observed on the Sunday following the Paschal Moon (first full moon of spring). However, certain denominations use their own unique dating methods. Interestingly, in 2010 and 2011, Easter will be observed on the same date by all Christian sects and denominations. Most denominations will celebrate Easter on April 19, 2009; April 4, 2010; April 24, 2011; and April 8, 2012.

5.4 ORIGINS AND FOUNDER

Martin Luther

Protestants claim a recovery of the earliest meaning and forms of Christianity that lead directly back to Jesus Christ. The leader of this reformation was Martin Luther.

Martin Luther

Martin Luther was born on November 10, 1483, in Eisleben, Germany. His father found success in copper and rose from a peasant to a wealthy merchant. As a result, Luther's father wanted him to create a successful life in some form of civil service. To ensure that his son received the best education possible, Luther's father sent him to a number of prestigious schools.

By the time Luther was 17 years old, he had enrolled at the University of Erfurt. He earned his Bachelor's degree only a year later. Three years after that, he acquired his Master's degree. At the insistence of his father, Luther then enrolled in the University of Erfurt's school of law.

However, Luther's career in law proved to be a short one. In 1505, during his very first year of law school, it is said that a lightning bolt struck the ground next to him one day as he was returning to the campus. Shocked and terrified by the experience, he suddenly cried out a prayer for help to St. Anne, promising that if he was allowed to live, he would become a monk. After returning safely to his campus quarters, Luther almost immediately left law school and entered a nearby monastery.

Luther's life as a monk was not a peaceful one for him. He found no spiritual fulfillment in acts such as fasting and other rituals of self-denial. He also found himself at odds with many of the church's practices, such as indulgences. Luther went to a senior monk for counsel. The monk concluded that Luther needed more work to distract him from his inner struggles. Luther was ordered to continue his academic career.

Luther became an ordained priest in 1507. A year later, he became a professor of theology at the University of Wittenberg. Luther earned his second Bachelor's degree, this time in Biblical Studies, on March 9, 1508. The next year, he received a third Bachelor's degree, this one in the study of *The Sentences*, a medieval theological text. Four years later, Martin Luther received his doctorate in theology, and on October 21, 1512, he became a member of the senate for the theology faculty at Wittenberg.

In addition to his duties as a professor, Luther served as a preacher and confessor at the Castle Church, which was also a repository of a large collection of holy relics. The Castle Church served as the place of worship for both the monastery and the university. During this time, Luther found himself increasingly disgusted by how the sale of indulgences affected the lives of the people. These indulgence certificates were meant to absolve people of sins they had already confessed, and the church claimed that they reduced the amount of time that a person's soul would have to stay in purgatory.

Luther believed that the sale of indulgences was a practice that would mislead people into believing that indulgences alone could save their souls. He felt that parishioners would increasingly neglect confessions and forget the need for feelings of repentance. From 1516 to 1517, Luther gave three sermons in which he spoke of his displeasure with the trafficking of indulgences. The Church was none too happy with what he was saying.

On October 31, 1517, Luther is reported to have answered his critics by nailing his *Ninety-Five Theses on the Power of Indulgences* to the door of the Castle Church. In addition, he included an open invitation to any person who wanted to debate the work. At the time, he received no takers.

Pope Leo X quickly moved to discredit Luther, calling his *Ninety-Five Theses* the ramblings of a drunk. He then ordered a Dominican named Mazzolini, who was also a professor of theology, to travel to Germany and discover what Luther was up to. The Dominican priest reported that Luther denied the authority of the pope and was preaching against papal decree. He declared that Luther was a heretic and then wrote a work that attempted to challenge Luther's writings. For the most part, all that Mazzolini claimed in this writing was that the pope's authority was absolute and any assertions to the contrary were heresy.

Within two weeks, Luther's *Ninety-Five Theses* had spread across Europe. While the church denounced it as heresy, the nonclergy received it with great enthusiasm. Prince Frederick III, elector of Saxony and prince over Martin Luther, outlawed the sale of indulgences in his lands. Since Pope Leo hoped that Prince Frederick would be the next Holy Roman ruler, he chose not to pursue punitive action against Luther. Over the next few years, Luther continued to defend his beliefs against his critics in a number of public debates. With each victory, Luther became increasingly bold, until eventually he voiced his denial of the pope's authority. This was the last straw for Pope Leo X.

On June 15, 1520, the Pope threatened Luther with excommunication unless he agreed to recant 41 of his *Ninety-Five Theses,* which the pope claimed were incorrect, within the next 60 days. In October, Luther responded by sending the pope an essay he'd written titled *On the Freedom of a Christian.* In this essay, Luther proclaimed, "I submit to no laws of interpreting the word of God."

Having refused to recant the 41 points as ordered by the pope, Luther was excommunicated on January 3, 1521, and ordered to appear before the Diet of Worms, an assembly of the highest clergy of the Roman Catholic Church, to answer for his "crimes." Prince Frederick III, however, would not agree to let Luther go until he'd secured a legitimate agreement from the church that Luther would have safe passage. In the past, such Diets had resulted in executions, and Frederick wanted Luther to be able to return

At the Diet of Worms he was asked to recant his statements concerning the papacy and the Roman Catholic Church. The following is his response:

> Here it is, plain and unvarnished. Unless I am convicted [convinced] of error by the testimony of Scripture or (since I put no trust in the unsupported authority of Pope or councils, since it is plain that they have often erred and often contradicted themselves) by manifest reasoning, I stand convicted [convinced] by the Scriptures to which I have appealed, and my conscience is taken captive by God's word, I cannot and will not recant anything, for to act against our conscience is neither safe for us, nor open to us. On this I take my stand. I can do no other. God help me.

After this the current Holy Roman Emperor, Charles V, issued the Edict of Worms, which declared Luther a heretic and an outlaw. The edict also banned all of Luther's writings and even made it illegal for anyone to give him food or shelter. Finally, the edict announced that anyone could kill Martin Luther without fear of legal consequences.

Despite the church's promise to Prince Frederick of safe passage home for Luther, a warrant was issued for his immediate arrest. Foreseeing this, Frederick had Luther intercepted during his return journey and placed him under protective guard. Luther was taken to Frederick's castle in Wartburg, where he remained hidden until the Edict of Worms was renounced in 1526. During his exile, Luther translated the New Testament from Greek to German. Though the Edict of Worms was reinstated in 1529, the strong support for Luther among the people of Germany now made it impossible to enforce.

Luther died of natural causes on February 18, 1546, in Eisleben, Germany.

5.5 HISTORICAL DEVELOPMENT

John Calvin

The Plymouth Settlement

The Wesley Brothers

The Evangelicals

The Reformation and the reformers slowly began to change the religious and political landscape of Europe. Perhaps it is of no surprise that Protestant Christianity became the most widely practiced religious perspective in the United States. Following the American Revolution, the newly independent country sought to separate from its European past. The highly tolerant policies of the United States allowed for the development of new forms of Christian practice.

John Calvin

John Calvin was born July 10, 1509, in France, to a Roman Catholic family. Calvin's father worked as an administrator in the local cathedral and wanted his son to eventually join the priesthood. Interestingly, Calvin wanted to become a lawyer.

In 1523, when Calvin was 14 years old, his father sent him to study at the College de la Marche in Paris, where he majored in Latin. By the end of that year, he had transferred to the more prestigious College de Montaigne. In spring 1528, Calvin graduated from Montaigne with a Bachelor's degree in philosophy and theology.

After graduating, Calvin went to the University of Orleans, France, to study law. He then studied Greek at the University of Bourges. However, Calvin was forced to leave his studies and return home when his father fell gravely ill in 1530. Within a year, his father died.

In 1532, Calvin found himself unexpectedly forced to flee the city of Paris when he was accused of being an associate of certain reformation enthusiasts who had been declared enemies of the Roman Catholic Church due to their writing and lectures. In 1533, a year after leaving Paris, it is said that Calvin experienced a kind of personal revelation that eventually led him to split from the Roman Catholic Church.

By 1536, Calvin had begun to openly oppose the Roman Catholic Church. He now intended to leave France and travel to Germany. However, war broke out between France and Strasbourg, Germany. As a result, Calvin redirected his journey to the city of Geneva, Switzerland.

When Calvin arrived in Geneva, he was met with an unexpectedly enthusiastic welcome. He was invited to stay in Geneva by Farel, a local reformer, who (in a friendly manner, one would assume) threatened that he would suffer God's wrath if he refused. Calvin began to work in Geneva as a lecturer and preacher. However, he soon found himself at odds even with the clergy of Geneva. In 1538, Calvin was asked to leave Geneva as a result of these theological disagreements.

Calvin decided to finish his journey to Strasbourg, Germany. Arriving in 1538, he remained there until 1541. While in Strasbourg, Calvin worked as a chaplain for war refugees who had come to Germany from France. In 1541, however, the Council of Geneva requested that he return to Switzerland and resume his duties as a lecturer and preacher. Though he did not want to leave his duties in Strasbourg, which he found very fulfilling, Calvin decided that it was his duty to return to Geneva.

Calvin remained in Geneva until the day he died, on May 27, 1564. For over two decades, Calvin lectured, gave sermons, and wrote a multitude of works on the reformation. His most significant contribution by far, however, is his *Institutes of the Christian Religion*. It is in this work that he claims to set forth the true nature of Christian faith as taught by Augustine (354-430 C.E.) before it was corrupted by Roman Catholicism. This work became a "guiding light" for a great deal of non-Lutheran reformed theology and thinking in the centuries to follow.

The Plymouth Settlement

Probably the most common misperception of the Plymouth Pilgrims is that they were Puritans. However, they were actually a group of Protestants who had split from the Church of England. The Puritans did not settle in America until 10 years after the arrival of the Protestant Pilgrims at Plymouth Rock settlement in the region later dubbed New England.

From between roughly 1605 and 1617, this group of religious separatists first attempted to make a new place for themselves in the Netherlands, having left England due to religious persecution and political/social hostility. However, they found that life in the Netherlands came with a new set of hardships—job scarcity, the temptation of vices, and so on. They soon petitioned a number of English investors to allow them to establish a colony in the New World.

After years of preparation and waiting (and at least one failed attempt to reach the New World illegally, resulting in a number of Pilgrims being imprisoned for a year), the Pilgrims finally received word that it was time to depart in 1620. They were unaware, however, that their investors had not yet received all of the necessary land patents. The trip was primarily funded and crewed by a small investment group called the Plymouth Council for New England, which had failed in a previous attempt to establish a colony in 1606. They now hoped that the Protestant separatists would succeed, and the Plymouth Council owned the land on which they were expected to settle.

Originally, they departed on two ships, the *Speedwell* and the *Mayflower*. Unfortunately, the *Speedwell* turned out to be less than seaworthy and had to be sold. As a result, all of the settlers, as well as their supplies, had to cram onto the *Mayflower* for the remainder of the difficult voyage.

Despite many hardships, the Pilgrims came to be known as the ancestors of American Christianity—namely, Protestantism.

The Wesley Brothers

The Wesley brothers, John and Charles, were born in 1703 and 1707, respectively. They began their spiritual careers as leaders of an evangelical movement within the Church of England. Both attended Oxford University, and there they assembled a small but dedicated congregation that practiced a strict regimen of worship and disciplined adherence to the *Book of Common Prayer*. As a result of their rigidly structured behavior, they came to be called Methodists. Both also became ordained priests in the Church of England, John in 1725 and Charles in 1735.

After they both had received their ordinations, the Wesley brothers traveled to the Georgia colony in 1735. John intended to work as a missionary in the New World and Charles had received an appointment as a governor's secretary. Most accounts agree that they did not enjoy their experience in America at all. This is further confirmed by the fact that they returned to England after only a few years. Upon their return, it is said that they both experienced personal epiphanies, or "conversions," only three days apart.

Following this experience, John soon joined up with a religious organization called the Moravian society in Fetter Lane. In 1738 he traveled to Herrnhut, in Saxon Germany, where the Moravian Society's headquarters was located. After his return, he began to hold frequent meetings with the Moravian Society, as well as a number of other new religious societies in London. However, he did not preach during this year, as his recent religious activities had now made the parish churches of the Church of England off-limits to him.

In 1739, John Wesley decided that it was time to separate himself from the Moravian Society. He felt that, over time, the Moravians had fallen into the trap of complacency. Methodist societies soon began to be established all over Europe, as John Wesley; his brother, Charles; and a group of close followers began to travel and preach. It is said that these traveling Methodists, most of whom rode on horseback, journeyed an average of almost 8,000 miles a year. However, their journey was by no means a safe one.

According to John Wesley, three primary doctrines set Methodist beliefs apart from the teachings of the Church of England:

1. Humans are all born into sin, and therefore are children of wrath.

2. Men can be saved by faith alone.

3. Faith produces both inward and outward holiness in men.

5.5

As they traveled, Wesley and the Methodists were constantly persecuted by clergymen and threatened by regional magistrates. They were attacked by constables while giving sermons. In print, they were often the target of libelous writings, accusing them of being fanatics, cultists, and even Roman Catholic loyalists. On more than one occasion, they found themselves on the run from violent mobs.

The Evangelicals

In the early twentieth century, Protestantism in America began to wane as liberal theology made its way into the Church at large. Fundamentalism offered conservative theology but tended to be separatist in orientation. From within the Protestant tradition a new theological tradition developed that claimed to return to the same commitments of the reformers and early Christianity. The emphasis was placed on evangelism and the need for salvation (personal conversion through faith in Christ). There was a high regard for biblical authority and the core doctrines of New Testament Christianity were reaffirmed. This movement, which crossed a wide variety of denominations, sought to engage the world in a positive manner. There was agreement in this group to set aside nonessential doctrinal differences for the work of spreading the gospel message. There was also a recognition that Protestants needed to engage the world in more direct ways through socially responsible activity. The most famous member of this group is the evangelist Billy Graham, who worked across denominations and even across non-evangelical denominations preaching and doing social work to spread the gospel throughout the world. Evangelicals would eventually come to dominate the American landscape. Today 26 percent of the United States population are self-identified as Evangelicals. This is the largest single group of Christians in the nation, followed by Roman Catholics at 22 percent.

5.6 PRESENT-DAY FACTS

Since there are so many denominations of Protestant Christianity, finding an exact number of adherents can be difficult. Some denominations do not even consider themselves to be Protestant. However, most global estimates state that there are currently between 450 million and 550 million Protestant adherents worldwide.

The United States currently has the largest number of Protestant Christians, which make up over 50 percent of the population, with adherents of varying denominations. The two largest denominations are currently Baptists, with roughly 17 million members, and Methodists, with just short of 10 million members. Since denominational memberships in Protestant organizations tend to change from year to year, keep in mind that these numbers may be different at the time of publication.

6

DEISM

6.1 FUNDAMENTAL TENETS

Basic Information on Deism

The Core Beliefs of Deism

Almost as much a philosophy as a religion, Deism has only been around for roughly 400 years. Many of this religion's ideas had significant impact on a number of key historical figures during the seventeenth and eighteenth centuries. During a time of rebellion, followed by both social and political reforms, Deism was the religion of many who fought against the established order. Though Deism is not as widely influential in modern times, there are still adherents of this religious philosophy in the world today.

Basic Information on Deism

- ▶ Origin Date: Seventeenth century C.E.

- ▶ Founder/Originator: Lord Edward Herbert of Cherbury.

- ▶ View of God: Monotheistic.

- ▶ Dietary Restrictions: None, but stresses moderation in food consumption.

- ▶ Life/Death View: Deism makes no specific claims regarding the events that follow one's death. However, Deism does state the belief that humans are judged for good and evil in the afterlife.

- ▶ Lifestyle Foci: Stresses moderation, reason, freethinking, tolerance (racial, social, and religious), self-reliance, and the equality of all human beings.

- ▶ Worship Restrictions: None, save that one's faith is tempered with reason.

The Core Beliefs of Deism

- ▶ A monotheistic belief in creator god, but one that is based on reason

- ▶ Belief that the existence of God is made evident through observing both the order and complexity of nature and the universe

- ▶ Belief that God's nature is unfathomable, due to the limitations of the human mind and language

- ▶ Belief that God gave humankind the ability to reason so that they could create moral and ethical principles (this also applies to the human conscience)

- ▶ Belief that every individual should be allowed the freedom to find, know, and worship God in whatever manner he or she deems fit

▶ Belief that all humans are created equal under God, with the same basic inalienable rights

▶ Belief that all views of God (whether they are Deistic or not) are to be respected, under the condition that they do not cause harm to or oppress the views of others

6.2 SACRED TEXTS

Thomas Paine's *Age of Reason*

Voltaire's *Dictionnaire Philosophique*

For the deist, of course, there are no sacred texts; only reason. We can identify, however, two major texts that present the main ideas of deism. These works are Thomas Paine's *Age of Reason* and François-Marie Arouet's *Dictionnaire Philosophique*, or "Dictionary of Philosophy." François-Marie Arouet is more commonly known by the name under which he wrote, Voltaire.

Thomas Paine's *Age of Reason*

Thomas Paine's work, *The Age of Reason*, is a detailed criticism of organized religion. The work also boldly challenges the literal validity of the Christian Bible. Paine wrote the first installment of the three-part in 1793, while he was serving a sentence in a Paris prison as a result of his allegiance to a political group known as the **Girondists.** Before this, he had served as a member of the National Convention of France, despite the fact that he couldn't speak French. The three parts of *The Age of Reason* were published separately, over the span of more than a decade:

- ▶ Part One: Published in 1794
- ▶ Part Two: Published in 1795
- ▶ Part Three: Published in 1807

Britain, now at war with France after the execution of King Louis XVI and Marie Antoinette in 1791, feared a resurgence of the political radicalism that gave rise to the French Revolution. As a result, Paine's work was not well received in Britain. In the still newly independent United States, however, *The Age of Reason* was a bestseller.

Deists view *The Age of Reason* as the primary text in which the sum of arguments for Deism are made. The church is heavily criticized in the work, for both corruption and attempts to gain political power. The work strictly supports the separation of church and state.

One of the main theological themes in *The Age of Reason* is the replacement of divine revelation with reason. Miracles are rejected as falsehoods in Deism, and according to Paine, and the Christian Bible is treated in his work as nothing more than a work of literature or collection of ancient mythology. Ideas such as these led some critics to the mistaken conclusion that Paine was an atheist (and that Deists, in general, are). However, the ideas expressed in *The Age of Reason,* and in Deism, are not atheistic. In fact, Paine argues that God does exist and that this God created the universe.

Prior to the publication of *The Age of Reason,* Paine's views had already long been available; however, only a small group of highly educated intellectuals had been given access to them. The distribution of *The Age of Reason* now made Paine's ideas available to the general public, and the work was written in a rather blunt, nonintellectualized narrative style. This writing style gave the work an irreverent mood that appealed greatly to the American public at the time, people who had only recently rebelled against, fought, and defeated the British Empire and gained their independence. In addition, the book was printed in an inexpensive format, which meant that the majority of people could afford to purchase it.

While Paine's *The Age of Reason* enjoyed great success in the United States, the British authorities and aristocracy were none too pleased with how well it was being received by the lower classes. They viewed Paine's work as a dangerous glorification of ideas that could spark yet another revolution, only this time in the heart of Britain itself. Afraid that Paine's work would incite civil unrest, the British government outlawed *The Age of Reason.* Printers who dared to publish Paine's book were arrested, as were any booksellers who attempted to distribute it. While *the Age of Reason* resulted in a short period of Deist enthusiasm in the United States, it led to a period of harsh censorship in the British Empire.

Voltaire's *Dictionnaire Philosophique*

Beginning with the section entitled "Adultery" and ending with "Why?," Voltaire's *Dictionnaire Philosophique* is a mock dictionary of philosophy that heavily criticizes the institutions and proclamations of organized religion.

In *Dictionnaire Philosophique,* Voltaire provides the reader with a series of short essays. Aside from its attack on organized religion, the *Dictionnaire Philosophique* criticizes a number of other entities, such as Voltaire rivals and critics, certain political institutions, the Christian Bible, and the Roman Catholic Church. In the work, Voltaire lays out the details of what he believed the ideal religion should consist of. Voltaire claimed that the ideal religion should consist of a strong set of moral and ethical principles, while remaining void of dogmatic declarations or claims of divine revelation.

Voltaire's controversial work, while celebrated as genius by the Deist community, was not very well received by many of the world's governing bodies at the time. In fact, his *Dictionnaire Philosophique* was even outlawed in the traditionally tolerant regions of Amsterdam, Geneva, and Paris. For a number of years, Voltaire denied having even written the work, fearing that his authorship might make him the target of violence.

WORDS TO GO . . .WORDS TO GO . . .WORDS TO GO

Girondists were a political group of the French National Assembly who shared certain political and social opinions and principles. The name was first given to them because most members among them were initially deputies from Gironde, a region in Southwest France.

6.3 RITUALS AND HOLIDAYS

Deists believe that all days are of God's creation and that no single day is any more holy than another. Also, Deism is heavily critical of ancient superstitions, upon which a number of traditional holidays are based. Therefore, Deists celebrate no specific holidays (aside from more widely observed holidays, in which some Deists may choose to participate on a purely social level, such as Christmas).

6.3

6.4 ORIGINS AND FOUNDER

The first man credited with expressing the ideas that later formed the foundations of Deism is Lord Edward Herbert of Cherbury. Born on March 3, 1582, he attended Oxford after being tutored by the self-taught Welsh scholar Edward Thelwall.

In 1619 C.E., Lord Herbert was appointed as the English Ambassador to France. In 1629, after a long and unexplained delay, he was made Baron of Cherbury. Unfortunately, he had yet to receive any payment for his service as Ambassador to France. After finding that his tendency to speak his mind was an undesirable attribute in political circles, Lord Herbert dedicated himself to study. This pursuit eventually led him to write out his revolutionary ideas on theology.

Lord Herbert wrote two major works on the subject of religion, *De Veritate* (meaning "The Truth") in 1624, and *De Religione Gentilium* (roughly translated, this means "Pagan Religion") in 1645. With these works, Lord Herbert's primary intention was to illustrate the similarities between world religions, by revealing the common ground they shared.

Lord Herbert claimed that all religions shared a number of universal ideas, which he called Common Notions:

▶ There is a God.

▶ God should be worshipped.

▶ Virtue, ethics, and morality are essential to any religion.

▶ Sin and vice may be forgiven through some form of repentance.

▶ Human beings are judged after death for the good and evil committed during their lives, resulting in either rewards or punishments.

HISTORICAL DEVELOPMENT

The Rise and Fall of Deism

Deism and the Founding Fathers

At its peak, Deism became known somewhat as the religious view of the rebellious intellectual. Some adherents wished to rebel against theocracy, others against social norms, and still others wished to end the church's persecution of science. Deists, unlike atheists, were not arguing against the existence of God. They were simply arguing against the wrongdoings that they felt were the result of ordered religion.

The Rise and Fall of Deism

The absolute authority of the church was first challenged in what is historically called the "Age of Enlightenment." This was also a time when scientists and philosophers questioned the ancient Greek philosophers' ideas about science. It is a turbulent period in which faith and science clash. The rise of Deism is largely a response to this culture clash. Deists reject revealed religions, that is, religions based on sacred texts containing reports of miracles, prophecies, and so forth. They embrace a position that reason ultimately leads one to certain basic religious truths. The rejection of Judaism, Christianity, and Islam and the embrace of reason alone set this position apart.

Early Deists were often persecuted. On more than one occasion, Deist writings were publicly burned. Early Deists, fearing what might happen if their true beliefs became known, often met in their homes or in secluded cafés. Many Deists continued attending their local churches/assemblies regularly, so as to avoid coming under suspicion.

The height of Deism was short, between the mid-eighteenth and early nineteenth centuries.

Deism lost its momentum and ceased to be an influential mode of religious thought around the turn of the nineteenth century. While the word *Deism* may have ceased to be used, the ideas of the movement heavily influenced nineteenth-century British theology, as well as the religion of Unitarianism, which absorbed a number of Deist ideas.

Deism and the Founding Fathers

The Deist idea that all men are created equal in the eyes of God was one catalyst that sparked the American Revolution in 1776 and later the French Revolution in 1791. Both uprisings occurred when Deism was a popular system of belief among the more educated men of the period, most of whom were involved in political or social activism. Many of the men who are considered "Founding Fathers" of the United States of America were Deists. The following founders of America were all Deists, or at least agreed with the majority of Deist ideas:

▶ George Washington

▶ James Madison

▶ Benjamin Franklin

▶ Thomas Jefferson

Abraham Lincoln was also known to have been heavily Deistic in his beliefs for much of his early life. However, most historical records agree that Lincoln experienced a religious conversion to Christianity shortly after the tragic death of his son.

6.6   PRESENT-DAY FACTS

The exact number of Deist adherents is unknown, as many do not claim it as a religion in the census. Some do not claim it because they realize that Deist ideas are not popular among adherents of mainstream Christianity. Other Deists believe that Deism is not a religion, by the traditional definition, and therefore do not claim it.

For the last 200 years, Deists have learned to keep their beliefs to themselves, telling only those of like mind about their beliefs. As a result of this, Deism is often mistakenly referred to as a "dead religion." However, the rise of the World Wide Web has brought adherents of Deist beliefs back together in recent years. Also, society has become more tolerant of alternative religious views, thus making it safer for Deists to openly speak about their beliefs.

In the modern world, the main home for Deism is an Internet-based entity known as the World Union of Deists, which may be found on the web at www. deism.com.

7

ISLAM

7.1 FUNDAMENTAL TENETS

Basic Information on Islam
The Core Beliefs of Islam
The Five Pillars of Islam

Islam is the second-largest religion in the world with approximately 1.5 billion adherents. Many unfamiliar with this religion are surprised to learn that the vast majority of adherents do not live in Arab or Middle Eastern countries but in Africa and Asia. One of the most impressive facets of this religion is the unity of practice around the world. While Muslims don't agree on everything regarding their religious perspective, they do all pray at the same times of the day and toward the same place, fast in the same month, pilgrimage to the same place, and make the same profession of faith.

Basic Information on Islam

▶ Origin Date: 610 C.E. (though Muslims do not often think of this as the origin of Islam, as they view that their roots are those of the Judeo-Christian Genesis).

▶ Founder: Muhammad, called "The Prophet" (also spelled Mohammed, Mohammad, and Muhammed).

▶ View of God: Monotheistic; the one God of Islam has revealed His name to be Allah.

▶ Dietary restrictions: Muslims are forbidden from eating meat from animals killed in sacrifice to a pagan deity, as well as pork, carrion (dead animals), or any carnivorous animal (including birds of prey). A number of additional "unclean," called *haram* animals were later included, such as monkeys, elephants, and donkeys. The consumption of alcohol, non-medicinal drugs, and blood is also forbidden. In addition, animals that are not slaughtered according to the *halal* instructions of Islamic law are also *haram*.

▶ View of Life/Death: Believe in an afterlife in which one goes to either Heaven or Hell.

▶ Lifestyle Foci: The daily activities of Muslims are primarily dictated by the Five Pillars of Islam and obedience to the Qur'an.

▶ Worship Restrictions: None, other than submission to the One God (Allah) and acceptance of Muhammad as the prophet of God.

◄ SEE ALSO 2.1, *"Fundamental Tenets of Judaism"* ▶

The Core Beliefs of Islam

The core beliefs of Islam are as follows:

▶ Belief that there is only one God (Allah).

▶ Belief that Muhammad is God's final Prophet.

▶ Belief that God has sent a number of Prophets prior to Muhammad to communicate His message. These include but are not limited to the following: Noah, Abraham, Moses, and the "virgin born" Jesus Christ. Muslims do not believe that Jesus is the divine "Son of God" but that he was one of the greatest Prophets of God.

▶ Belief that the Qur'an is God's final and perfect message to the world about Himself and His expectations of humanity.

▶ Adherence to the Five Pillars of Islam.

The Five Pillars of Islam

The Five Pillars of Islam are as follows:

1. *Shahadah:* Literally, "bearing witness," which means both the belief and verbal testimony that "There is no God but God (Allah), and Muhammad is his prophet."

2. *Salat:* "Prayer." Muslims are expected to pray five times a day, and at specific periods—dawn, midmorning, midday, afternoon, and midevening— while facing in the direction of Mecca **(Qiblah)**. On Friday the midday prayer is to take place at a **mosque** in community with other Muslim believers.

3. *Zakat:* "Almsgiving." This pillar applies primarily to those who have the necessary financial means to give alms. Those who are poor are not required to do so. In countries with Islamic systems of government, the *Zakat* is collected at a fixed percentage in the form of a tax. However, giving to the poor is considered a Muslim's duty, whether or not the government under which he or she lives requires it.

4. *Sawm:* "Fasting." During the month of Ramadan (ninth month of the Muslim calendar), the most extensive required fast of any religious perspective takes place. The fast is intended to allow Muslims to concentrate on their faith and spend less time on the concerns of everyday life. During this period Muslims are to abstain from eating, drinking, smoking, and sexual intercourse during the daylight hours. They are to pray, read the Qur'an, and do good deeds. This is in remembrance of the month that Muhammad received the first verses of the Qur'an from Gabriel. If a Muslim is sick, traveling, a nursing mother, or a small child, there is an exception granted.

5. *Hajj:* "Pilgrimage." This pillar is also meant to apply to Muslims who can both afford it and are physically capable of making the trip. The *Hajj* specifically refers to the pilgrimage to Mecca, traditionally made during the month of *Dhu'l-Hijjah* (the twelfth month in the Islamic Lunar calendar.

WORDS TO GO . . .WORDS TO GO . . .WORDS TO GO

The Arabic term **haram** (which is pronounced *Hah-rom* and should not be confused with the term *harem*) refers to "forbidden" and/or "unclean" items that are not to be consumed by those of the Muslim faith. Such items are often forbidden for reasons of physical and mental health. For example, the law that forbids drugs and alcohol may be extended to apply to any substance that confuses one's mind or might cause a Muslim to stray from pious behavior due to impaired judgment.

Halal means "permitted" or "acceptable" in Islam. It is often used to identify permissible foods according to Islamic law. For example, animals that are not *haram* (forbidden) must still be slaughtered according to an Islamic prescription. Some sects of Islam allow a substitution of kosher meats when halal meats cannot be found. In some parts of the United States, it is becoming more common to see meat packaged as "100% Halal."

Qibla is the Arabic term for the direction a Muslim faces when praying. All Muslims pray toward Mecca and the Ka'bah during the various times of prayer throughout the day. Mosques quite often contain a niche (also called a *mihrab*) that indicates the direction of Mecca.

A **mosque** is an Islamic place of worship. It is primarily a place of prayer, but many activities within the life of the community are fulfilled there as well (for example, education, certain community holy day celebrations, and so forth). On Friday, in lieu of the midday prayer time, Muslims are required to attend a prayer service and there will often be a message.

SACRED TEXTS

The Qur'an

The *Sunnah*

Nearly all of the teachings of Islam can be found within two primary texts—the Qur'an (often spelled *Koran* in the West) and the *Sunnah*. The Qur'an is a compilation of the revelations Allah bestowed upon Muhammad through the voice of Gabriel. The *Sunnah*, however, is a text containing customs and religious practices that are based upon the acts and words of Muhammad. The majority of *Sunnah* is said to have been recorded by Muhammad's early followers. However, some is believed to have been written by individuals who had never even been in the man's presence.

The whole of Islamic law, called the *Shari'ah*, was derived primarily from the texts of the Qur'an and *Sunnah*. While the *Shari'ah* is not necessarily viewed as being of divine or prophetic origin, it is highly revered as a guide for Muslims to walk a path of living the way in which Muhammad intended. While Muhammad is not considered divine in and of himself, his position as both the founder of Islam and the last prophet of Allah means that he is highly revered and respected. However, it is important to note that Muslim reverence for Muhammad stops short of worship.

The Qur'an

The Qur'an is the centerpiece of Islam. It is held in such high regard that some Muslims memorize the entire text (it is slightly shorter than the length of the New Testament). The Qur'an is considered the eternal, absolute, and irrevocable word of God. Christians and Jews consider their holy texts divinely inspired but acknowledge human authorship. Muslims believe that the Quran is divinely inspired and authored. There is literally a copy of the Quran in heaven that Gabriel read to Muhammad and he is reciting so as to make sure that it is perfect.

Islam also views the Hebrew Scriptures and Gospels as inspired texts, although they are considered inspired to a lesser degree than the Qur'an. Much of the Quranic teaching assumes the theology of the Judeo-Christian biblical texts. For example, belief in monotheism, sin, angels, demons, Satan, judgment, afterlife, are assumed from these texts and verified by the Qur'an. The Qur'an also accepts the historicity of the biblical stories, miracles, and messengers. A number of prophets that precede Muhammad, including Jesus, are acknowledged. At times the Qur'an disagrees with the Hebrew or Christian texts, and in those cases the Qur'an as the final revelation and perfect revelation is considered the true presentation while the other texts have been corrupted.

The teachings of the Qur'an were (for the most part) written down during Muhammad's lifetime by his followers. Some believe that most were written down by Ali, whose written compilation (called *mus'haf*) had a different arrangement than the existing Qur'an. Initially, Muhammad's teachings were conveyed through an oral tradition. The Islamic rulers (called *Caliphs*) went to great lengths to ensure that a score of "reciting officials" or "memorizers" were well versed and made available throughout the lands of Islam. However, they also discovered a small but potentially troublesome flaw in this system.

In December of 632 C.E. (62 AH), shortly after Muhammad's death, the Caliph's army fought the followers of a self-proclaimed non-Islamic prophet at the Battle of Yamama. Though the Islamic forces were victorious, approximately 70 of the Qur'an "memorizers" were killed in the fighting (please note that Muslims who die in battle for the sake of Islam are commonly considered martyrs of the faith).

After seeing the deaths of so many reciting officials, who made up the backbone of Islam's oral tradition, *Caliph* Abu Bakr had all of the existing writings collected, arranged, and repeatedly copied. Few of the copies were identical, however. In 650 C.E. (80 AH), the third *Caliph*, Uthman **ibn** Affan, ordered that a standard version be compiled, and all differing versions discarded. This is the origin of the Qur'an as it exists today. The text is arranged into 114 chapters (not counting the opening chapter), called *suras*.

Many Muslims claim that translations of the Qur'an into another language will always result in corruption. Therefore, the only way one can be sure that they are studying an uncorrupted copy of the Qur'an is to study Arabic, the original language of the Qur'an, and read it in its original language. Its beauty and rhetorical brilliance are viewed as further evidence of its divine origins since it is believed that Muhammad was illiterate. The miracle of the Qur'an is believed to prove that Muhammad is the true prophet of Allah.

The *Sunnah*

The word *sunnah* means "the walked path" and refers to the path of the prophet Muhammad. The *Sunnah* text was based on a loosely compiled collection of stories about the life of Muhammad, called **hadiths,** which means "news reports." The *Sunnah* is a collection of basic Islamic laws and universal codes of behavior, and is considered second in authority only to the absolute laws stated in the Qur'an.

However, the *Sunnah* is considered superior (or, at least, more sacred) to the third basis for the formation of Islamic laws, called *Qiya*, which means "reason." One common example of how *Qiya* is applied to Islam is that the Qur'an and *Sunnah* both forbid the consumption of wine. If one applies *Qiya* to this rule, one realizes that this rule exists because wine clouds one's judgment. Therefore, the rule extends to any nonmedicinal substance that clouds one's mind.

Qiya is considered imperfect, in that it relies upon the use of human reason (which can be flawed). This has resulted in controversies and disagreements surrounding the interpretation and/or modification of the *Sunnah*. While certain Muslim sects might disagree with one another on the exact interpretations of parts of the *Qur'an*, none of them would ever dare attempt to modify such a sacred writing. The *Sunnah*, however, can and has been altered from one sect to another (often as a result of the application of *Qiya*). As a result, the *Sunnah* text that is followed by members of the Shi'a sect differs from that used by the Sunni sect.

7.2

WORDS TO GO . . .WORDS TO GO . . .WORDS TO GO

The term **ibn** is one that you see rather frequently throughout this chapter. The term was used in Arabic names to identify a man's father. Technically, the term can be translated in English as "son of." Therefore, when one sees the word *ibn* within an Arabic name (especially in historical texts), one should understand that although this term is part of a name, it is not itself an Arabic name. For example, in English-speaking terms, the name Uthman **ibn** Affan would be said "Uthman, son of Affan."

The term **hadith**, on its own, means "news report." However, in the context of Islam, it refers to stories about the life of the prophet Muhammad (meaning that these stories are not in the Qur'an). These stories are very informative, telling much about who Muhammad was as a man and/or offering practical life lessons. These *hadith* tales were the basis for the *Sunnah*.

7.3 RITUALS AND HOLIDAYS

Understanding the Islamic Calendar

Ashura

Mawlid al-Nabi

Ramadan

Eid-Ul-Fitr

Eid-Ul-Adha

Al-Hijri

A number of the Islamic holidays differ from year to year, as their dates are based on the position of the moon in the Islamic lunar calendar. Sometimes the dates also differ from one sect to another (primarily either Shi'ia or Sunni). Please remember that, technically, all Muslim holidays begin at sunset of the previous day. However, actual observance is commonly performed on the days listed in this chapter. Please understand, however, that these dates may vary as the later years draw closer, and that one should annually consult with local Islamic religious organizations in order to confirm the dates for the exact year in question.

Understanding the Islamic Calendar

Muslims follow their own 12-month Islamic calendar, sometimes called the *Hijri* calendar, which begins dating years from the date and year when Muhammad made the journey from Mecca to Medina (July 16, 622 C.E. in the Gregorian calendar was the first day of the first year on the *Hijri* calendar). This calendar is based on the lunar cycle and each year (aside from leap years) has a total of 354 days. Therefore, 2009 is 1430 AH in the Islamic calendar. Because of the 11-day difference between Islamic and Gregorian years, it is difficult to give an exact match of both systems. Islamic calendar years are often designated with the initials AH, which stands for *Anno Hegirae*, Latin for "In the year of Hijri."

Most Islamic months are named for either the season in which they occur or their religious significance. The 12 lunar months of the Islamic calendar are as follows, in chronological order:

1. *Muhurram:* Means "forbidden." Traditionally, fighting and war (and most violence in general) are forbidden during this month.

2. *Safar:* The "Yellow" or "Empty" month, which often takes place in autumn.

3. *Rabi'a Awwal:* The month of the "First Spring."

4. *Rabi'a Thani:* The month of the "Second Spring."

5. *Jumada Awwal:* The month of the "First Freeze."

6. *Jumada Thani:* The month of the "Second Freeze."

7. *Rajab:* Means "respect." This is another month during which most violence (primarily fighting and war) is prohibited.

8. *Sha'ban:* Means "to distribute." This month is named because it is said to have initially marked the separation of true Muslims from those tribes who still worshipped in the pagan traditions. During this month, members of pagan-worshipping, non-Islamic tribes would travel outward in different directions in a search for water.

9. *Ramadan:* Means "the parched thirst." This month is considered perhaps the most sacred of the Islamic calendar.

10. *Shawwal:* Means "to carry vigorously" or "to carry as though light." This month is so named because it was traditionally the time during which female camels became pregnant. Thus, they were "carrying" their unborn fetuses.

7.3

11. *Dhul-Qi'dah:* Means "a month for rest." This is yet another month during which, traditionally, fighting and warfare were forbidden.

12. *Dhul-Hajj* (sometimes *Dhul-Hijjah*): Means "a month for the Hajj." This is the month during which most Muslims traditionally make their pilgrimages to Mecca.

Ashura

In the Islamic calendar, *Ashura* is observed on the tenth day of Muharram. For Muslims of the Shi'ite sect of Islam, *Ashura* is a festival that marks the martyrdom of Hussein, Muhammad's grandson. However, it is observed as a holiday by most Muslims.

- ▶ January 7, 2009
- ▶ December 27, 2009 (in the Islamic calendar, a new year has already arrived by this date of the 2009 Gregorian calendar)
- ▶ December 16, 2010
- ▶ December 5, 2011
- ▶ November 24, 2012
- ▶ November 14, 2013
- ▶ November 3, 2014

Mawlid al-Nabi

This festival marks the birthday of Muhammad, the first Islamic Prophet of Allah. Shi'ite Muslims celebrate *Mawlid al-Nabi* five days later than do those of the Sunni sect. Some members of the Muslim faith disagree with the idea of celebrating Muhammad's birthday altogether, as they feel it venerates him in a way that is appropriate only for Allah. The Gregorian dates of *Mawlid al-Nabi* from 2009 to 2014, for both Sunnis and Shi'ites, respectively, are as follows:

- ▶ 2009: March 9 (Sunni), March 14 (Shi'ite)
- ▶ 2010: February 26 (Sunni), March 3 (Shi'ite)
- ▶ 2011: February 14 (Sunni), February 19 (Shi'ite)
- ▶ 2012: February 3 (Sunni), February 8 (Shi'ite)
- ▶ 2013: January 24 (Sunni), January 29 (Shi'ite)
- ▶ 2014: January 13 (Sunni), January 18 (Shi'ite)

Ramadan

Ramadan is the Muslim month of daytime fasting and is a very sacred month. *Ramadan* is one of the Five Pillars of Islam and is therefore very special to Muslims. The dates for *Ramadan*, from 2009 to 2014 on the Gregorian calendar, are as follows:

- ▶ August 22, 2009
- ▶ August 11, 2010
- ▶ August 1, 2011
- ▶ July 20, 2012
- ▶ July 9, 2013
- ▶ June 28, 2014 (due to the moon's location, those in North America will celebrate Ramadan on June 29, 2014)

Eid-Ul-Fidr

Eid-Ul-Fidr (sometimes spelled *Eid-Ul-Fitr*) is the "Celebration of the Feast." This holiday is a celebration that marks the end of the daytime fasting of *Ramadan*. Muslims celebrate *Eid-Ul-Fidr* with feasts and give praise to Allah for helping them to endure the month of fasting and retain their self-discipline. The dates for *Eid-Ul-Fidr*, from 2009 to 2014 on the Gregorian calendar, are as follows:

▶ September 21, 2009

▶ September 10, 2010

▶ August 30, 2011

▶ August 19, 2012

▶ August 8, 2013 (due to the moon's location, those in North America will celebrate Eid-Ul-Fidr on August 9, 2013)

▶ July 29, 2014

Eid-Ul-Adha

Eid-Ul-Adha is the "Celebration of the Sacrifice," a two- to four-day holiday (depending on the country in which it is observed) celebrating Allah's forgiveness of Abraham (in the Qur'an, he is called Ibrahim). As in the Judeo-Christian texts, Ibrahim is tested with an order by Allah to kill his own son, Ishmael (called Isaac in Judeo-Christian texts), as a sacrifice. The dates for Eid-Ul-Adha, from 2009 to 2014 on the Gregorian calendar, are as follows:

▶ November 27, 2009

▶ November 16, 2010

▶ November 6, 2011

▶ October 26, 2012

▶ October 15, 2013 (due to the moon's location, those in North America will celebrate Eid-Ul-Adha on October 16, 2013)

▶ October 4, 2014 (due to the moon's location, those in North America will celebrate Eid-Ul-Adha on October 5, 2014)

Al-Hijri

Al-Hijri means "New Year," but it is more commonly referred to in Arabic as R'as A'sana (a transliteration of the Hebrew Rosh Hashanah, the name for the Jewish New Year). In Islam, this holiday commemorates the journey from Mecca to Medina that was made by Muhammad, his family, and his followers. The dates for Al-Hijri, the Islamic New Year, from 2009 to 2014 on the Gregorian calendar, are as follows:

▶ December 18, 2009

▶ December 7, 2010

- November 26, 2011
- November 15, 2012
- November 5, 2013
- October 25, 2014

7.4   ORIGINS AND FOUNDER

The First Pilgrimage to Mecca

Mecca's Assassination Plot

Two Cities at War

Mecca's Submission

In the year 610 C.E., a mysterious voice spoke to Abu al-Qasim ibn Abdullah, the son of a poor but noble family in the city of Mecca. This voice, which later identified itself as that of the archangel Gabriel, gave Muhammad a simple but insistent order: "Recite!" Muhammad was 40 years old at the time, standing on Mount Hira (located just outside of Mecca). Muhammad often came to Mount Arafat in search of peace and quiet, a serene escape from the chaos of the city where he could be alone in his meditations.

Fifteen years prior to the arrival of Gabriel's voice, Muhammad had encountered a rather wealthy widow by the name of Khadijah. She had been, ironically enough, 40 years old at the time and 15 years Muhammad's senior. When they'd met, Khadijah had been so impressed with Muhammad that she asked him to marry her. He had agreed, and their marriage provided him with enough financial stability to entirely devote himself to spiritual affairs. Well aware of the fact that, without Khadijah, such a situation would have been impossible, and loving her sincerely for it, Muhammad took no other wives while Khadijah was alive.

When the voice of Gabriel first spoke to Muhammad, he was confused by it and feared he was losing his mind. An intense panic soon gripped him, provoking such a terrible fear of insanity that Muhammad considered committing suicide. However, Khadijah did not believe that her husband was going insane. She believed that the voice he heard was of divine origin, and this belief was encouraged by her cousin. Khadijah began to comfort Muhammad's fears with the idea that he was experiencing not mad hallucinations, but divine revelations. In fact, Khadijah soon became Muhammad's first spiritual follower and is thus considered the first Muslim. Soon after, Muhammad's pre-adolescent cousin (who lived in Muhammad's home) also joined him and, for the rest of his days, remained one of the prophet's most loyal followers. Next to join was Uthman ibn Affan, a less-than-influential member of the powerful Umayyad clan. After Uthman, a successful but soft-spoken merchant named Abu Bakr converted to the teachings of Muhammad.

Muhammad's revelations continued to occur regularly for the rest of his life, nearly all of which he is said to have written down (often on whatever ready material was at hand, from paper to bark). Some historians claim that it is impossible that Muhammad wrote down the words he was ordered to "Recite!" This is due to a long-held belief that Muhammad could neither read nor write (which was not uncommon at the time, even for members of noble clans).

The First Pilgrimage to Mecca

In 620 C.E., six men made a pilgrimage from Yathrib to Mecca in order to listen to Muhammad's teachings. They were overwhelmed by his message and saw in Muhammad a man who could bring peace and order to the chaotic city from which they had come. At the time, Yathrib was a city at war with itself. Tribe fought against tribe, and no single entity exercised any actual control over them. As a result, bloodshed and chaos had become the norm in Yathrib. These six pilgrims returned home, but they returned to Mecca two years later.

This time, they brought with them a far larger group of men. Upon arrival, every Yathribi pilgrim pledged undying allegiance to Muhammad. They swore to both fight and die for him. Suddenly, Muhammad had an army of loyal warriors willing to defend his teachings to the death. As a result, Muhammad immediately began relocating his family and followers to Yathrib. Upon their arrival, Yathrib came to be called *Madinat al-Nabi,* or "City of the Prophet," now simply referred to as Madina. While the majority of Muslims went to Madina, Muhammad, Ali, and Abu Bakr remained behind in Mecca.

Mecca's Assassination Plot

Eventually, the Meccan authorities became aware of the Muslim emigration and began to view Muhammad as a threat. They soon hatched a plot to assassinate the Islamic prophet. Before they could carry out their plans, however, Muhammad disappeared. Both he and Abu Bakr slipped out of Mecca under the cover of night.

For three days, the pair hid in a nearby cave just outside the city. When it was safe, they traveled via camelback for nine days until they reached Madina. This exodus from Mecca to Madina is referred to as *hijrah,* which translates roughly as "a breaking of kinship." Those Meccans who abandoned the city to emigrate to Madina came to be called *Muhajirun,* the plural form of an Arabic term (*Muhajir*) meaning "refugee," "emigrant," or "immigrants."

Two Cities at War

For the next 10 years, Muhammad led his Madina army in war against Mecca (in addition to several expansion campaigns). Two years after arriving in Madina, Muhammad sent out a small war party with a sealed letter of instructions. Once the men were out of the city, they opened the letter to find instructions for hitting a Meccan caravan. However, this was at a time during which a truce was supposed to have been in effect. Despite this, the war party followed their prophet's orders and attacked, successfully taking the caravan by surprise.

Not much later, a Madina force of 300 soldiers intercepted a caravan belonging to the powerful Umayyad clan (from which Utham ibn Affan, one of Muhammad's first followers, descended). Mecca sent a large army out of the city to reinforce the caravan, but to no avail. The caravan still fell to the Madina Army. Both Muslims and non-Muslim Meccans alike began to believe that such victories were evidence that Allah was on the side of Muhammad and his Madina forces.

The Battle of the Trench

In 627 C.E., the Meccan tribes made one final push to defeat Muhammad and his followers by attacking Madina with the total of their combined forces. Most estimates number the Meccan Army at around 10,000 strong (greatly outnumbering the Madina forces). As the vast army marched upon the city, a Persian slave suggested to one of Madina's military leaders an unprecedented tactic—dig a deep trench around the city in the areas that were not already naturally fortified by hills. The Madina Army dug the trenches and, in so doing, rendered impotent the power of the Meccan cavalry.

For two weeks, the Meccan Army tried to find a place through which their forces could cross. They never succeeded. The Meccan forces, now tired, hungry, demoralized, and running short of water, were left with no choice but to turn around and return home. This came to be known as the Battle of the Trench (which is interesting, since no battle actually took place).

Mecca's Submission

As a result of Mecca's defeat at the Battle of the Trench, more and more Arab tribes began converting to Islam and joining the ranks of Madina's army. Muhammad now launched a wide-scale offensive against Mecca. In 630 C.E., Muhammad led his Madina Army into Mecca. The Meccans surrendered after very little fighting. Muhammad opted to grant amnesty to the Meccan authorities who once tried to have him killed. However, this amnesty came with the following two conditions:

1. Conversion to Islam.

2. The destruction of all pagan idols in the **Ka'bah,** a cube-shaped structure that housed a sacred black stone.

Mecca's submission to Islam following the Battle of the Trench proved to be a pivotal victory for the Islamic forces. While Mecca was one of the most powerful cities of the region, so was the great city of Ta'if. Shortly after the fall of Mecca, Ta'if voluntarily surrendered, opting to convert to Islam and swear allegiance to Muhammad without a fight.

The year that followed is referred to as the Year of Delegations, during which tribal leaders from every region came to swear their allegiances to Muhammad and Islam. Though many of the **Bedouin** tribes converted to Islam only on paper, their allegiances allowed the ranks of the Madina Army to swell. The power of Muhammad's forces now appeared unstoppable.

However, in 632 C.E. (62 AH), Muhammad was struck with a sudden fever. He retired to the quarters of his most beloved wife, A'ishah (daughter of Abu Bakr). With his head resting in her lap, the great prophet of Allah took his final breath at the age of 62. His holy message now firmly recorded, and an Islamic state now well secured, one Islamic tradition states that Muhammad's soul ascended into Heaven (some claim that both his soul and body were taken into Heaven), escorted by Gabriel and a host of angels. In the Islamic calendar, the year 10 AH is sometimes referred to as the year of *mijra*, or "ascension."

WORDS TO GO . . .WORDS TO GO . . .WORDS TO GO

The **Ka'bah** is a cube-shaped structure that has a black stone on its eastern corner that is about twelve inches in diameter and surrounded by a metal frame. It is the holiest place in Islam and also the place that all Muslims face during prayer throughout the world (*qibla*). Islamic tradition says that the black stone fell from heaven during the time of Adam and Eve and that Adam built the first Ka'bah. According to the Qur'an, Abraham and Ishmael rebuilt the Ka'bah and it reflects a house in heaven. The *hajj* pilgrimage (fifth pillar of Islam) is to be taken to Mecca, the home of the Ka'bah, during the last month of the Islamic year. This place also later became part of the *umrah* (Lesser Pilgrimage). Pilgrims traditionally circle the structure seven times and kiss the stone. If the crowds are too large, the adherent may walk around the Ka'bah and point to the stone on each circuit. One story claims that when Muhammad first saw the *Ka'bah* stone, tears fell from his eyes and he touched and kissed its surface. It has stood as a powerful symbol of the Muslim faith ever since.

The **Bedouin** were the warlike, nomadic tribes of the Arabic world. These tribes often traveled a constant but annually cyclical migratory route. The *Bedouin* existed all over the Arabic world, and their routes expanded along with the expansion of the Islamic territories. At one point, *Bedouin* tribes could be found from the Arab regions, to Syria, to as far west as North Africa.

7.5 HISTORICAL DEVELOPMENT

Shi'a
Sunni
Sufism

After the death of Muhammad, Islam soon experienced a schism as a result of a disagreement over who should now assume the position of *Caliph*, the leader of the religion as well as ruler of the Islamic territories. Initially, the *caliphate* was given to Abu Bakr, who, through Muhammad's marriage to one of his daughters after the death of Khadijah, had become the prophet's father-in-law.

However, some disagreed with this and felt that Ali, not Abu Bakr, should have been made *Caliph*. The main point of their argument was that Ali was directly related to Muhammad by blood, not simply marriage (as was Abu Bakr), and should therefore have been the rightful heir to the *caliphate*. Some believed that Muhammad had intended for Ali to succeed him, pointing to the fact that he had been allowed to marry one of the Prophet's most beloved daughters, Fatimah. Ali had also been the first member of Muhammad's tribe, the Quraysh, to declare that he was a Muslim. However, Abu Bakr remained as the *Caliph*.

You see, a group of city officials from both Mecca and Madina had quickly held an election after Muhammad's death. They had elected Abu Bakr as the *Caliph*. Ali, however, had not been given a say in this electoral body. In fact, all members of Muhammad's immediate family, many of whom believed Ali was the rightful successor, had also been excluded. The officials of Mecca and Madina, however, had already sworn their allegiance to Abu Bakr. They now attempted to use the threat of force to convince Ali to endorse Abu Bakr as *Caliph*.

Later, following the death of the second *Caliph*, Uthman ibn Affan of the Umayyad clan, in 656 C.E., Ali finally gained election as *Caliph*. The still-powerful Umayyad clan, however, was extremely displeased that a member of their clan had not been chosen. Therefore, they rose up against Ali and established their own Umayyad *caliphate*. Since the Umayyad clan was the most influential and powerful entity in almost all regional governments, they now took control of the *caliphate*, and Ali was expelled.

This disagreement over the right of Ali as *Caliph* continued to escalate, until the religion of Islam finally split into two main sects—Shi'a and Sunni.

Shi'a

The Muslims who supported Ali called themselves the *Shi'a Ali,* or "Partisans of Ali." While the sect is simply called Shi'a, the term *Shi'ite* refers to the actual followers of the sect. This sect of Islam was begun by four members of the electoral body that elected the first *Caliph,* Abu Bakr, who voted for the appointment of Ali. These four men came to be known in Shi'a as the four **Sahabah,** or "Companions." Over time, Shi'ites came to be predominantly found in the countries of Iran and Iraq.

After the expulsion of Ali by the Umayyad *caliphate,* he was appointed the equivalent title of **Imam.** In Shi'a, the *Imams* were chosen by bloodline heredity. This idea became the core of the Imamate system of Shi'a. Ali was the first Imam.

Ali's son, Husayn al-Husayn, was murdered by the *caliphate* in 680 C.E. when he refused to swear his allegiance to the *Caliph.* His death is viewed by the Shi'a as his martyrdom, and the Shi'ites view his execution as a symbol that many early Muslims did not follow the true teachings of Muhammad. Today the Shi'a Muslims are in the minority in Islam.

7.5

Later, however, even the Shi'a eventually split into three subsects—Twelvers, Fivers, and Seveners. The majority of Shi'ites belong to the Twelver sect (roughly 80 to 90 percent). The Twelvers are called by this name because they endorse the legitimacy of the traditionally recognized Twelve *Imams.* The Twelvers also believe that the twelfth and final Imam, Muhammad ibn Hasan (also called Mahdi), has been hidden in a kind of immortal seclusion since the ninth century. However, they also believe that he will return during Earth's last days as an agent of justice, and deal out Allah's final judgment upon the wicked and unfaithful.

When the time came for the appointment of the fifth *Imam,* a conflict arose within the ranks of the Shi'a. The Imam had two sons—Zaid (the oldest) and Muhammad (whom he'd named after his great-grandfather). Zaid, a talented warrior, led a revolt against the powerful Umayyad clan. He paid for this act with his life. However, some Shi'ites felt that since Zaid was the rightful heir and had died before he could sire a son, the line of Imams had officially ended. These Shi'ites recognize no *Imam* after Zaid; for this reason, the *Zaidi* (meaning "those of Zaid") are often referred to as Fivers.

Another similar occurrence took place with the seventh *Imam.* Isma'il ibn Jafar was the oldest son of the sixth *Imam,* Jafar. He was born in 719 C.E. Fearing that his son would be the target of assassination attempts, Jafar sent his son to be raised in seclusion and had him publicly declared dead. However, it is uncertain whether this declaration was in fact a ruse, because Isma'il did not return after Jafar's death in 765 C.E. Some (especially among the Twelvers) still believe that Isma'il truly had died before his father, while others believed at the time that he would eventually return to take his place as *Imam*.

Without a definite successor present to assume the position of the *Imam*, the second-eldest son of Jafar, Abdullah ibn Jafar, was appointed. Unfortunately, he had no sons and died only weeks after his appointment. Therefore, the next-oldest of Jafar's sons, Musa al-Kazim ibn Jafar, was appointed *Imam*. As had happened with the fifth *Imam*, many among the Shi'a saw Musa's appointment as a corruption of the Imamate system, and they refused to acknowledge any *Imam* following Isma'il, whom they gave the post-mortem title of seventh *Imam*. For this reason, members of the *Ismaili* are often referred to in the West as Seveners.

Sunni

Sunnis make up the majority of Muslims, approximately eighty-five percent. They believed that Muhammad died without appointing an heir and that the *Caliphs* (under whom they were governed from 632 C.E. until 1924) should be the legitimate governing body of Islam. Though *Caliphs* were often chosen by an electoral body of Islamic clerics, they were not believed to have divine right, nor were they thought to be infallible (unlike the *Imams* of the Shi'a).

The Sunnis are committed to following the Qur'an and the traditions known as *hadith*. The *hadith* are the words and actions of the Prophet Muhammad. The *hadith* often expand upon the teaching of the Qur'an. These two texts are the basis of all Sunni religious education and jurisprudence. The Sunnah or Muslim way of life has a number of schools of interpretation within its tradition. Since Islam is a worldwide religion, the amount of weight given to the Qur'an, *hadith*, and human reason varies across geographic regions. Every Sunni is a member of one of these schools. The four Sunni schools of law are as follows:

▶ Maliki

▶ Shafi'i

▶ Hanafi

▶ Hanbali

Sufism

Sufism (which is called *Ta'wouf* in Arabic and *Tasawouf* in the Persian dialect) is a mystical branch of Islam, founded on the pursuit of spiritual truth as a means by which to discover the absolute truth of all reality. Sufism arose as an opposing force to the structured, law-centered Islamic theology of the ninth century C.E. While Sufism was originally derived from Islam, it is important for readers to note that the vast majority of traditional Muslims have long considered Sufism to be a heretical and blasphemous practice.

The root term for Sufism is **Sufi,** which means "clad in wool" and has come to be used to refer to the followers of Sufism. The word *Sufi* came from another Arabic term, *suf,* or "wool." This term stemmed from how the early Sufis wore simple wool garments. This was done in protest of the increasingly extravagant dress, excessive vices, and other such indulgences of the *caliphate*. Sufis lived much like Buddhist monks, Hindu Brahmas, or Jain ascetics, opting for a frugal and simple communal lifestyle. In fact, a number of concepts in Sufism were borrowed from Buddhism, Hinduism, and Zoroastrianism.

SEE ALSO 11.1, *"Fundamental Tenets of Buddhism"*

SEE ALSO 13.1, *"Fundamental Tenets of Hindu Dharma"*

SEE ALSO 14.1, *"Fundamental Tenets of Jainism"*

SEE ALSO 16.1, *"Fundamental Tenets of Zoroastrianism"*

The early **Shaykhs** (often spelled *Sheikh* in the West), a title given to the highest of Sufi scholars, were rather intrigued by the customs of Christian sects of mysticism. These small (and often short-lived) sects of Christianity (such as the Manichean sect) were heavily influential in the initial development of Sufism. Mystical love and oneness with God (*tawhid*) form the basic tenets of the Sufi faith.

Sufis consider guidance from wise teachers essential to prevent straying from the Path. These sheikhs, who are venerated as saints, are believed the only ones able to provide access to the knowledge of God. However, Sufi teachers discourage others from becoming their disciples because the goal of Sufism is for each believer to acquire his personal wisdom independently and develop a line of communication with the Beloved.

According to the writings of the Sufi scholar Shaykh Idries Shah, a Sufi must successfully traverse through four paths of existence:

7.5

1. *Fana:* Meaning "annihilation," this is the initial stage during which a **Sufi** becomes aware of objective reality and begins to pursue the path of Sufism in an effort to achieve a unification of the self with consciousness. This stage is often associated with ecstatic experiences of divine bliss.

2. *Baq'ha:* Meaning "to remain" or "permanent," this is the stage during which a Sufi develops into a *Qutub*, or "teacher." At this stage, a Sufi often transforms from student to teacher, and those of the *Fana* stage will often turn to him or her (though, traditionally, Sufi teachers are male) for learning. A Sufi who has reached this stage has surrendered his consciousness to God, and thus attained a form of perfection. Some refer to a Sufi of the *Baq'ha* or higher as being a "Perfect Man."

3. The Third Path: This stage can be seen as the next level of *Baq'ha*. During the Third Path, the *Qutub* goes from being simply a teacher to being a spiritual guide to all people (which often requires travel). A *Qutub* of the second-path *Baq'ha* stage is restricted to teaching locally only.

4. The Fourth Path: The *Qutub*'s duties are now extended to being a guide for those who are experiencing the transition from this life to the next. However, Sufis view this not as "death," but as just a new stage of the individual's spiritual journey. Sufis believe this journey to be visible only to the eyes of one who has attained the Fourth Path. Those who have not are blind to it. In Sufism, the attainment of the Fourth Path is considered an extremely rare occurrence and is possible for only a few special individuals.

WORDS TO GO . . . WORDS TO GO . . . WORDS TO GO

The term **Sahabah** means "Companions." This term can be used to refer to the close or early followers of Muhammad who followed him to Madina from Mecca. *Sahabah,* in very specific contexts, can also refer to the four members of the *caliphate* electoral body who supported the election of Ali as first *Caliph.* Today this term is sometimes used loosely to refer to the Muslim religious community as a whole.

An **Imam** is the Islamic leader of a mosque or community. Sunni Muslims give this title to any recognized leader or teacher of Islam. Imams typically lead prayers at the mosque. The title Imam, however, has been given a technical usage by the Shi'a to identify individuals chosen by God to be special examples. Twelvers are the most common sect (80 percent). According to Twelvers, there are "Twelve Imams" that have been identified as appointed by God and have a status parallel to the Prophet Muhammad. Many Twelvers are awaiting the "Twelfth Imam" or the "Mahdi" who will one day return and establish Islam worldwide.

The Arabic term *suf* means "wool" and is the root word from which Sufism developed. **Sufi** means "clad in wool" and originates from the early Sufi practice of wearing wool garments as a protest against the extravagances of the Caliphs.

Sufis are expected to follow their **Shaykh** with undying loyalty, often for the rest of their physical lives. A *Shaykh* is thought to be one who has attained the higher paths of wisdom and therefore possesses a greater understanding of Allah. *Shaykh* are referred to in Persian as *Pir,* meaning "elderly man." An alternative Arabic term is *Mush'a'hid,* meaning "guide" or "director." Before a *Shaykh* accepts a pupil, that person is commonly required to swear a strict oath of allegiance, obedience, and selfless devotion.

7.6 PRESENT-DAY FACTS

Today Islam is the world's second-largest religion, and in 15 different countries Muslims make up more than 99 percent of the population. Currently, the country of Indonesia claims the largest number of Muslims, at more than 170 million. While only just over 10 percent of China's population is Muslim, it is home to more than 36 million Islamic adherents.

The United States currently has one of the lowest Muslim populations in the world, with between two million and three million Islamic adherents. Percentage-wise, Muslims make up roughly one half of one percent of the population of the United States. However, please note that some organizations have claimed that there are as many as seven million Muslims in the United States. The estimates provided here are not meant to claim that such higher estimates are incorrect. However, no concrete statistical data currently supports them.

8

BAHA'I

8.1 FUNDAMENTAL TENETS

Basic Information on Baha'i
The Core Beliefs of Baha'i

The word Baha'i isn't exactly the name of the faith, but for the sake of clarity it is used in this book. The word Baha'i actually refers to a follower of the teachings of Baha'u'llah. Baha'i is one of the world's youngest religions, being roughly a century and a half old (it was founded in 1844). This religion, while acknowledging other prophets like Abraham, Zoroaster, Moses, Buddha, Jesus, Muhammad, and so forth, claims that its prophet has the most recent prophetic message from God, which contains a call for the **"unification of all of humanity."** According to the teaching of Baha'u'llah, these earlier messengers of God presented specific messages for their time and culture. Their messages are true and have value but are incomplete (which explains why even today in small groups of Baha'i adherents various holy books will be read in support of some noble ideal). The Baha'i view is that as human beings grow in spiritual maturity, successive evolutionary stages are reached and new messengers are sent out with new messages. The message of Baha'u'llah is the most recent message.

Basic Information on Baha'i

▶ Origin Date: 1844 C.E.

▶ Founder/Originator: Mirza Husayn Ali Nuri (later known as Baha'u'llah, or "Splendor of God").

▶ View of God: Monotheistic.

▶ Dietary restrictions: Baha'i adherents are not allowed to consume alcohol or use any drugs (except for medicinal purposes).

▶ View of Life/Death: Belief that the soul continues on after physical death, traveling toward God on a journey that spans multiple planes of existence, among which are Heaven and Hell.

▶ Lifestyle Foci: To serve in one's work and treat all others as equal, regardless of race, color, sex, or creed. Baha'i adherents are encouraged to actively improve themselves and grow spiritually through daily prayer and meditation.

▶ Worship Restrictions: None; anyone may practice Baha'i. Even those of other religions are considered worshippers of the same God to those of the Baha'i faith.

The Core Beliefs of Baha'i

The core beliefs of Baha'i are as follows:

▶ Belief that all religions come from the same source.

▶ Belief that Baha'u'llah is the most recent messenger from God.

▶ Belief that the *Kitab-i-Aqdas* (Most Holy Book) is revelation from God.

▶ Belief that a life's purpose is to seek out, form a relationship with, and worship God.

▶ Belief that one should cultivate virtue and thereby promote the unity of humankind, which, in turn, will move human civilization forward.

▶ Belief in the equality of humankind under God, that humans were created by a single, all-powerful God, and that all people are members of a unified human race.

▶ Belief that the soul is created at the moment of conception and destined to reach the afterlife, where it will continue to progress across the planes of existence until eventually reaching the plane of God's presence.

▶ Belief that work performed in service to others is itself a form of worshipping God.

8.1

WORDS TO GO . . .WORDS TO GO . . .WORDS TO GO

The **"unification of all of humanity"** is God's message given to Baha'u'llah. This theme of unity (oneness) and equal opportunity pervades the religion of Baha'i. The world should be one as God is one. Unification would at a minimum include the following: there is a need for harmony of people of all religious perspectives. There is a need for a harmony of religion and science. There is a need for harmony among nations through international justice. This unification would bring about one world government, one world religion, and one world language.

8.2 SACRED TEXTS

The **Kitab-i-Aqdas,** meaning "Most Holy Book" (though it is sometimes referred to as the "Book of Laws"), is the central text of the Baha'i faith. Written in Arabic script sometime before 1873 (the exact year of its composition is unknown), this book states the basic tenets of the Baha'i religion as revealed to Baha'u'llah in his divine revelation. The text appears to have been somewhat influenced by the ideas of Babism, a religious movement of which Baha'u'llah was a key figure before he established Baha'i.

The book consists of the following four primary laws for adherents of the Baha'i faith:

1. Prayer: All Baha'i between the ages of 15 and 70 are required to perform a daily prayer while facing the direction of **Qiblih,** which is a shrine located in Israel that was identified by the **Bab** (founder of the Babi movement, a precursor to Baha'i) as the place of the Chosen One (Baha'u'llah).

2. Fasting: From March 2 to 20, all adherents who are in good health are obligated to fast during the period between sunrise and sunset. While fasting is expected during this time, it is not restricted to it.

3. Laws of Personal Matters: This section of laws deals with matters such as the giving of alms, dealing with gossip, marriage, divorce, and the managements of inheritance.

4. Ordinances: This is a section of miscellaneous laws, ordinances, and requirements. Within this section is the law that every Baha'i must recite the "Holy Name" of *Allahu Abha.*

In addition to the *Kitab-i-Aqdas,* there are also two other texts in the Baha'i faith—*Kitab-i-Aqdas* and *Kitab-i-Asma. Kitab-i-Aqdas,* which means the "Book of My Covenant," is the last will and testament of Baha'u'llah, which he wrote and sealed himself before his death. It was unsealed on the ninth day after his death and revealed his choice of successor. *Kitab-i-Asma* means the "Book of Names," and is a work that was written by the Bab, who was Baha'u'llah's predecessor. It is primarily a commentary on religious unity. However, it is the *Kitab-i-Asma* that is the source of the Baha'i calendar.

WORDS TO GO . . . WORDS TO GO . . . WORDS TO GO

Kitab-i-Aqdas is the title of the "Most Holy Book" in the Baha'i faith, which is the book of laws. This book was revealed by Baha'u'llah in 1873.

Qiblih means "The Point of Adoration." This is the direction in which Baha'i adherents turn during prayer. Geographically speaking, it is in the direction of a shrine to Baha'u'llah in Bahji.

Bab literally means "Gate," and it is the title assumed by Siyyid Ali-Muhammad, Prophet-Founder of the Babi movement and forerunner of Baha'u'llah.

8.3 RITUALS AND HOLIDAYS

Ayyam-i-ha

Ridvan Festival

Other Baha'i Holy Days

The Baha'i faith has its own unique calendar, which comes from the *Kitab-i-Asma* text. Unlike the 12-month Gregorian calendar, the Baha'i calendar has 19 months. The calendar contains 19 months with 19 days plus 4 days in a solar year. Each month is named after a different attribute of God. This, in part, explains the Baha'i worship schedule as well. The beginning of each month marks the time for meeting, prayer, and celebration in homes. The 19 months of the Baha'i calendar are as follows:

1. Baha: "Splendor"
2. Jalal: "Glory"
3. Jamal: "Beauty"
4. Azamat: "Grandeur"
5. Nur: "Light"
6. Rahmat: "Mercy"
7. Kalimat: "Words"
8. Kamal: "Perfection"
9. Asma: "Names"
10. Izzat: "Might"
11. Mashiyyat: "Will"
12. Ilm: "Knowledge"
13. Qudrat: "Power"
14. Qawl: "Speech"
15. Masa'il: "Questions"
16. Sharaf: "Honor"
17. Sultan: "Sovereignty"
18. Mulk: "Dominion"
19. Ala: "Loftiness"

Ayyam-i-ha

The festival feast of Ayyam-i-ha is celebrated annually; it begins at sunset on February 26 and ends at sunset on March 1. The purpose of the feast is as preparation for the long period of fasting that all healthy Baha'i between the ages of 15 and 70 must practice March 2–20 of each year (sunrise to sunset). The preparation takes place in the intercalary days (either four or five days in a Leap Year) before the last month of the Baha'i year. During the Ayyam-i-ha festival, adherents of the Baha'i faith are often especially charitable to one another, delivering gifts to relatives and friends. Often feasts are held in the form of elaborate social gatherings for the local Baha'i community. Some have called this the equivalent of the "Baha'i Christmas."

Ridvan Festival

The Ridvan festival begins on April 21 and ends on May 2. Ridvan refers to the garden in which Baha'u'llah spent 12 days before he was exiled from his home-land of Tehran to Constantinople. During this time, he announced to his family and companions that he was the Chosen One of whom the Bab had prophesied. To adherents of the faith, Ridvan marks the birth of the Baha'i religion.

Other Baha'i Holy Days

The two previously mentioned holidays are the most significant in the Baha'i faith. However, there are also other holidays that are observed, though not as elaborately. Adherents of the Baha'i faith observe the following holidays:

▶ May 29: The Anniversary of Baha'u'llah's Ascension. This day commemo-rates the death of Baha'u'llah in 1892. On this day, no Baha'i adherents are supposed to attend work or school.

▶ October 20: The Bab's Birth. This day commemorates the birth of the Bab, who was both a spiritual mentor to and prophesier of Baha'u'llah.

▶ July 9: The Bab's Martyrdom. This day commemorates the firing-squad execution of the Bab by the Shah government in 1850.

8.3

8.4 ORIGINS AND FOUNDER

Mirza Husayn Ali Nuri, who later come to be known as Baha'u'llah (the glory of God), was born in Tehran, Iran, in the year 1812 C.E. Baha'u'llah began his spiritual journey as one of the leading figures of the Babist religious movement.

The movement called for sweeping religious and social reforms within the Shi'ite Islamic community including, for example, raising the status of women. The spread of the Babist movement across Iran resulted in violent persecution from the established Islamic religion. The Babis' founder, known as the Bab (which means "Gate"), was arrested and later executed. Before he died, however, the Bab predicted that he had prepared the way for one who would come and bring a universal religion to the world.

Baha'u'llah was also arrested and brought back to Tehran. Influential members of the Islamic clergy wanted him sentenced to death. However, they did not get their wish. The high status of Baha'u'llah's family caused the court to receive protests from the Western embassies and other high-ranking families. As a result, his life was spared. However, this did not mean he was set free.

Baha'u'llah was sentenced to four months in one of the most terrible prisons in the Persian Empire, *Siyah-Chal,* or "The Black Pit." Both court officials and the Islamic clergy expected that even a four-month sentence, if served in such a horrible prison, would likely result in Baha'u'llah's death. However, he not only survived, but emerged from the prison with even more religious enthusiasm. While imprisoned, Baha'u'llah had experienced a divine revelation and now went to share what he'd learned with others.

After serving his time in prison, however, Baha'u'llah was banished. His period of exile took him all over the Persian Empire and lasted for 40 years. He was first sent to live in exile in Baghdad. After about a year, however, he left Baghdad for the mountains of Kurdistan. He spent the next two years in meditative solitude, considering how he should approach the divine endeavor to which God had called him.

In 1856, Baha'u'llah left Kurdistan and returned to Baghdad. The Babis now asked that he assume leadership of the religion. Baha'u'llah proved very capable in this task, and soon word of his spiritual teachings began to spread.

Unfortunately, this caught the attention of the Shah government (the ruling body of Persia at the time), which feared that Baha'u'llah's rising popularity might lead to yet another religious movement in Persia. The Shah sent envoys to the authorities from the Ottoman Empire (which ruled Baghdad at the time) and convinced them that it would be best to relocate Baha'u'llah to a place that was much farther from Persian borders.

In April 1863, just before leaving Baghdad, Baha'u'llah and some of his fellow Babists made camp on the banks of the Tigris River. During this time, he revealed to one of them that he was the "Promised One," whose arrival the Bab had prophesied. This garden later came to be called *Ridvan*, or "Paradise."

By May 1863, Baha'u'llah had departed from Baghdad and began traveling toward Constantinople. Despite his being an exile, his popularity continued to grow, and many of the most prominent citizens of Baghdad were displeased that he was forced to leave.

After four months in Constantinople, Baha'u'llah's popularity had not waned satisfactorily to the comfort of the Persian Empire. In fact, his following had continued to flourish. Therefore, he was ordered to the city of Adrianople to live out a period similar to that of house arrest. By December 1863, Baha'u'llah had reached Adrianople. He remained there for five years.

Continued agitation from opponents caused the Turkish government to send Baha'u'llah and the other Babist exiles to the horrid "Prison City" of Acre, Palestine. Baha'u'llah, along with his family and fellow Babist exiles, entered the walls of Acre on August 31, 1868. Acre was meant for the most dangerous and violent of criminal offenders—murderers, rapists, robbers, political insurgents, and the criminally insane. Acre was basically a city that had been walled up. It had no form of sewage system, no source of water, and no proper methods of waste disposal. Needless to say, Acre was a foul-smelling hell that was rampant with disease, and it was the last stop of Baha'u'llah's exile.

He spent the last 24 years of his life within the horrible walls of Acre. However, in Acre, Baha'u'llah composed one of his most important works, the *Kitab-i-Aqdas*, or "Most Holy Book." This text became the foundation of the Baha'i faith.

By the late 1870s, Baha'u'llah was allowed to walk outside the walls of Acre as he pleased. He and his companions soon took up residence in an abandoned mansion nearby. Baha'u'llah passed the last of his days immersed in writing.

Baha'u'llah died on May 29, 1892. His body was buried in the atrium of the mansion, a place now called *Bahji*. To adherents of the Baha'i faith, the *Bahji* is considered one of the most sacred locations on the planet.

8.5 HISTORICAL DEVELOPMENT

Abbas Effendi was the given name of Baha'u'llah's eldest son, known later by the title of Abdu'l-Baha, meaning "Servant of Baha." Baha'u'llah appointed Abdu'l-Baha as his immediate successor and designated him as the "Centre of the Covenant." This appointment made Abdu'l-Baha the sole authority on the truth of his father's writings, as well as leader of the Baha'i faith.

Abdu'l-Baha, who had spent much of his life as an exile, continued living as such until 1908, when an uprising known as the Young Turk Revolution resulted in his release. Once free, he dedicated his life to teaching, speaking out against war and violence, developing the principles of Baha'i, and maintaining the spiritual community of the faith.

Abdu'l-Baha died on November 28, 1921, at the age of 77, just a year after being awarded a knighthood by the British Mandate of Palestine for his efforts toward ending war and promoting religious tolerance. He appointed his oldest grandson, Shoghi Effendi, as his successor under the title of "Guardian of the Baha'i Faith."

Shoghi Effendi spent much of his life translating the sacred texts of Baha'i. He also led an expansion campaign for the Baha'i community and established the Baha'i World Center. Perhaps most important, Shoghi Effendi established the "Spiritual Assembly," which consisted of regional Baha'i representatives who were responsible for electing officials to serve in the first central Baha'i governing body, which he named the Universal House of Justice. Shoghi Effendi died suddenly and unexpectedly in 1957, and so was unable to appoint a successor.

Each Baha'i community elects its own members to a Spiritual Assembly, which runs the regional affairs of the religious community and elects members to serve in the Universal House of Justice. However, the members of the Spiritual Assemblies and the Universal House of Justice should not be misunderstood as clergy. The Baha'i Faith does not have an established clergy.

The first election of members to the Universal House of Justice took place in 1963. To this day, it is considered the last successor of the Baha'i Faith. Every five years, the members of the Spiritual Assemblies hold elections. Any male Baha'i who is at least 21 years of age may be elected to the Universal House of Justice. The Spiritual Assembly positions may be held by both male and female Baha'i adherents.

8.6 PRESENT-DAY FACTS

Throughout the past century, the sphere of unity encompassed by the Covenant of Baha'u'llah has steadily widened as the Baha'i community has grown and spread around the world. Today, more than 150 years after the birth of the Baha'i Revelation, millions of followers in hundreds of countries and territories all over the world remain united through the provisions of Baha'u'llah's Covenant. Adherents of the Baha'i faith exist throughout the world. With more than eight million adherents worldwide, the Baha'i faith is most widely practiced in the following five countries:

▶ Asia: Over 3 million

▶ India: Over 2 million

▶ Africa: Near 2 million

▶ Latin America: 900,000

▶ Iran: 350,000

▶ United States: 150,000

There is one magnificent "templelike" house of prayer on each continent around the world. Each building is nine sided in reverence to the number that Baha'i adherents venerate. The world center of Baha'i is on Mount Carmel in Haifa, Israel. Despite the fact that the Baha'i faith is most obviously still being practiced, it has yet to find a national home. Currently, there is no country in the world in which Baha'i adherents are in the majority. However, most Baha'i believe that, as Baha'u'llah once said, "The world is but a country, and humankind its citizens." So perhaps they do have a home after all.

9

TAOISM

9.1 FUNDAMENTAL TENETS

Basic Information on Taoism
The Core Beliefs of Taoism

The syncretism that is allowable among Chinese religions is often difficult for the Western mind to comprehend. The Chinese have no qualms with being Taoist, Confucian, and Buddhist all at the same time. This is possible because often all these perspectives have common beliefs that can be harmonized. Taoism is one of the two main indigenous religions of China, the other being Confucianism, with which it shares a number of core beliefs and philosophies. Taoism is as much a philosophy of life as it is a systemized form of religion, focusing upon the *Tao,* meaning "the Way," and emphasizing that human beings should align themselves with the natural flow of the universe in order to achieve harmony and perfection. Founded upon the ancient teachings of the sage Lao Tzu (also spelled Lao Tze), Taoism focuses upon the quest to find and become one with the harmonious balance between the opposing forces of the cosmos.

Basic Information on Taoism

▶ Origin Date: Sixth century B.C.E. (unconfirmed).

▶ View of God: Pantheistic.

▶ Dietary Restrictions: While some sects have dietary restrictions, such as avoiding the consumption of grain, Taoism as a whole has no dietary restrictions.

▶ Life/Death View: Taoists do not consider death or the afterlife to be an issue they need to address. They believe that concerns about death or the afterlife waste energy better exerted toward following the proper path in life.

▶ Lifestyle Foci: Pursuit of **wu wei,** a lifestyle that emphasizes quietism and non-aggression, personal hygiene, meditation, dietary moderation, mental control, and physical discipline.

▶ Worship Restrictions: Taoists may worship at temples or home altars, and there are no restrictions or requirements for becoming a Taoist (aside from a desire to follow "the Way").

The Core Beliefs of Taoism

▶ Belief in the teachings of Lao Tsu and his disciple Chuang Tsu

▶ Belief that humans are at their very best when they live in harmony with nature

▶ Belief that those who live the most simply are those who learn to go with the flow of the Tao

▶ Belief that the journey of life is of far more value than the destination (*Tao* can also translate as "journey" in certain contexts)

▶ Belief that the Supreme Being is not present or active in human affairs; however, the Supreme Being does manifest in the form of lesser figures and deities who are active in human affairs

▶ Belief that all things in creation, whether natural, supernatural, or spiritual, are one

▶ Belief in the harmony of opposites within the peaceful flow of the Tao **(yang and yin)**

▶ Belief that physical existence is finite and that only the Tao is eternal

---

WORDS TO GO . . .WORDS TO GO . . .WORDS TO GO   9.1

Tao (pronounced *Dao,* and sometimes spelled as such) means "the Way," and is impossible to define precisely. It is sometimes called "the way of the universe" or "nature's way." The Taoist term **wu wei,** though somewhat difficult to accurately translate into English, means "nonaction" and stresses a nonforced lifestyle that moves in harmonious accord with the forces and impulses of nature. It is the idea that many things happen quietly and effortlessly; for example, plants grow, seasons change, nature reproduces.

Yang and yin is in the background of all Chinese religious thought. To put it another way, the Chinese assume the truth of yang and yin whether Taoist, Confucian, or Buddhist. The Chinese yang and yin are simultaneously complementary and opposing principles in nature. These two principles generate all forms of reality. These are not the same as good and evil. One is not expected to win over the other. They are opposed forces providing a dynamic balance to the universe. The emblem of yang and yin provides an improved understanding of the Chinese perspective. It is typically a circle what looks like two intertwined commas that represent two opposing forces. One half is light, representing yang, and the other is dark, representing yin. Inside each division is a small dot that contains the seed of its opposite. The dot indicates that everything contains its opposite and will eventually become its opposite. Yang is the positive force in nature: brightness, warmth, maleness, and so forth. Yin is the negative force in nature darkness, coolness, femaleness, and so forth. From the Chinese view, when these two forces are in harmony life is as it should be.

9.2 SACRED TEXTS

Tao Te Ching

I Ching

Chuang Tzu

Taoism has three primary texts: the *Tao Te Ching, I Ching,* and *Chuang Tzu.* Though they are all part of the Taoist canon, each text serves its own unique role. The *Tao Te Ching* is the foundation of the Taoist religion. The *I Ching,* which was not originally intended to be a Taoist text, was absorbed by Taoist practitioners of mysticism. Lastly, the beautifully poetic *Chuang Tzu* text offers a number of allegorical lessons told in the form of stories.

Tao Te Ching

Lao Tzu (who lived in the sixth century B.C.E.) has long been credited as the author of the *Tao Te Ching,* which means "Way of Power." The earliest-known manuscripts of Lao Tzu's teachings, however, are estimated to have been transcribed during the third century B.C.E. The *Tao Te Ching* is considered the first of two primary sacred texts in Taoism, the other being the *Chuang Tzu.*

Although the teachings of the *Tao Te Ching* share some common ideas with Confucianism, they mark a significant departure from a number of Confucius's teachings. For example, Lao Tzu stressed the equality of human beings and expressed the need for a classless, caste-free society. He also introduced the concept of **wu wei,** meaning "nonaction," which stressed a nonforced lifestyle that allowed one to live in accordance with instincts and other natural impulses.

To the Western mind, many of the ideas of Taoism appear, at first glance, somewhat paradoxical and/or contradictory in nature. However, this is often because the unfamiliar mind does not understand that confusion is a large part of the *Tao,* in that the very first step for any Taoist adherent is the realization that one knows nothing about the *Tao.* For many, this first step proves to be the most difficult. Until one acknowledges that one does not know the *Tao,* one cannot begin to seek it out. This idea is expressed best by the opening lines of the *Tao Te Ching:*

> The *Tao* that can be walked upon is not the enduring and unchanging *Tao.* The name that can be spoken is not the enduring and unchanging name.
>
> Having no name, it is the Originator of Heaven and Earth; having a name, it is the Mother of all things.

Always free of desire we must be found, if we would speak of the deep mysteries. But if desire is always within us, then all we shall see is the outer borders [of those mysteries].

Once one recognizes one's ignorance of the *Tao*, one must come to the difficult realization that no one but one's self can ever lead one to the true *Tao*. This is yet another idea that many find difficult to truly grasp, in that it eventually requires an adherent to seek out the truth of the *Tao* without a guide and to learn it without a teacher. This idea is perhaps expressed best by the teaching of section 56 of the *Tao Te Ching*:

He who knows the *Tao* does not speak of it; he who speaks of the *Tao* does not know it.

He who knows the *Tao* will know to keep shut both his mouth and his nose. He will blunt the sharp edges of his self and unravel the most difficult of mysteries; he will increase his luminescence, bringing himself into an agreement with obscurity. This is called the "Mysterious Pact."

Meditation of various sorts is a critical part of getting into harmony with the *Tao*. Current Taoists use a variety of techniques to aid in this process. For example, *t'ai-hsi* seeks to produce inward vision using "embryonic breathing" techniques. It is thought to not only cure diseases but confer to immortality. *Shou-i* is a meditation technique that Taoists use in an attempt to come into a mystical union with the *Tao* and with the Cosmos.

9.2

I Ching

The *I Ching* (also spelled *Yi Jing*), which means "The Book of Changes," is one of the most ancient Chinese classical texts. However, it was not originally intended as a sacred text for Taoism. In fact, the ideas within it are believed to date back to prehistoric China (as far back as 5000 B.C.E.), greatly predating the lifetime of Lao Tzu, possibly by more than 2,000 years. Although estimates vary, the mystical ideas of the text were compiled and written down under the title of *I Ching* sometime around 2900 B.C.E. Authorship of the text is credited to the legendary Chinese Emperor Fu Xi, who is reported to have lived from 2953 B.C.E. to 2838 B.C.E. (which would mean he lived to be 115 years of age). Later, the Chinese ruler King W'en inserted additions into the *I Ching* sometime during the Zhou Period in the eleventh century B.C.E. A supplementary section of commentaries in the text, called the *Shi Yi*, or "Section of Ten Wings," is said to have been written by Confucius sometime in the sixth or fifth century B.C.E.

Although the *I Ching* was not originally a Taoist text, it came to be a part of the religion nonetheless. As a result of certain mystical elements in Taoism, a number of sects of Taoist mysticism arose. Some of these sects sought out the secrets of immortality, but nearly all of them practiced the arts of magic, healing, demon exorcisms, and divination. Since the *I Ching*, at its core, is a book of ancient divination practices, the text came to be adopted into many such sects of Taoism.

The *I Ching* illustrates and explains 64 different combinations of broken and unbroken lines, each line with four possible values, in groups of six (hexagrams). Sometimes these lines are seen grouped by threes (trigrams). Each combination of these lines had its own physical, numerical, chronological, astrological, and elemental values. These lines are believed to represent what were originally broken and unbroken sticks that were cast randomly to the ground, the combinations of which were thought to offer specific signs for divination purposes, much like the casting of bones in certain ancient Western cultures.

Chuang Tzu

The *Chuang Tzu* text (also spelled *Chuang Tze* or *Zhuangzi*) was named for its author. This text was written by the most wise adherent of Lao Tzu's teachings, a poet named Chuang Tzu. The *Chuang Tzu* text combines the ideas and knowledge of the man Chuang Tzu, sometimes by repeating or elaborating upon Lao Tzu's teachings, primarily through stories that often teach moral and/or philosophical lessons.

Perhaps the most touching section of the text tells a story of the funeral of Lao Tzu, whom Chuang Tzu refers to in the text by the pseudonym Lao Tan. Chuang Tzu even refers to the character representing himself in the story by the name Chin Shih. The story is meant to convey that death is a fundamental and inevitable part of the natural order and that it is not something to be feared or lamented. The point of the story seems to be that the Tao produces both life and death and that even these features of yang and yin should be embraced by the Taoist.

9.3   RITUALS AND HOLIDAYS

The Lantern Festival

The Dragon Boat Festival

The Chinese New Year

Taoism has roughly 55 holidays a year, 3 to 5 for each of the 12 lunar cycles on the calendar, each in reverence to a different deity or figure in Taoist and/or Chinese cosmology. To list and explain all of these holidays could take up an entire book. Therefore, the three most widely celebrated holidays are explained in detail: the Lantern Festival, the Dragon Boat Festival, and Chinese New Year. The dates of Chinese events follow their lunar calendar, which changes in the dates of the Western Gregorian calendar from one year to the next. Therefore, only the dates for 2009 through 2011 are provided.

The Lantern Festival

The Lantern Festival, which Taoists call *Shan-Yuan*, has been celebrated in China for more than 2,000 years. For Taoists, the Lantern Festival is primarily a celebration that honors the deity known by the title of "Heavenly Officer." The celebration is so called because of the fact that families decorate and light lanterns around their homes, and children carry paper lanterns on the night of the festival. While originally these lanterns were lit by candles, most are now lit with electricity, due to modern concerns about fire safety. It is also customary that people eat a sweet treat called *Yuan-Xiao* during the lantern festival, which is made from sweetened rice flour rolled into balls that are often filled with red bean paste, sesame sauce, or peanut butter.

The dates of the Lantern Festival from 2009 to 2011 are as follows:

- ► February 9, 2009
- ► February 28, 2010 (the date is later due to a lunar leap month)
- ► February 17, 2011
- ► February 6, 2012

The Dragon Boat Festival

The Dragon Boat Festival, interestingly enough, is often more popular and widely celebrated in countries outside of China. Although this event may have had a different purpose originally, the festival is now observed in honor of the life of a deified provincial leader named Chu Yuan. A respected poet and political official during the third century B.C.E., Chu Yuan's life ended tragically.

Due to a mishap, Chu Yuan fell out of the king's favor, and his homeland of Chu was taken from him and handed over to be governed by corrupt officials. No longer able to gain an audience with the king, he could not change anything, and soon the entire country fell victim to foreign invasions and internal corruption. Unable to bear the sadness, and powerless to stop the deterioration of his beloved homeland, Chu Yuan threw himself into the *Mi-Lo* river in the land of Chu. The residents of Chu, who revered Chu Yuan, rushed to his aid. Unfortunately, they were too late to save him.

In honor of Chu Yuan, on the fifth day of the fifth lunar month of each year, people hold races in which they paddle in boats decorated as dragons. These races are said to be re-enactments of how the Chu villagers rushed so desperately (although vainly) to save the drowning Chu Yuan from the *Mi-Lo* river.

The dates of the Dragon Boat Festival from 2009 to 2011 are as follows:

- ▶ June 27, 2009 (the date is later due to a lunar leap month)
- ▶ June 16, 2010
- ▶ June 6, 2011

The Chinese New Year

Chinese New Year, whether celebrated by Taoists or not, always takes place on the first day of the first lunar month on the Chinese calendar. In Taoism, this day marks the ascension of the Kitchen Lord to the celestial realm of the 33rd Heaven, where he makes his annual report on the realm of humankind to the Jade Emperor (who resides there), lord of Heaven and Earth. On this festival, one sees many people practicing both Taoism and Buddhism simultaneously, much as many people do in Japan with Shinto and Buddhism.

The dates for Chinese New Year from 2009 to 2011 are as follows:

- ▶ January 26, 2009
- ▶ February 13, 2010 (February 14 in China, due to lunar position)
- ▶ February 3, 2011
- ▶ February 23, 2012

9.4   ORIGINS AND FOUNDER

Lao Tzu and Chuang Tzu

Taoism: From Philosophy to Religion

The founding of Taoism, as already mentioned, is credited to a man named Lao Tzu (also spelled Lao Tsu, Lao Tze, and Laozi). Biographical information on Lao Tzu is difficult to find and/or confirm, so some historians have come to question whether he ever actually existed. Most of the information on who Lao Tzu was comes from legends. All legends, interestingly enough, are very consistent in their geography (consistency is an unusual occurrence in fabricated legends), placing him in the province of Luoyang (located along the Luoyang River, south of Beijing and west of Shanghai).

According to Taoist legends, Lao Tzu was an archivist for the Chinese Imperial Court during the latter half of the sixth century B.C.E. As Lao Tzu grew older, he became increasingly disenchanted with the corruption and debauchery he witnessed in men. Overcome with sadness that men were unwilling to follow the path to natural goodness, Lao Tzu decided to leave China and began a journey to the country's western border (near what is now known as Tibet). The legend states that when Lao Tzu reached the border, he met a guard named Yin Xi, a thoughtful man who wanted to live a good life. Yin Xi asked Lao Tzu to write a book containing his most important life teachings. As a result, Lao Tzu took to writing the text that would one day become the *Tao Te Ching,* and the very foundation of Taoism.

9.4

Lao Tzu and Chuang Tzu

While some Taoist legends claim that Chuang Tzu was a direct disciple of Lao Tzu and was tutored by him, the truth of this is very questionable. The main problem with the idea of them sharing a teacher/pupil relationship is that the two men are not believed to have been alive at the same time. For example, Lao Tzu is known to have lived in the late sixth and early fifth centuries B.C.E. However, Chuang Tzu, born under the given name of Zhou, is known to have lived during the fourth century B.C.E., from 370 to 301. However, the fact that the two men never met should not in any way be thought to devalue the Taoist lessons written in the *Chuang Tzu* text.

Taoism: From Philosophy to Religion

The writings of both Lao Tzu and Chuang Tzu were extremely influential on the development of the philosophical and religious ideas that would later form the core of Taoism. However, there were no formal Taoist religious organizations (at least, none that are known) during either man's lifetime. In fact, Taoism did not become a recognized religion in China for several hundred years. However, despite this, the ideas of Lao Tzu and Chuang Tzu spread throughout the land until they could no longer be denied.

9.5 HISTORICAL DEVELOPMENT

The Great Age of Taoism

The Quanzhen Sect

The Zhengyi Sect

Taoism finally was recognized as a formally established religion during the second century C.E., in the latter years of the Eastern Han Dynasty (which lasted from 25 C.E. to 220 C.E.).

During the time of the Northern and Southern Dynasties (lasting from 386 C.E. until 589 C.E.), Taoism ceased to be viewed as strictly mysticism and came to be viewed as a legitimate and common religion in China, such as Buddhism. This view likely arose because Taoism began to gain support from a number of emperors who hoped to utilize the religion for political reasons. This period marked the beginning of one of the greatest ages for Taoism in China.

The Great Age of Taoism

Taoism experienced a great surge during the years of the Tang Dynasty (lasting from 618 C.E. until 907 C.E.) and again during the Northern Song Dynasty (lasting from 960 C.E. until 1127 C.E.). A multitude of new Taoist sects began to spring up all across China during these periods. Taoist shrines, statues, and temples were a common sight in almost every area of the country. Also, Taoist philosophers, ascetics, and masters began teaching students of their own, forming schools in astounding numbers. After the fall of the Yuan Dynasty (lasting from 1271 C.E. until 1368 C.E.), however, Taoism suffered a sort of reverse schism, as a result of a renewed sense of national unity that caused many sects to merge. It became divided into two main sects: Quanzhen and Zhengyi.

Benefiting from the support of so many powerful dynasties, Taoism continued to develop and spread. However, during the turbulent years of the Ming Dynasty (lasting from 1368 C.E. until 1644 C.E.), the Ming Imperial Court had few resources to spare toward religious cultivation, including Taoism. As a result, Taoists began to suffer from financial hardships and internal conflicts. To make matters worse, during the Qing Dynasty (lasting from 1644 C.E. until 1911 C.E.), the Manchu rulers chose to honor Buddhism, ignoring Taoism completely. This marked the end of Taoism's support from the ruling dynasties, as well as the close of a great age for the development of the religion. Sadly, this was only the beginning of a difficult period for the adherents of Taoism.

After Taoism lost its support from the ruling body, it seems to have returned to mysticism, becoming a secret religious organization with far fewer members. During the Opium Wars, also called the Anglo-Chinese Wars, Taoism suffered an even worse decline as a result of political oppression, a surge in drug addiction (mainly to opium that was being trafficked into Canton by the British East India Company), and the corruption of Western influences. As a result, many Chinese people abandoned their pursuits of religious studies, including Taoism.

The Quanzhen Sect

The Quanzhen Sect (Quanzhen means "completely true") was founded by a man named Wang Chongyang, a talented martial artist who decided to become a military officer after failing an official's exam when he offended his examiner. In his late 40s, it is said that he encountered a Taoist *immortal* at the Ganhe River. After this encounter, the legend says that Wang Chongyang abandoned his military position and left his family in the care of his father-in-law so that he could go into religious and meditative seclusion on Zhongnan Mountain.

When Wang Chongyang reached his place of meditation, he immediately dug a grave for himself. He lived in this grave for three years, contemplating the truth of the *Tao*. At the end of three years, he arose from the grave and filled it in with earth. He then left the mountain and established the Quanzhen sect of Taoism. Later, the students of Wang Chongyang erected a temple on the spot on Zhongnan Mountain where their teacher once dug himself a "grave of the living dead." Among Wang Chongyang's multitude of students, seven were called the *Quanzhen-qi-zhi*, "The True Quanzhen Seven." A number of amazing Taoist folktales and legends about Wang Chongyang and "The True Quanzhen Seven" are told to this day.

The Zhengyi Sect

Zhengyi Taoism was founded through a merger of the Wudoumi Sect and the older Tianshi Sect. The naming of the new sect as Zhengyi is believed to have been the result of some unspecified policy on religion that existed during the rule of the Yuan Dynasty. During the reign of Emperor Chengzong, a man named Zhang Yucai, known as the "38th Tao Master" and head of the *Tianshi* Sect of Taoism, was the leader of the Zhengyi Sect. From that point forward, *Tianshi* Taoism was given the new, state-approved name of "Zhengyi" Taoism. Later this new sect absorbed the Wudoumi Sect. The main thing that separates the Zhengyi from the Quanzhen Sect is that the adherents of Zhengyi Taoism have a choice of whether they want to practice the religion solely and completely as Taoists. Zhengyi Tao includes, or later absorbed, a number of other Taoist sects—Zhenwu Xuanwu, Qingwei, and Jingming, to name just a few.

9.6   **PRESENT-DAY FACTS**

Taoism is still alive and well, with some 20 million exclusive practitioners and more than 200 million others who practice the religion in conjunction with another (such as Buddhism or Confucianism). Although it is not practiced openly as a religion in today's Communist China (as of 1949, when Chinese Communist Party leader Mao Tse-tung assumed leadership of the country), the people still observe many of its holidays ceremonially. The religion is currently practiced in more than 30 countries, but it has its strongest presences in Hong Kong, Taiwan, Korea, Vietnam, Laos, and Thailand.

9.6

10

CONFUCIANISM

10.1 FUNDAMENTAL TENETS

Basic Information on Confucianism

The Core Beliefs of Confucianism

Importance of Relationships in Confucianism

The Chinese are remarkably syncretistic in their religious orientation. It is not uncommon for an individual to align themselves with the teachings of Taoism, Buddhism, and a position identified in the West as Confucianism simultaneously. In actuality, there is no such form of religious practice called "Confucianism" because this is not the true title of the original Chinese system. Only in the West is this term used to refer to the practice based on the teachings of Confucius. Confucius is actually a Latinized version (created by Jesuit missionaries) of the founder's true Chinese name, K'ung Fu Tsu (also spelled K'ung Fu Tze or Kungfuzi), which means "K'ung the Teacher" or "K'ung the Master." In Chinese, the system of practice based on Confucius's teachings is referred to as *Ju-chia,* which translates as "Scholarly Tradition" or "School of Scholars."

A debate has long raged over whether the ancient Chinese practice of Confucianism is, in fact, a religion. Some argue that it *is* a religion, in that it deals with matters of both Heaven and Earth. Others, however, argue that Confucianism is *not* a religion and claim that it is primarily a philosophical point of view, a moral and ethical code, or simply a guide for a righteous way of life. Still others argue that since Confucius based his teaching on the pre-existing cosmology of Taoism, Confucianism is simply an expansion of the Taoist religion (even Confucius seems to have voiced his own belief that he was not creating a new religion, simply elaborating on the truth of the *Tao*). It seems, however, that the two perspectives have differing focuses. Taoism is focused on the individual in the natural realm while Confucianism is focused on the individual within society. In the end, it appears that this debate will continue for some time. Scholars continue to disagree concerning the status of Confucianism as a religious perspective.

Basic Information on Confucianism

▶ Origin Date: Sixth century B.C.E.

▶ Founder: Confucius/K'ung Fu Tsu.

▶ View of God: Pantheistic.

▶ Dietary Restrictions: None, except to avoid excess.

▶ View of Life/Death: Consideration of the afterlife is discouraged. Instead, the focus should be on living a life in harmony with family, society, and authority.

▶ Lifestyle Foci: Living a sincere life, improving one's self, actively seeking out knowledge through education, and being fair, civil, and wise in one's dealings with other people.

▶ Worship Restrictions: None. Anyone may practice Confucianism.

The Core Beliefs of Confucianism

The core beliefs of Confucianism are as follows:

▶ Belief in and adherence to the teachings of Confucius, as written in the texts of the Confucian Canon.

▶ Belief that every person should aspire to achieve the status of **Junzi** translated "superior man/gentleman."

▶ Belief in and practice of *ren* translated "humanity." Confucius was concerned with the individual development of humaneness within the context of relationships. This is seen in the practice of love, compassion, human kindness, and so forth. It is also visible in the rule of reciprocity **(shu)** better known as the *Silver Rule*.

▶ Belief in *li* translated "propriety," "rites," or "courtesy." This is the public expression of courtesy and honor that is given by the "Junzi." It is knowing one's place in society.

▶ Belief that human nature is inherently good and that evil is an unnatural occurrence that disrupts the harmony and order of existence.

▶ Belief that the microcosm affects the macrocosm; for example, Confucius voiced the belief that the family is the basic unit of the human world and that, by supporting and educating one's family in *ren* and *li*, one also supports the state and contributes to the existence of government.

◀ SEE ALSO 9.1, *"Fundamental Tenets of Taoism"* ▶

◀ SEE ALSO 3.1, *"Fundamental Tenets of Christianity"* ▶

Importance of Relationships in Confucianism

In Confucianism, filial devotion (called *xiao*) is considered one of the most noble virtues. It stresses that respect must be paid to all people, not only to those living, but also to the dead. The term *filial* is used to refer to the respect and obedience that a child, always discussed by Confucius as a son, should show to his parents (to his father, in particular). Confucius extended this base relationship by varying degrees, eventually creating a "filial network" of sorts, made up of five crucially interconnected relationships. These five relationships are as follows:

1. Father and Son (Parent and Child)

2. Husband and Wife

3. Older Siblings and Younger Siblings

4. Friend to Friend (may also be seen as "Colleague to Colleague" or "Co-worker to Co-worker")

5. Emperor and Subject

These paired sets of relationships were said to apply even to the dead, in the sense that living men existed as sons to their deceased relatives. This belief further popularized the Chinese/Taoist tradition of the religious veneration of one's ancestors.

Eventually, this concept even found its way into the Chinese system of criminal justice for a time. For example, a convicted criminal's punishment was far more severe if the committed crime was a transgression against a parent. This is not surprising, considering that Confucius once held the position of a Minister of Criminal Justice.

WORDS TO GO . . .WORDS TO GO . . .WORDS TO GO

In Chinese, the word **Ju-chia** refers to what Westerners call Confucianism. The word translates as "Scholarly Tradition" or "School of Scholars."

A **Junzi** literally means "nobleman" but the term was morphed by Confucius into the idea of the "superior/perfect man." A Junzi is much like Aristotle's "magnanimous man" concerned with living virtuously and cultivating benevolence throughout society. His is a standard not just for the nobility but for all of society.

The **Silver Rule**, in Confucianism, states: "What one does not want done to one's self, one should not do to others." A similar idea is found in a number of world religions but famously is stated positively by Jesus in the Sermon on the Mount and is known as "the Golden Rule."

Li, in reference to the writings of Xun Zi, refers to certain purifying rites which he claimed a person had to undergo before they could understand the true natures of goodness and righteousness.

10.2 SACRED TEXTS

The Confucian Canon

The Analects

The Five Classics

For centuries it was mistakenly thought that most of the texts in the Confucian Canon—that is, the primary texts studied by adherents of Confucianism—were written by Confucius himself. It is now believed that the Confucian canon is made up of writings that preceded Confucius and texts that were subsequently edited and added later by Confucian scholars.

The Confucian Canon

The text titled *The Analects* contains the teachings of Confucius as written down by his disciples during the final days of his life and shortly after his death. This is the only existing Confucian text that is believed to contain any of the direct ideas or teachings of Confucius himself.

Including *The Analects*, the texts of the Confucian Canon are as follows:

▶ *The Analects:* Called *Lun Yu* in Chinese. The words of Confucius, written by his students from the lessons he taught in Lu during his final days, as well as some that were written by memory shortly after his death.

▶ *M'eng Tzu:* The writings of the Confucian scholar called Mencius, which is a Latinized version of his Chinese name, M'eng Tzu, from which the book is titled. Though Mencius wasn't even born until over a hundred years after the death of Confucius, he became one of the greatest champions of Confucian virtues during his time.

▶ *Ta Hsueh:* Means "The Great Learning." The authorship of the work has been debated for centuries. The essay was originally thought to have been written by either Confucius's grandson or one of his disciples, commonly Tseng Tzu. However, it is now believed to have been written sometime around 200 B.C.E. by an unknown author. This essay later became part of the *Li Chi*, one of the Chinese "Five Classics" (see the next section).

▶ *Chung Yung:* "The Doctrine of the Mean." The date of this work's composition, as well as the name of the author, are unknown. This text is undoubtedly the most mystical in nature among the texts of the Confucian Canon, often addressing the rituals and relationships of Heaven and Earth.

The Analects

Because *The Analects* is a record of Confucius's teachings as remembered by his students, it is more sporadic in its subject matter than the other books of the Confucian Canon. Believed to have been written during and after the last few years of Confucius's life, this book addresses many issues—political, social, and religious. Following are a few excerpts from the text, to give you a more familiar understanding of the work.

"When at home, a young man should be filial, and when he is abroad, he should be respectful to his elders. He should be honest, frank, and earnest. His love should flow to all around him, and he should cultivate friendships with the virtuous. When he has both the time and opportunity, after he has done all these things, he should employ them politely in his studies."

Analects Section 1

"If the people are led by laws, and uniformly and consistently punished for transgressions against the law, they will seek to avoid being, but they have no sense of shame. If the people are led by virtue, and uniformly and consistently encouraged by the rules of propriety, they will have a sense of shame, and moreover they will become good people."

Analects Section 2

"When a prince conducts himself correctly in his personal life, his government will be effective without the need for him to even issue orders. If a prince conducts himself incorrectly in his personal life, he will soon find that even though he issues orders, they are not being carried out by his subordinates."

Analects Section 13

"A public servant who in the face of danger is ready to lay down his life, who when tempted by gain considers first what is righteous, who when making sacrifices focuses on remaining reverent, who when mourning the dead focuses on his grief, should definitely know success."

Analects Section 19

The Five Classics

The "Five Classics," called *Wu-Jing* in Chinese, contain many Confucian writings and ideas, though they are not considered exclusively Confucian texts. These books, however, were at the core of education for most of the Asian world, from China to Korea to the islands of Japan, for hundreds of years. The Five Chinese Classics are as follows:

▶ *Shu Ching:* "The Book of Historical Records." Written during the Eastern Han Dynasty (25 C.E. to 220 C.E.), this text claims to be a record of events that date back to as far as 3,000,000 B.C.E.

▶ *Shih Ching:* "The Book of Odes." This is a collection of poetry written between the years 1000 B.C.E. and 500 B.C.E.

▶ *I Ching:* "The Book of Changes." This text explains ancient Chinese divination practices dating back to 3000 B.C.E. The Chinese believed that because of the unity of the universe the future could be predicted through the study of patterns found in nature. The *I Ching* is a text that contains sixty-four hexagrams used for the interpretation of patterns that emerge from the casting of coins or stalks of a plant. The outcome of this process was believed to give one insight into the future.

◀ *SEE ALSO 9.2, "Sacred Texts of Taoism"* ▶

▶ *Li Chi:* "The Book of Rites." This is a record of approximately 300 years of Chinese religious practices, from the eighth century B.C.E. to the fifth century.

▶ *Ch'un Ch'iu:* Also called the *Lushi Ch'un Qiu,* "The Annals of Spring and Autumn." This well-organized text reads much like an encyclopedia or almanac. This text deals with a number of subjects in great details, including music, agriculture, the conduct of a ruler, and even divination practices. The vast nature of this text may be the reason why, of all Five Classics, this is the most difficult to find translations of.

10.2

10.3 RITUALS AND HOLIDAYS

Confucius Day

Birthday of the Jade Emperor

Ritual vs. the Nature of Humankind

Most of the holidays observed by adherents of Confucianism are the same as those observed in Taoism. This is not surprising, considering that both practices are based upon the same cosmology. The ideas of Confucius are believed to have been heavily influenced by those of Taoism, so he would have seen little to no reason for challenging or changing the extant Taoist perceptions of divinity with his teachings.

◀ SEE ALSO 9.3, *"Rituals and Holidays of Taoism"* ▶

Confucius Day

Confucius Day is celebrated in a number of different countries, usually on September 27, 28, or 29. The variations in date may have been caused by the fact that, due to the lunar variations that decide the dates in which traditional Chinese holidays are celebrated each year, this holiday sometimes coincides with the Mid-Autumn Full Moon Festival.

Though this holiday was originally designated to honor the birth and life of Confucius (he is said to have been born on September 28, 551 B.C.E.), it is now commonly also referred to as "Teacher's Day." Some countries do this in order to honor teachers, since Confucius was himself considered one of the greatest teachers in history. However, in some Communist Asian countries, such as mainland China, this name change may have been done to remove any religious connotations from the holiday.

Birthday of the Jade Emperor

The Jade Emperor's birthday is celebrated on the ninth day of the first lunar month, which usually coincides with the first day of spring. While this holiday is also considered a Taoist holiday, it is important in relation to the ideas of Confucianism.

Confucius believed that people flocked to virtuous leaders and rulers, and that the mythological Jade Emperor was a divine example of the perfect leader/ruler because he ruled over both Heaven and Earth. This idea was manifested by a concept called the **Mandate of Heaven,** which stated that a dynasty must rule wisely, fairly, and virtuously to maintain Heaven's endorsement. When a ruling body fell into corruption or ruled unwisely, it would lose the *Mandate of Heaven* and be replaced by a new Dynasty that the Jade Emperor had chosen.

The night before the holiday, people begin a fast. When midnight approaches, the patriarch of a household (or whoever the head of the household is) leads everyone in the home to the nearest shrine, where they all burn incense and pay respect by bowing or prostrating themselves. Offerings then are made to the Jade Emperor in the form of red rice cakes shaped into the form of tortoise shells. At this time, prayers are made to the Jade Emperor, asking him for forgiveness as well as protection from sickness, harm, evil, natural disasters, and other such misfortunes.

Next, the patriarch of the household offers an invitation to the Jade Emperor, asking that the divine ruler visit the family's home when the next Chinese New Year arrives, as he sometimes comes to Earth to take stock of good and evil people after receiving his report from the Kitchen Lord. Finally, more incense is burned and further offerings of food are placed before the shrine. At this point, other deities may be addressed in prayer if one wishes, as long as they are not placed above the Jade Emperor in respect and importance.

◀ *SEE ALSO 9.3, "Rituals and Holidays of Taoism"* ▶

Ritual vs. the Nature of Humankind

Confucius considered the honoring and observance of traditional Taoist rituals as a way of demonstrating focus, morality, and a respect for order, as well as contributing to order and harmony. This was in line with his belief that human order was a reflection of the divine order of Heaven and that, to achieve this, the people of his time needed to return to the traditional virtues of Taoism, which had fallen into neglect during the war-torn period of his life (see the next section).

Just as he believed that the proper performance of rituals demonstrated a respect for moral, social, and political order, he viewed the neglect or improper observance of rituals as a demonstration of social/political chaos, moral bankruptcy, and spiritual corruption. The patriarch of a household oversaw many rituals and holidays (as seen with the Jade Emperor's birthday). Therefore, if the patriarch of the house did not lead these rituals, he was not ensuring that virtues were being practiced in his own home. Since the home was considered the basic unit of order in Confucius's thought, a household without virtue would eventually lead to a village without virtue. Like an infection, such a thing could spread throughout entire regions, in the eyes of Confucius.

WORDS TO GO . . .WORDS TO GO . . .WORDS TO GO

The **Mandate of Heaven** *(t'ien-ming),* in Confucianism, refers to a concept that is similar to the Western ideas of Divine Right or Divine Principle, in which a ruler is believed to have been chosen by some divine entity. However, unlike the Western concepts of divinely chosen rulers, the *Mandate of Heaven* could and would be changed if the Jade Emperor deemed a ruler unworthy to rule the people.

10.4 ORIGINS AND FOUNDER

From Administrator to Teacher

Confucius Comes Home

Confucius was born in 551 B.C.E. in the Chinese province of Lu, which is now called Shantung. His family is said to have been rather poor, likely because his father (though he had been a successful official in his lifetime) died when Confucius was only about 3 years old. Though he did not have much money, Confucius had a burning desire for knowledge. He was extremely well read and knowledgeable, despite being primarily self-educated. During his youth, Confucius worked as a stable manager and granary bookkeeper for the local ruler. Though the job was of low status, the experience opened his eyes to the injustices of peasants heavily taxed to support the leisure and luxury of the small ruling class.

Confucius married at the age of 19 and soon became a local administrator. He quickly proved himself to be a moral, wise, fair, and diligent administrator. In 501 B.C.E., Confucius left the land of Lu when he received an appointment as governor of the Chung-tu province. Less than a year later, he was promoted to the position of Minister of Criminal Justice.

From Administrator to Teacher

The exact age at which Confucius began his teaching career is unknown. However, most sources agree that is was sometime shortly before he reached the age of 30. One Chinese legend states that Confucius encountered the wise sage Lao Tzu, whose teachings made up the foundation of Taoism, sometime in the year 518 B.C.E. The legend also claims that Lao Tzu harshly rebuked Confucius for his unnecessary adherence to formality and for his arrogant, "know-it-all" nature.

Confucius eventually returned to Lu in 515 B.C.E. Upon his return to Lu, most sources state that he did not return to government, but occupied himself with study. He also began teaching to an increasing number of students. No one can be certain of exactly what Confucius was teaching at this time. However, we can guess from the writings about him that the curriculum likely included Chinese history, musical studies, Taoist rituals, the Five Classics, and poetry.

Sometime near the turn of the century, when Confucius was in his late 40s or early 50s, he was finally fed up with the corruption, immorality, and debauchery that he witnessed in politics. So he left his homeland of Lu and began wandering the lands of eastern China, with a number of his pupils in tow. However, some historians believe that Confucius more likely left Lu because of threats to his life.

Confucius was loyal to the Zhou Dynasty (which had been extremely pro-Taoist). The ruling clan of Lu at this time, the Chi clan, owed its power and authority over the province to the fact that they were no longer bound by the rule of the Zhou Dynasty.

◀ *SEE ALSO 9.5, "Historical Development of Taoism"* ▶

Confucius and his band of pupils traveled (in no particular order) through the Chinese provinces of Ch'en, Wei, and Sung. On more than a few occasions, the group members' lives were jeopardized as a result of their teachings. In fact, as they traveled through the province of Sung, Confucius narrowly avoided assassination.

Yet although Confucius had violent enemies, the rulers of each province through which he traveled protected him and treated him respectfully. Some rulers even paid the knowledgeable teacher for his counsel in matters of politics, criminal justice, and even agriculture.

During these travels, Confucius seems to have focused much of his energy on developing his ideas on the proper conduct of government. With each province, the number of students traveling with Confucius became greater. Because of this, it is commonly believed that the Confucian school of thought was officially established during these years.

Confucius Comes Home

Though some students followed Confucius until the end, many of his initial pupils chose to stay behind. In fact, a number of them were actually awarded positions of administration and governance for the Chi clan. When Confucius was invited to return to Lu in his late 60s, many believe that the influence of his former students played a large part. Confucius continued to teach in Lu for three or five more years (sources vary), until his death at the age of about 72, in approximately 479 B.C.E.

When Confucius died, it is said that he did so with a heavy heart. He did not witness the "golden age" for which he had hoped and worked, a return to the Taoist virtues of the Zhou Dynasty. Even more, he is said to have died disen-chanted with his own life, believing that all of his hard work, idealism, and optimism had been for nothing and that the world was no better than it had been before his teachings. However, no matter what Confucius believed when he died, his students did not share his belief that it was all for nothing. After his death, they began transcribing his teachings into written works (refer back to the section "The Sacred Texts of Confucianism," in this chapter).

10.5 HISTORICAL DEVELOPMENT

The Hundred Schools of Thought

Mencius and Xun Zi

Burning Books and Burying Scholars

The Han Dynasty and Beyond

The Cultural Revolution

Second perhaps only to Taoism, Confucianism is closely tied to Chinese history. In a land where dynasties often rose and fell, Confucianism experienced a roller coaster of treatments from the ruling clans of China, from favoritism to neglect to persecution. However, whether or not a ruling dynasty endorsed Confucianism, like a seed that grows, it was ever present among the scholars of China who followed the life and teachings of Confucius ... some of them following its teachings to their deaths.

The Hundred Schools of Thought

The first organized systems of Confucianism are now believed to have been created by Confucius's disciples following his death. Some are even thought to have been created by the disciples of Confucius's disciples. During a period called the "Hundred Schools of Thought" (lasting from approximately 722 B.C.E. until about 221 B.C.E.), there was a great surge in the spread of philosophical ideas. Interestingly enough, this "golden age" of reason in China took place simultaneously with two of the most chaotic and violent periods of Chinese history, known as "The Period of Spring and Autumn" (lasting from 722 B.C.E. until 481 B.C.E.) and "The Warring States Period" (lasting from 480 B.C.E. until 221 B.C.E.).

During this great philosophical age, a number of talented thinkers and debaters arose as champions of Confucian thought. Two key figures among them were Mencius (known as M'eng Tzu in Chinese, and the author of a primary Confucian text that bears his name as the title) and Xun Zi. These two men were the first to begin developing Confucianism into more than just a lifestyle philosophy—into an ethical and political doctrine as well. Through vicious debates and competitions of rhetoric, the two men were able to gain the favor of the noble clans and even dynastic rulers.

10.5

Mencius and Xun Zi

Mencius's treatment of Confucianism focused on the dualistic form of human nature. His teachings offered concrete definitions of morality, addressed what was needed to improve the government of his time, and explained that human nature is inherently good (an idea that Confucius had expressed as well).

Xun Zi, on the other hand, deviated more from the original teachings of Confucius. He also vehemently opposed a number of Mencius's ideas. Xun Zi's treatment of Confucius's teachings was far more structured in nature than was Mencius's. In contrast to both Confucius and Mencius, Xun Zi's teachings were based upon the belief that human nature is inherently evil. Therefore, a human being must become educated and must be exposed to the purifying rites (a concept called *li*) before he or she can understand the true natures of righteousness and goodness.

Some of Xun Zi's disciples, including Han Fei and Li Si, continued their teacher's path of deviation from Confucius by joining a group known as the Legalists. This group exercised a form of law-based totalitarianism, preaching the righteousness of actively seeking out and punishing the wicked, who (by Mencius rationale) were "everywhere." Such ideas contrasted greatly with the virtue-based teachings of Confucius.

However, the Legalist group provided the means by which the ruthless warlord Qin Shi Huang Di unified the land of China under the Qin Dynasty. He used the ideas of the Legalists to maintain strict control over the country, primarily by placing extreme state-sponsored regulations upon just about every human activity one could imagine.

Confucius's dream of a unified China, a country free from war and chaos, was (quite ironically) achieved by a school of thought that stood in polar opposition to his own teachings on human virtue. Han Fei and Li Si, disciples of Xun Zi, became advisors to Qin Shi Huang Di. Li Si soon became one of the top advisors. In approximately 221 B.C.E., Li Si, a self-proclaimed "Confucian scholar," brought an end to the period of the Hundred Schools of Thought and used his influence with Emperor Qin Shi Huang Di to plunge all other Confucian scholars into a new period of darkness, plagued by censorship, violence, tyranny, and fear.

Burning Books and Burying Scholars

The period in Chinese history during which the land fell under the tyrannical rule of the Qin Dynasty is often called "The Burning of Books and the Burying of Scholars." This period began when, in 221 B.C.E., Li Si suggested to Qin Shi

Huang Di that scholars were a threat to the security of his rule. When the ruler asked Li Si how to deal with the matter, Li Si basically told him that free speech must be outlawed and all unapproved political opinions silenced. Claiming that the scholars (most of whom were Confucians) of the time were breeding dissent and promoting unrest among the people by spreading false information and publishing libelous writings, Li Si carried out his campaign against the Hundred Schools of Thought.

The true horror began in 213 B.C.E., when Li Si ordered the confiscation and burning of all books, pamphlets, and other such writings from any scholars of the Hundred Schools of Thought. Of course, his own writings were excluded from this. Qin Shi Huang Di then went a step further, ordering the seizure and burning of all Chinese history books. He feared that the Confucian-endorsed Zhou Dynasty concept of the Mandate of Heaven (*t'ien-ming*) might eventually become a threat to the legitimacy of his rule. He then had them rewritten to legitimize his position as emperor.

The madness of Qin Shi Huang Di's and Li Si's campaign went even further, and they soon ordered that all books within the imperial archives—a treasure trove of histories, poetry collections, classical writings, and even religious materials—that were not written during the Qin Dynasty be handed over for incineration. Only books on subjects of technological, medicinal, or agricultural value were excluded from destruction. Even the discussion or mention of a burned text was an offense punishable by death. Anyone who published unapproved materials during this period of time was also subject to execution.

Qin Shi Huang Di, paranoid man that he was, began to fear the approach of death as he grew older. He eventually hired and generously paid two alchemists who swore that they could bring him an elixir that would grant him immortality. When, of course, they were unable to deliver on their promise, Qin Shi Huang Di was enraged by their deception and soon took out his wrath on every scholar in the land.

Qin Shi Huang Di ordered hundreds of scholars (the majority of whom were Confucians) arrested, brought by force to the capital, and buried alive. Fusu, son of Qin Shi Huang Di and heir of the Qin Dynasty, begged his father to see reason, claiming that such an act would lead to unrest and anger among the people. Unfortunately, Qin Shi Huang Di would not be swayed. Original reports claimed that over 450 scholars were buried alive. However, later reports by the Chinese historian Wei Hung revised the number to well over a thousand. Interestingly enough, many historians believe that the downfall of the Qin Dynasty began with this act of unnecessary cruelty.

As Confucius would likely have said, the Qin Dynasty lost the Mandate of Heaven, which passed to the Han Dynasty.

The Han Dynasty and Beyond

The Han Dynasty (206 B.C.E. to 220 C.E.) marked a revival of Confucianism. The teachings of Confucius and Confucian scholars became the approved state philosophy and basis for governance, during the Western (or Early Han Dynasty, 206 B.C.E. to 24 C.E.) as well as early Eastern (or Later Han Dynasty, 25 C.E. to 22 C.E.) Han Dynasties. In fact, the Confucian classics were used to create a government examination system for administrators and government officials, and were at the center of the curriculum for the Han Dynasty's education system. Shrines to Confucius were constructed all over the country, to encourage the spread of Confucius's teachings.

During the Tang Dynasty (618 C.E. to 907 C.E.) a new sect of Confucian scholars, called Neo-Confucians in the West, sought to revive interest in Confucianism, which had begun to wane since the fall of the Han Dynasty and had been overshadowed by the state endorsement of Taoism during the Southern and Northern Dynasties (386 C.E. to 589 C.E.). They further increased their efforts during the Song Dynasty (960 C.E. to 1127 C.E.). Neo-Confucian scholars such as Zhu Xi expanded the metaphysical aspects of Confucianism and focused less upon the moral virtues that were the original basis of Confucius's teachings.

◄ *SEE ALSO 9.5, "Historical Development of Taoism"* ▶

The Cultural Revolution

During the 1960s, Confucianism came under fire from the "Cultural Revolution" that was then taking place in the Communist state of the People's Republic of China. Confucianism was seen as a naïve philosophy of the old world of mysticism. The Communist regime had long championed the view that "religion is poison," and Confucianism was not spared its wrath. The People's Republic claimed that the superstitious ways of "old" China had now become obstacles to the country's modernization and expansion efforts.

10.6 PRESENT-DAY FACTS

The influence of Confucian ideas can still be seen in the world of today. While few countries would claim Confucius as an influence on their governments, the country of Singapore still proclaims itself as the only true "Confucian State" still in existence. One may also still witness the influence of Confucian ideas in South Korea. This is not surprising: the entire country of Korea was itself once a "Confucian State" from the fourteenth century C.E. right up to the early twentieth century.

A number of modern, Confucian-inspired philosophical movements have arisen in modern times, such as that of New Confucianism. Such sects seek to discover new ideas to remedy governmental and social problems by studying the ideas, concepts, and systems of Confucius and the Confucian scholars who followed him.

As with Shinto, many adherents of Confucianism practice it in conjunction with other religions (such as Taoism or Buddhism). Therefore, the available estimates on the number of Confucian adherents vary greatly, from as few as 5 million to as many as 350 million adherents worldwide. Today Confucianism is most strongly practiced in the countries of China, Burma, Thailand, and Japan.

◀ *SEE ALSO 9.6, "Present-Day Facts of Taoism"* ▶

10.6

11

BUDDHISM

11.1 FUNDAMENTAL TENETS

Basic Information on Buddhism

The Core Beliefs of Buddhism

The Three Jewels

The Four Noble Truths

The Eightfold Path

More than any other religious perspective, Buddhism has had the greatest impact on the evolution of Asian civilization. Originating in India, the religion of Buddhism spread to China, Korea, Japan, and eventually into regions of Southwest Asia through missionary activity. Buddhist missionaries sought to demonstrate the similarities of their religion to the religions of other Asian cultures in order to proselytize. In doing so, over time, some syncretism of religious perspectives took place. This has led to a family of religions that is Buddhist. Theravada, Mahayana, and Tibetan Buddhism clearly have the same family of origin, but much like siblings in a family they each have their own uniqueness. In this chapter we will seek to present the features of similarity across the Buddhist perspective.

Basic Information on Buddhism

▶ Origin Date: Sixth century B.C.E. (unconfirmed).

▶ Originator: Siddhartha Gautama (later called the Buddha).

▶ View of God: Primarily nontheistic, with somewhat polytheistic views in some sects.

▶ Dietary Restrictions: Primarily vegetarian. However, while not *all* practicing Buddhists are vegetarians, all Buddhist monks are.

▶ Life/Death View: Belief in **samsara,** the cycle of reincarnation caused by the accumulation of **kharma.**

▶ Lifestyle Foci: Stresses a belief in the sanctity of *all* life, as well as a disciplined practice of prayer and/or meditation.

▶ Worship Restrictions: Dependent on which sect of Buddhism a person follows. However, there are no restrictions or requirements to practice Buddhism.

The Core Beliefs of Buddhism

▶ Belief in the teachings of the Buddha, and adherence to the Four Noble Truths and the Eightfold Path.

▶ Belief that all suffering arises from the ego, that is, from a sense of a permanent self which is ultimately an illusion.

▶ Belief that **nirvana** (enlightenment) is available to all regardless of social status or gender.

▶ Belief that achieving *nirvana* is the means to ending the wheel of rebirth.

Buddhism is in large part a response to the Hindu religious perspective of Gautama's era. It rejects the caste system and the authority of the Vedas on some significant issues. It is important to note, however, that Buddhism affirms the core doctrines of Hinduism: *samsara* and *kharma*; and redefines other notions like **Dharma**. It would be accurate to say that Buddhism is a fresh attempt to solve the same problems that Hinduism and Jainism had already attempted to solve.

◁ SEE ALSO 13.1, *"Fundamental Tenets of Hindu Dharma"* ▷

◁ SEE ALSO 14.1, *"Fundamental Tenets of Jainism"* ▷

The Three Jewels

In some sects of Buddhism, it is believed that reciting and accepting the Three Jewels officially makes one a legitimate Buddhist. The Three Jewels, called the **triratna** in its original Sanskrit, is also sometimes called the "Triple Jewel" or "Triple Gem." This encompasses three basic proclamations of the Buddhist faith. There are two basic forms of the Three Jewels, depending on the sect. The traditional Three Jewels of Theravada Buddhism, which is most widely practiced in India, encompasses very straightforward and simple proclamations of faith:

11.1

1. *Buddham saranam gachammi:* I go to take refuge in the Buddha.

2. *Dharmam saranam gachammi:* I go to take refuge in the law of *Dharma*.

3. *Sangham saranam gachammi:* I go to take refuge in the community of the **Sangha.**

Mahayana Buddhism, which is more widely practiced in China and Japan, varies slightly from the Theravada version. Though the initial proclamations of the Three Jewels remain the same, secondary, explanatory passages have been added to the Mahayana version:

1. I will take refuge in the Buddha, and wish that all sentient beings come to understand the great way and will also make this greatest vow.

2. I will take refuge in the law of *Dharma*, and wish that all sentient beings will study deeply the **sutras,** and in so doing gain an ocean of understanding.

3. I will take refuge in the *Sangha*, and wish all sentient beings to lead the community onwards, harmoniously and without obstruction.

The Four Noble Truths

The Four Noble Truths make up the foundation of Buddhist belief. They are four statements regarding the nature of human suffering and are revelations experienced by the Buddha during a very long period of meditation. The Four Noble Truths are as follows:

1. Life is suffering. (This is sometimes translated as "There is suffering.")

2. Suffering is caused by ignorance and desire.

3. Suffering can end only when *nirvana* has been achieved, which can occur only when ignorance has been overcome and desire has been defeated.

4. The Eightfold Path is the way to *nirvana*, thereby bringing an end to suffering.

Many scholars debate that *suffering* is too simple a term to replace the original Sanskrit word, **Dukkha,** used in the first version of the Four Noble Truths. Many Sanskrit terms have multiple and/or integrated definitions. As a result, many Sanskrit terms do not have English-language equivalents. While *Dukkha* can be defined as suffering, the integrated definitions for the word are "suffering," "hard to endure," "intolerable," and "insatiable."

The Eightfold Path

The Eightfold Path is technically considered the fourth Noble Truth. Sometimes called "The Middle Way" or "The Noble Path," the Eightfold Path of Buddhism is the method by which one is meant to eliminate the suffering of *dukkha* and negative *kharma*, achieve *nirvana*, and escape the wheel of *samsara*.

The Eightfold Path, as its name suggests, consists of eight disciplines that lead to nirvana. Once one realizes the impermanence of the self and how grasping at the transitory only leads to frustration and disappointment, there is a realization of interdependence rather than self-absorption. These practices are intended to encourage goodwill and peace, as well as promote a balanced harmony with one's environment and fellow living beings. The eight points of the Eightfold Path are as follows:

1. **Right Understanding/View:** Maintain a simple outlook by seeing things for what they are. Understand and accept reality joyfully, with neither fear nor hope.

2. **Right Intent/Thought:** Once one has assumed Right Understanding, one must apply it to life with proper Intent. This is achieved by renouncing desire for selflessness, being properly motivated by goodwill instead of greed, and choosing a peaceful life by rejecting the temptation to act in ways that are harmful to others.

3. **Right Speech:** When one has a proper view and pure intentions, one's speech should reflect this. Speak plainly and honestly. Do not try to fool, bully, or manipulate other people with deceitful or angry words. Speak only the words that need to be said, and do so with simplicity and sincerity.

4. **Right Action/Discipline:** Practice a frugal and simple lifestyle. Abandon needless indulgences and frivolous possessions. Such things complicate one's life and relationships, leading to desire, jealousy, increased debts, and unnecessary financial hardship.

5. **Right Living:** Earn an honest living by assuming an occupation. Be joyful and hardworking in your job, whatever it may be. Do not waste your working hours by bemoaning how you wish to be home or desire a job that is more "important" or "glamorous." Every job is important, from a janitor to a soldier to a world leader, as each contributes to the whole of humanity in its own way. However, do not assume illegal, dishonest, or harmful occupations, such as slave trading, drug dealing, or killing for profit.

6. **Right Effort:** Put all the previous precepts into every effort or task you undertake. Negative thoughts cannot be eliminated. Therefore, when negative thoughts enter your mind, accept and recognize them, and find positive aspects to counter them. By doing so, one will act with love, compassion, and kindness in all one does.

7. **Right Mindfulness:** Live in and be mindful of the present moment. Do not waste time or energy dwelling upon the past or worrying about the future. Avoid entering situations with preconceived notions, as they hinder one's ability to see the truth of matters with Right Understanding. In dealing with other people, try to see things from their points of view and avoid being judgmental.

8. **Right Concentration:** Simply put, *pay attention* to and be mindful of one's place in the cosmos. Meditate often and seek inner harmony. In meditation/prayer, do not allow oneself to become distracted by preconceived expectations or selfish desires.

The first two disciplines (right understanding and thoughts) are thought to lead to wisdom about the self and reality. The practices of right speech, action, and livelihood emphasize the need for the cultivation of morality. The final three disciplines (right effort, mindfulness, and concentration) are thought to lead to mental discipline and the goal of stillness of mind.

WORDS TO GO . . .WORDS TO GO . . .WORDS TO GO

Samsara is the cycle of life, death, and rebirth that will continue until an individual achieves enlightenment through *nirvana.*

Nirvana is the blissful state of enlightenment, in which one is freed from the cycle of *samsara. Nirvana* is a state in which one is completely free from all desires and material attachments.

Dharma (law), in Buddhism, refers to the teachings of the Buddha and later traditions and interpretations that are developed by the various sects within Buddhism.

Kharma is the accumulation of either positive or negative energies in one's lifetime, which are the result of one's thoughts, words, and actions.

Roughly translated, the word **Sangha** means "gathering" or "assembly." In Buddhism, it refers to the "spiritual community" of Buddhists. Depending on the sect or country, the word is used to refer to either all Buddhist practitioners, monks or nuns, or those who are thought to have achieved *nirvana.*

Triratna is the original Sanskrit name for the Three Jewels.

Sutras, in Buddhism, are narrative sections of Buddhist texts. Often this word is used in Buddhism to refer to the dialogues of the Buddha in sacred texts.

Dukkha is a Sanskrit term that refers to the pain and suffering (either in body or mind) that are the result of desire and ignorance.

11.2 SACRED TEXTS

The Pali Canon

The Mahayana Sutras

There are two main sects of Buddhism, from which all other sects derive—
Theravada and Mahayana. Both of these sects have their own primary text. The
Theravada sect primarily uses the Pali Canon text, while the Mahayana sect
uses the Mahayana Sutras. Therefore, we focus on these two texts here. It is
important to note that the following should in no way be considered a complete
summary of Buddhist texts. There exists a plethora of texts on the ideas and
beliefs of Buddhism, some of which were written as early as the last few decades.

The traditional Pali Canon belongs to the Theravada sect of Buddhism, also
called Southern Buddhism. The Mahayana sect of Buddhism considers the Pali
Canon somewhat outdated, but not all non-Theravada sects agree with this
claim. Many non-Theravada sects of Buddhism grant the Pali Canon equal status
with other, more recent interpretations and commentaries, such as the Mahayana Sutras. Adherents of the Mahayana sect of Buddhism believe that the
Mahayana Sutras are more accurate and believe that some were directly handed
down by the Buddha.

The Pali Canon

Initially, the Buddha conveyed his teachings orally. It is known that he did not
write any of the current Buddhist texts. The teachings he conveyed were passed
down orally until they were finally written down, roughly 400 years after his
death. As a result of the large time gap between the Buddha's life and the writing
of his teachings, it cannot be said for certain how much of the Pali Canon accurately conveys his original teachings. Nevertheless, the Pali Canon is considered
the "Word of the Buddha." However, the Pali Canon also contains a number of
works that originate from later **bodhisattvas.**

The traditional Pali Canon is divided into three parts, which are referred to as
pitakas. Roughly translated, *pitaka* means "basket." Since there are three "baskets" to the Pali Canon, it is sometimes called the **tripitaka,** meaning "three
baskets." It is commonly believed that the word "basket" is used to indicate a
basket being delivered by a messenger or carrier, as each category offers its own
unique collection of philosophical and spiritual insights.

11.2

The Vinaya Pitaka

The *Vinaya Pitaka*, or "Basket of Monastic Discipline," is the first section of the Pali Canon and focuses upon the behavioral and ethical codes that should be followed by the *Sangha*, used here to refer specifically to Buddhist monks and nuns. Many of the guidelines contained within the *Vinaya Pitaka* are preceded by stories that explain the origins of each and/or provide a validation of the Lord Buddha's declarations. According to the stories of the *Vinaya Pitaka*, the Buddha developed the rules within as rational and necessary reactions to the behaviors and issues of his early disciples.

The Sutta Pitaka

The *Sutta Pitaka*, or "Basket of Threads," offers firsthand written accounts of the Lord Buddha's teachings. This section of the Pali Canon is the most important, as it is the only section of the text that all Buddhist sects, both Theravada and non-Theravada, consider to be the authentic teachings of the Buddha. In non-Theravada sects, it is sometimes referred to by a different title, but the content remains the same.

The *Sutta Pitaka* is arranged in five subsections, called **nikayas.** The first four sections are written in prose form and consist of stories that follow general themes. The fifth and final section of the *Sutta Pitaka* is a compilation of assorted works, some written in prose and others in poetic verse.

The Abhidharma Pitaka

The third and final "basket" of the Pali Canon is the *Abhidharma Pitaka*, or "Basket of Higher Dharma." This section contains the basic elements of the *Sutta Pitaka*, only with further elaboration. This collection consists of seven books, focusing only on the principles that dictate the nature of the mind, spirit, and matter, as introduced by the *Sutta Pitaka*.

The Mahayana Sutras

Most historians agree that the bulk of the Mahayana Sutras were written down sometime between 100 B.C.E. and 200 C.E. However, the authors of most of the sutras are unknown. These sutras are central to Mahayana Buddhism, and different sects often focus on different sutras. For the most part, the Sanskrit texts upon which they were originally based have been lost. The Mahayana Sutras survived only through their translated versions, which are mainly in Chinese and Tibetan.

The Lotus Sutra

The Lotus Sutra is one of the largest among the Mahayana Sutras. Most modern historians agree that the Lotus Sutra was written in India, sometime between 100 B.C.E. and 150 C.E. The Mahayana Sects of Buddhism believe this Sutra to be Lord Buddha's most important teaching regarding the highest state of enlightenment (sometimes referred to in Western speech as "Buddhahood"). The Lotus Sutra has much to say about the *bodhisattva* path, which is of primary importance in the Mahayana school of Buddhism.

The Lotus Sutra focuses on faith and religious discipline. It represents the central idea of Mahayana Buddhism, that the path to Buddhahood is not restricted to those who practice monastic asceticism, but open to all who worship the Buddha, in any form. This Mahayana concept is given great praise and attention in the second section of the Lotus Sutra, which states that all paths eventually lead to the enlightenment of the Buddha.

The Vimalakirti Sutra

The Vimalakirti Sutra is considered one of the most well constructed of the Sanskrit/Indian Mahayana Sutras. The sutra elaborates upon one of the main principles that separates Mahayana Buddhism from the beliefs of Theravada Buddhism. This principle has to do with nonduality, that all things are one in their separations to the enlightened mind—yin and yang. This sutra was originally addressed to high-ranking Buddhist disciples by a *bodhisattva* named Vimalakirti, who wanted to explain the concept of **Sunyata** (which, roughly translated, means "emptiness") to them in depth. Eventually, the sutra ends with silence.

11.2

WORDS TO GO . . .WORDS TO GO . . .WORDS TO GO

Bodhisattva (future Buddha) is used differently within Theravada and Mahayana Buddhism. The Lord Buddha refers to himself as a bodhisattva or someone "bound for enlightenment." This is seen in some of the stories of his previous lives found in the *Jataka Tales*. It simply means "someone on the path to liberation." In the Mahayana tradition there are many bodhisattvas. These are individuals who during their lives made vows to become bodhisattvas, postponing their achievement of nirvana in order to aid other human beings to enlightenment and release.

Pitaka means "basket" and, in Buddhism, refers to a section of the Pali Canon.

Tripitaka means "three baskets" and is a Sanskrit term often used to refer to the Pali Canon.

Nikayas are the five subsections of the *Sutta Pitaka.*

Sunyata means "emptiness." In Buddhism, it refers to the concept of nonduality.

11.3 RITUALS AND HOLIDAYS

Buddha Day

Dharma Day

Anapanasati Day

Sangha Day

Some holidays are universal to Buddhism, and observed by all adherents. However, the manner in which these holidays are observed often differs from one country to the next. Also, there are some holidays that are specific only to certain sects of Buddhism. For example, Tibetan Buddhists observe a number of holidays that are not observed by Buddhists of other sects.

Buddha Day

Buddha Day, also known as *Vesak* or *Visakha Puja*, celebrates the birth, enlightenment, and death of the Buddha. This holiday is considered the most sacred of the Buddhist calendar. In most countries, Buddha Day is celebrated on the first full moon of May. However, in most Japanese sects of Buddhism, the holiday is celebrated in three parts:

1. **Buddha's Birth:** Celebrated on April 8.

2. **Buddha's Enlightenment:** Celebrated on December 8 (in other countries, this day is celebrated as a separate holiday, called Bodhi Day").

3. **Buddha's Death:** Celebrated on February 15.

The celebration of Buddha Day varies from one country to another. However, a number of common practices still take place regardless of the country in which it is celebrated.

The observance of Buddha Day begins before dawn, when Buddhists assemble in the early morning hours at their local temples or shrines to meditate. Often Buddhist monks are present, chanting sutras.

A practice known as "Bathing the Buddha" often occurs throughout the celebration of Buddha Day. Monks pour water over the shoulders of Buddha statues. This is done as a reminder that Buddhists must seek to purify their bodies, minds, and spirits. Offerings of fruit, rice, or coins are often made to the monks, temples, or shrines, laid out on an altar. This is done as a way of showing respect to the Lord Buddha and paying homage to the sanctity of his teachings.

Dharma Day

Dharma Day celebrates the beginning of the Buddha's teaching. The first teaching of the Lord Buddha to his first five disciples is called **Dharmachakra,** "The Turn of the Dharma Wheel." Dharma Day is a chance to express gratitude to the Lord Buddha and the *bodhisattvas*, who shared their knowledge of enlightenment with humankind.

Dharma Day is celebrated mainly by reading Buddhist sutras and texts. Buddhists view this day as a time for meditating upon the teachings of the Buddha. For Buddhist monks, nuns, and/or layman, Dharma Day is usually celebrated in their respective temples or monasteries.

Anapanasati Day

At the end of one of his retreats during the rainy season, the Buddha was overjoyed with the progress of his monks. As a result, he insisted that they extend their retreat for an additional month. On the day of the full moon that marked the end of their four-month retreat, the Lord Buddha instructed them all with a commentary on **anapanasati,** or "mindfulness of one's breathing," which is now a part of the Mahayana Sutras, found in the Anapanasati Sutra.

Sangha Day

Sangha Day is also known as the "Fourfold Assembly," or *Magha Puja* Day. This holiday is meant to honor the *Sangha*, the Buddhist community. This day is celebrated as an opportunity to reaffirm one's spiritual discipline to the *Sangha*, as well as one's commitment to the beliefs, practices, teachings, and traditions of Buddhism.

11.3

Historically, Sangha Day is a commemoration of the day when approximately 1,250 enlightened monks are said to have spontaneously assembled, without invitation, to hear the teachings of the Buddha at a sermon he gave at Veluvana Vihara (his place of residence, which was dedicated to him by the king, Raja Gaha). At this gathering, the Buddha gave his first sermon on the **Patimokkha,** which are the codes and regulations of the Buddhist monastic order.

At the nonmonastic level, Sangha Day is traditionally a day when gifts are exchanged between friends and family. Interestingly enough, Sangha Day is primarily observed by Buddhists in the West (Europe and the United States). In Asia and India, the festival of Sangha Day is somewhat obscure and is not widely celebrated.

The celebration of Sangha Day often includes group chanting sessions, lighting of oil lamps, and time for personal meditation.

WORDS TO GO . . .WORDS TO GO . . .WORDS TO GO

Dharmachakra, literally translated, means "Wheel of Law" (*Dharma* = law, *Chakra* = wheel/circle). In Buddhism, it refers to the first teaching of the Buddha to his original five disciples.

Anapanasati means "mindfulness of one's breathing" and is the title of a Mahayana Sutra regarding the same subject.

Patimokkha is the code of ethics and behavior for the *Sangha* monastic community, said to have been given in a sermon to 1,250 monks by the Lord Buddha himself.

11.4 ORIGINS AND FOUNDER

There are many accounts that have grown up around the story of the Buddha's life making it very difficult to separate fact from fiction. While there is no single authoritative biography, many of the stories follow a similar outline.

The Buddha was born the son of a prince of the Shakya clan (which is why he is sometimes referred to as *Shakyamuni,* or "Prince of the Shakya") in the ancient city of Kapilavastu in what is now Nepal. His birth in the ruling class afforded him wealth, education, and privilege. He was educated in classical Hinduism. Before his enlightenment, at which time he became the Buddha (meaning "Enlightened One"), his given name was Siddhartha Gautama.

Gautama lived a life of ease and luxury, never stepping beyond the walls of his father's palace. His father hoped that his son would never know suffering, and therefore kept the prince in blissful yet ignorant seclusion. One day, when Gautama was 29 years old, he slipped away from the palace. At this time, the young prince saw three (in some versions, four) passing sights:

1. A wrinkled and bent elderly person.

2. A man with a loathsome disease.

3. A rotting corpse.

4. Finally, in some versions of the tale, Gautama sees a peaceful monk or an ascetic.

Shocked by these revelations of suffering, which he had never known, Gautama sought to find the cause as well as how it could be stopped. These sights led to what is now called the "Great Renunciation." Gautama gave up his right to rule his father's kingdom, left his wife and child, and departed from the city of Kapilavastu in search of answers to questions about suffering, death, and release from the wheel of rebirth. The king, Gautama's father, intended to prevent his son's departure. However, one Buddhist tale states that the powers of Heaven made it so that his horse's hooves did not touch the ground, and therefore made no sound. As he approached the palace gates, the powers of heaven opened them without making a sound.

Gautama lived the life of an ascetic for six years in his quest for knowledge concerning release from *samsara.* His severe ascetic practices, however, did not bring the enlightenment he sought.

For a time, Gautama meditated under a tree until he had the epiphany that revealed what are now referred to as the "Four Noble Truths." *Bodhi* (enlightenment) is the name commonly given to the tree under which the Buddha sat and meditated. One Buddhist story tells of how the servants of darkness often threw rocks and other missiles at the meditating former prince. However, upon reaching him, they all transformed harmlessly into beautiful flowers.

After his enlightenment, the Buddha preached a message that announced that neither extreme asceticism nor indulgence will bring about salvation or release from the wheel of rebirth. He preached a "middle way" that was open to all regardless of caste or sex. At the time this was a revolutionary teaching in India. The Buddha's middle way is centered on deep meditation and detachment from the body and the world. Over the next 45 years of his life, the Buddha spread his message traveling around India and forming monastic *Sanghas*. The message was eventually taken to other Asian countries through missionary activity. India seems to have been turning Buddhist during the following centuries but eventually returns to Hinduism as the religion of the masses. The departure from Buddhism back to Hinduism was so complete that in India today there is virtually no Buddhist presence. The vast majority of Buddhists reside in countries outside the land of its origins.

11.5 HISTORICAL DEVELOPMENT

Theravada

Mahayana

Zen/Ch'an

Nichiren Buddhism

Pure Land Buddhism

Tibetan Buddhism

Buddhism spread relatively quickly and in a number of different directions, some-times causing the events of its development to occur in overlapping time periods that can be confusing if considered simultaneously. Therefore, it is far easier to understand the historical development of Buddhism by familiarizing oneself with a brief history of each main sect. Though Theravada and Mahayana are the two main schools of Buddhism, a number of other sects later arose—namely, Zen, Nichiren, Pure Land, and Tibetan Buddhism.

Theravada

Theravada, or "Way of the Elders," is considered the oldest sect of Buddhism. Theravada claims its origins date to the sixth century B.C.E., during the time of the Buddha. Theravada Buddhism claims to continue with the original teach-ings of the Buddha, as written down in the scriptures of the Pali Canon by his early disciples.

Theravada Buddhists believe that only an enlightened few can attain the state of Buddhahood, and only through undertaking a difficult and disciplined lifestyle of ascetic monasticism. Theravada values wisdom and discipline above all other virtues, and values meditation over ritual. In addition to the Pali Canon, the *Visuddhimagga*, written in the fifth century B.C.E. by the *bodhisattva* scholar Bud-dhaghosa, is a secondary but central text of Theravada Buddhism.

Mahayana

Mahayana Buddhism is often referred to as the "Buddhism of the people" because this sect opposes the Theravada belief that only a select few can attain the state of Buddhahood. In the first century C.E., Mahayana Buddhism split from Theravada. For the next few centuries, the sect spread quickly across Asia. It was enthusiastically accepted in Korea, Japan, China, and Tibet, and often integrated easily with the pre-existing religious philosophies of those countries, such as Taoism, Shinto, and other Eastern indigenous religions.

In contrast to Theravada Buddhism, Mahayana values compassion for others and a love for all creation over wisdom and ascetic practice. Mahayana also defied Theravada ideas by personifying the "Buddha Nature" into a figure that could be worshipped. Mahayana Buddhism is the root from which nearly all other forms of Buddhism sprouted. All the following schools of Buddhism originated from Mahayana.

Zen/Ch'an

Zen (Japanese), called *Ch'an* in Chinese, was founded in China by a monk named Potitamo (a transliteration of the Indian name Bodhidharma) sometime around the seventh century C.E. Potitamo integrated the ideas of both Buddhism and Taoism, creating a new sect of Buddhism that he called *Ch'an*. Simply put, Zen Buddhism is a path to enlightenment through simple living and meditation.

The most well-known *Ch'an* temple is that of Shaolin, the birthplace of the fighting style of Kung Fu. This is, perhaps, the reason Zen/*Ch'an* Buddhism has come to be thought of by some as "Warrior Buddhism." Many of the philosophies and stories of Zen Buddhism use warrior symbols, such as the sword, bow, and spear.

In the twelfth century C.E., *Ch'an* was introduced to the Japanese, who called it Zen. The main focus of Zen practice is to avoid complex thoughts in favor of achieving a state of "no-mind," in which one is free of all negativity, such as fear, doubt, and anger. This idea quickly became very popular among members of the Samurai class, especially those who wanted to improve as swordsmen. In fact, many Samurai frequently took retreats to Zen monasteries in pursuit of enlightenment or, at least, a better understanding of the state of "no-mind."

Soon Zen Buddhism in Japan split into two primary sects—Rinzai Zen, founded by a monk named Eisai, and Soto Zen, founded by a student of Eisai named Dogen. While Rinzai Zen did meet with wide acceptance, the Soto tradition became the more popular of the two. Soto Zen focused on mental discipline and integrated physical action with meditation (from calligraphy to the martial arts). Since many of the Zen practitioners at the time were Samurai, such practices would have been considered highly valuable.

Even today, Zen schools continue to teach painting, calligraphy, archery, and other art forms that are thought to allow an individual to practice the state of "no-mind." Unlike in Mahayana Buddhism, where it originated, the Buddha is not worshipped in Zen. Instead, the Buddha (often called by the name Shakyamuni in Zen) is regarded as the most perfect example of a human being's ultimate potential.

In the mid-twentieth century, Zen enjoyed a brief period of popularity in the West. This rise is attributed to the writings of the Zen scholar D. T. Suzuki, who wrote a number of English texts on the philosophies of Zen Buddhism.

Nichiren Buddhism

Founded in the twelfth century C.E. by the Zen monk Nichiren, this sect is also known as the Lotus Sect of Buddhism. Nichiren taught that the only genuine teachings of the Buddha were those contained in the Lotus Sutra. The central act of worship in the Nichiren sect is the repetitive chanting of the phrase *Namu-myoho-rengekyo*, which Nichiren created as a devotion to the Lotus Sutra. The Nichiren sect continually separated until there were close to 40 smaller sects of the religion. To this day, the most popular Nichiren subsect is called Nichiren Shoshu.

Pure Land Buddhism

The Pure Land school of Buddhism is devoted to the *bodhisattva* of the Pure Land, called Amitabha (Infinite Light) in China and India. In Japan, this form of the Buddha is called Amida. The adherents of the Pure Land sect seek to be reborn in the Pure Land, where they believe they will be able to gain enlightenment through Amitabha's mercy. Pure Land Buddhism focuses on worship, faith, and devotion to Amitabha. This sect of Buddhism is fairly recent and is considered by some to be a cult. It is also one of the most popular forms of Buddhism in Western cultures.

11.5

Tibetan Buddhism

Though Tibetan Buddhism derives from the Mahayana sect, it adheres to many of the original Indian traditions. Tibetan Buddhism believes in the existence of *bodhisattvas*, believes that the path to Buddhahood is slow and gradual, and believes that Buddhahood can be achieved only through a disciplined practice of ascetic monasticism.

Unlike monks in other sects of Buddhism, Tibetan monks are not required to shave their heads daily. The main school of Tibetan Buddhism is called *Gelugpa* and is headed by the Dalai Lama. The Dalai Lama, which means "Guru of the Ocean," is considered the reincarnation of a *bodhisattva* named Avalokiteshvara. Each Dalai Lama is chosen during childhood and is believed to be the reincarnation of his predecessor.

The line of the Dalai Lama ruled peacefully over the theocratic Tibet for centuries, beginning in the seventeenth century, until the invasion and occupation of the country by Communist China in the 1950s. In 1959, fearing assassination by the Chinese government, the current Dalai Lama fled to India. To this day, he lives in exile. Many Tibetan Buddhists still consider the Dalai Lama as the rightful ruler of Tibet and oppose the Chinese occupation.

11.6 PRESENT-DAY FACTS

Today Buddhism continues to thrive as one of the world's main religions. With somewhere between 300 million and 500 million adherents worldwide, Buddhism continues to thrive as a popular religious philosophy. Also, Buddhism is no longer a religion practiced solely in Asia and India.

▶ Roughly 500,000 to 700,000 practicing Buddhists reside in the United Kingdom.

▶ Between four million and seven million Buddhist adherents practice in the United States and Canada.

▶ Thailand and Cambodia have the highest population percentages of Buddhists, both at 95 percent, with over 61 million practicing adherents in Thailand and over 13 million in Cambodia.

12

SHINTO

12.1 FUNDAMENTAL TENETS

Basic Information on Shinto
The Core Beliefs of Shinto

Shinto is the nature-focused, "first" religion of Japan, and has had perhaps the greatest impact on the development of Japanese history, culture, beliefs, and modes of thought. Shinto, which was, for a time, the established "state religion" of Japan, stresses a strong sense of nationalism, racial unity, family, and community, all of which continue to be core beliefs in modern Japanese culture.

The word *Shinto* is a transliteration of the Chinese word *Shin-Tao* (which most experts agree translates to mean "Way of Divine Powers"). Shinto (originally called *Kami-no-Michi* in Japanese) was given this new, more unique-sounding name to make clear the distinction between the nature religion of the native Japanese people and the religious beliefs of the **gaijin** foreigners (such as Buddhism, Confucianism, and even Christianity).

Basic Information on Shinto

- ▶ Origin Date: The first Shinto writings were done in Japan during the early eighth century C.E., but the actual origin date of Shinto is unknown. However, the religion is believed to date back to prehistoric Japan.

- ▶ Founder: Unverifiable.

- ▶ View of God: Polytheistic, stressing that the **Kami** (gods or spirits) are found in Nature and that the workings of Nature are the workings of the Kami.

- ▶ Dietary Restrictions: None that are permanent; however, during certain purification holidays or rituals, followers of Shinto will abstain from the consumption of alcohol.

- ▶ View of Life/Death: Though Shinto is vague on details concerning the afterlife, its texts do speak of two worlds where a soul may go after death, the "High Plain of Heaven" for those who are good and "The Dark Land" for those who are evil. Since so little is presented on this topic from within Shinto, the concerns of the afterlife are often addressed by the absorption and application of Buddhist thought on this subject.

- ▶ Lifestyle Foci: Stresses respect and reverence for Nature, a focus on one's family and community, and good personal hygiene.

▶ Worship Restrictions: None. Anyone may practice Shinto, in almost any manner they wish, even in conjunction with other religions. Adherents, however, usually do participate in Shinto ritual practices and/or **domestic Shinto.**

The Core Beliefs of Shinto

▶ Belief in the **Kami-no-Michi,** the will and way of the *Kami*

▶ Belief in the divinity of *Nihon* (Japan) and the Japanese people

▶ Belief that divine and/or supernatural forces are expressed through the physical forces of the natural world and that, therefore, all things in nature are sacred

▶ Belief in purity of mind, body, and spirit, and that the cleanliness of each must be maintained

Shinto is a highly ritualistic religion. The need to frequently visit shrines is closely tied to the belief that humans are ritually unclean and in constant need of purification. There are over 100,000 shrines in Japan and the shrines are thought to be the home of the various *kami*. These shrines are almost always fronted by a **torii gateway** indicating an entrance into a sacred area. The many ritual practices of Shinto adherents serve to restore harmony between the spiritual and physical realms.

WORDS TO GO . . . *WORDS TO GO . . . WORDS TO GO*

The Japanese word **gaijin,** literally translated, means "barbarian." However, this word eventually came to be used in the Japanese language to refer to *all* non-Japanese peoples.

Kami is a Japanese word that is often mistakenly thought to be an equivalent to words such as "deity" or "god." However, this word is not restricted to these definitions and can also be used to refer to a nature spirit, demon, demigod, or even high-ranking and/or revered human being.

The practice of **domestic Shinto** is the maintenance of a personal altar or *kami-dana* (god-shelf) where daily offerings (for example, incense, food, drink, salt, and so forth) and prayers are made to ancestral *kami* and other *kami* that may be beneficial to the family. In Shinto salt is thought to be a purifying agent and is often present at the doorway of adherents' homes or perhaps on their *kami-dana* as an offering.

Kami-no-Michi is most easily translated into English as "Way of the *Kami*." However, in certain contexts, it can also mean something more along the lines of "Will of the *Kami*" or "Standards of the *Kami*." The term *Kami-no-Michi* is also used as an alternate word for Shinto, the title by which the religion is more commonly known.

A **torii gateway** is found at the front of almost all shrines in Japan and is used to mark the entrance into the sacred. Its distinctive appearance not only identifies the entrance of a shrine but also reminds adherents that they are in a place where a *kami* dwells.

◀ *SEE ALSO Chapter 11, "Buddhism"* ▶

12.2 SACRED TEXTS

Understanding *Kami*

The *Kojiki*

The *Nihongi*

The *Yengishiki*

Though technically Shinto does not have a set doctrine or ideology, two main texts tell the story of the religion—the *Kojiki* and *Nihongi*. These two primary Shinto texts are the basis of Shinto cosmology, explaining the tasks, achievements, and ideals of the *Kami,* as well as the creation story of the Japanese islands. These two texts are followed by the *Yengishiki*.

Understanding *Kami*

Before these texts can be discussed, one must take a moment to understand the concept of the *Kami*. Unlike the Western concept of words such as "god" or "deity," the Japanese word *Kami* should not be thought of as equivalent to these words in meaning. The literal meaning of *Kami* is "unseen" or "the hidden," and the word is used to refer to any being or entity that is divine, supernatural, and/or superhuman.

A number of primary differences exist between the Western concept of a god, or other divine being, and the Japanese concept of the *Kami:*

> ▶ The *Kami* do not dwell in a realm that is separated from the world of humans. Instead, they exist within the world of humans.

> ▶ *Kami* are not considered omnipotent.

> ▶ *Kami* are not portrayed as "perfect" beings.

> ▶ *Kami* are not all-benevolent. In fact, some *Kami* are evil.

> ▶ *Kami* may surpass humans in ability and power, but they are still forced to endure certain humanlike experiences, such as emotions, pain, and confusion.

There are three primary classes of *Kami:*

> ▶ *Mikoto:* These are the most powerful *Kami*. They wield tremendous powers, such as life, death, creation, and destruction.

> ▶ *Ujigami:* These *Kami* are the progenitors of the Japanese clans. Each family claimed a specific *Kami* as the originator of its bloodline.

12.2

▶ Nature *Kami*: A wide range of *Kami* fall into this category. At the bottom are lower-class nature spirits, such as the mountain demons/spirits called *Tengu* (Heavenly Dogs) and *Kitsune* (Fox Spirit). However, the higher-ranking *Kami* among this class are extremely powerful, wielding the forces of nature, such as the *Kami* of Lightning and Thunder, *Raiden*.

The *Kojiki*

The transcription of the **Kojiki** predates that of the **Nihongi** and was compiled by a nobleman of the Japanese Imperial court named Yasumaro Futo. The title of the book means "Record of Ancient Matters," and it has also been known by the title *Furukotofumi* (which is a different wording that translates similarly to the meaning of *Kojiki*). This text contains the earliest writings of the Shinto religion and also appears to have been heavily influenced by Chinese ideas.

In the chaos that existed before creation, Heaven and Earth separated. The *Kojiki* refers to the three *Kami* who sparked the beginning of creation, also named in the *Nihongi*—Kuni-toko-tachi, Kuni no sa-tsuchi, and Toyo-kumu-nu (all three are considered the progenitors of the *Mikoto* class of *Kami*). However, the act of creating land and life is credited to the divine couple of Izanami (Male-Who-Invites) and Inanagi (Female-Who-Invites), who were created by these first three deities. This pair is also credited with the creation of the islands of Japan, which they did by dipping a bejeweled spear into the ocean. The drops of brine that fell from the tip as they pulled out the spear became the islands of Japan. It is for this reason that salt is given such an important place in Shinto.

The *Nihongi*

Much of the initial sections of the *Nihongi*, meaning "Chronicle of Japan" (also known by the title *Nihon Shoki*, which translates similarly), is primarily summarizations, explanations, and/or recapitulations of the same stories that were initially told in the *Kojiki*. The *Nihongi* was compiled by Ono Yasumaro, beginning in the early eighth century, under the supervision of Prince Toneri, and was finally completed in the year 720 C.E.

Unlike the *Kojiki*, however, the *Nihongi* continues on to explain the lineage of the *Kami*, connecting them to the ruler of Japan at the time, Empress Jito. This record basically explains how the imperial family directly descends from the sun goddess Amaterasu-no-Mikoto (Amaterasu, for short), which provided validity to a divine right to rule for the Japanese imperial court. The ruler of Japan, for example, was long referred to as *O-Kami*, meaning "Great *Kami*."

The *Nihongi* claims to chronicle the first 41 rulers of Japan, beginning with Emperor Jimmu and ending with Empress Jito. Jimmu is said to have been the great-grandson of a *Kami* named Ninigi-no-Mikoto, who, in turn, was the grandson of Amaterasu. Ninigi was sent to Japan by Amaterasu in order to civilize, organize, and unify the people of Japan.

Scholars now believe that most of the initial emperors chronicled in the *Nihongi* were likely fictional. Though they may have existed, they were likely regional rulers. If they did exist, the years of their reigns are believed to have been exaggerated so that the chronology of the record would seem feasible.

For example, Chapter 4 of the *Nihongi*, called **Kesshi Hachidai,** chronicles the eight emperors, following Emperor Jimmu, in order of their successions to the **"Chrysanthemum Throne."** However, it does not give very much information about them, aside from the years they reigned, the dates when they were made crowned princes, and the locations of their burial tombs. Even more unusual is the fact the book offers absolutely no tales or myths about any of them. Shinto scholars now believe that the names and dates of these eight rulers were included simply to extend the timeline of the Japanese royal clan's lineage, so as to make the time of Emperor Jimmu's reign appear more impressively ancient.

In fact, after the tales of Emperor Jimmu, no more stories about the emperors are chronicled in the *Nihongi* until the book reaches the tenth successor, Emperor Sujin. Interestingly enough, he is often referred to as the first "national ruler" of Japan. The book offers a plethora of information about him, most of which is rather impressive (he seemed to have a knack for subduing troublemakers and putting down provincial lords who attempted to usurp him). In fact, Sujin was so beloved a figure that he was posthumously added to the line of Japanese Emperors who are connected to the same royal family that exists in Japan to this day (though no longer as a ruling body).

12.2

The *Yengishiki*

The **Yengishiki,** which means "Institutes of the Yengi Era," is a compilation of the **Norito** (Rituals of Shinto). This text is, most simply put, a book of Shinto rituals. It lays out in detail the proper ways in which to carry out certain rituals for certain seasons and/or in honor of specific *Kami*. Though the individual practitioner of Shinto is not required to have a working knowledge of this text, it is a crucial part of any Shinto priest's library.

The *Yengishiki* primarily details the proper methods for specific rituals. The seven main Shinto *Norito* rituals outlined in the *Yengishiki* text are as follows:

▶ *The Harvest Ritual:* This ritual is intended to secure the favor of agricultural *Kami* at the time of the harvest.

▶ *The Wind Gods Ritual:* This is a recitation meant to be spoken when giving offering to the higher-ranking wind/air *Kami*.

▶ *The Fire Ritual:* This ritual honors the balanced relationship between fire and water. A violent *Kami* of Fire was created by mistake in the first union of Izanagi and Izanami, so, next was born a female *Kami* of Water so that he might be controlled.

▶ *The Ritual for Evil Spirits:* As one might guess from the title, this is a ritual meant to ward off spirits of disease/pestilence, *bakemono* (demons/monsters), and/or destructive *Kami*.

▶ *The Ritual for the Road Kami:* This is a ritual meant to appeal to *Kami* of the road, to ensure safe travels. Also, it appeals to the *Kami* that traveling priests will not be tempted by the corruption of the outside world.

▶ *The Rituals to the Sun Kami:* This is a very important ritual in Shinto, as it is done in honor of Amaterasu, the female *Kami* of the Sun and progenitor of the Japanese royal clan.

▶ *The Ritual of Purification:* This is a ritual appealing to the *Kami*, by which the priest, through use of a symbolic broom, opens up a path to the High Plain of Heaven. This ritual is meant to purify the location in which it is performed, as well as the individuals present.

WORDS TO GO . . . WORDS TO GO . . . WORDS TO GO

The **Kojiki,** also known by the title **Furukotofumi,** which means "Record of Ancient Matters," is the oldest existing Shinto text.

The **Nihongi,** also called the **Nihon Shoki,** is the "Chronicle of Japan" and is a compilation of the works of the *Kojiki.* However, this text also includes as many existing versions of each story and myth as could be found in Japan at the time. Perhaps more important, the stories of the *Nihongi* seek to show how the Japanese royal family's lineage is connected to Amaterasu, the female *Kami* of the Sun.

The **Chrysanthemum Throne** is the title for the seat of the emperor of Japan. This term comes from the fact that the royal family's crest is a **kiku,** or "chrysanthemum."

The **Kesshi Hachidai** is the title for the fourth chapter of the *Nihongi* and is also known as "The Chronicle of the Eight Undocumented Emperors." This chapter of the text lists factual information for the second through ninth rulers of the "Chrysanthemum Throne."

Norito is a Japanese word for "ritual," used more specifically to refer to Shinto rituals. The existing record of Shinto rituals was compiled in the **Yengishiki** sometime during the early years of the tenth century C.E., a time period referred to as the Yengi Era.

12.3 RITUALS AND HOLIDAYS

The Shinto religion honors and/or celebrates a plethora of holidays. To explain them all in detail could make a book in itself. What follows is a list of the main Shinto holidays, with their dates (according to the Western calendar) and brief descriptions.

- ▶ *Seijin-no-hi:* January 15, the Coming of Age Festival.

- ▶ *Setsubun-no-hi:* February 3, the Closing of Winter Festival.

- ▶ *Hina-Matsuri:* March 3, the Doll Festival, which celebrates all the daughters in a village.

- ▶ *Shubun-sai:* March 21, Equinox Day. People visit the graves of the deceased on this day to pay honor to those who have passed on.

- ▶ *Haru-Matsuri:* End of March to end of April, the Spring Festival.

- ▶ *Koi-no-bori:* May 5, the Boys' Festival.

- ▶ *Natsu-Matsuri:* Entire month of June, the Summer Festival.

- ▶ *Nagoshi-no-Oharai:* June 30, the spring season's purification festival.

- ▶ *Akimatsuri:* September to November, the Fall Festival.

- ▶ *Shiwasu-no-Oharai:* December 31, the winter season's purification ritual.

- ▶ *Oshogatsu:* December, the End of Year Festival.

12.3

12.4 ORIGINS AND FOUNDER

Shinto has always been considered the original religion of the indigenous Japanese people; however, its origins predate the country's written history. As a result, there is no official record by which to historically and/or factually explain the origins or founder of the Shinto religion. Therefore, there is little else that can be explained in this section.

12.5 HISTORICAL DEVELOPMENT

Shinto and Buddhism

The Meiji Restoration

Hirohito's Proclamation

Shinto hit its highest period among the people of Japan during the era of Japanese history marked by the rule of the Tokugawa *Shogun,* which spanned from 1615 until roughly 1867. This was a fairly prosperous and peaceful time period and is often referred to in the West as the Tokugawa Peace Period. The years that preceded this period had been violent and bloody, marked by disease, famine, and constant warfare among the feudal lords, called *daimyo.* This era of chaos and war is often referred to as the Warring States Period.

Shinto and Buddhism

Tokugawa Ieyasu was able to end the Warring States Period by defeating the royal family and either defeating or unifying all the provincial lords under his banner. He then used his power to usurp all of the real political power from the imperial clan. Tokugawa allowed the royal clan to go on existing, and even paid tribute to them out of respect, but he refused to recognize their power to rule the country he had fought so long and hard to unite.

During the Warring States Period, Christian missionaries had begun to make some progress in their conversion campaigns. Unfortunately, one of the first proclamations of the new *Shogun* was to denounce and outlaw the practice of Christianity, as he considered the religion a corrupt foreign influence. Missionaries were sought out and expelled from the island by force whenever found.

12.5

◀ SEE ALSO *Chapters 3, 4, and 5, "Christianity," "Catholicism," and "Protestantism"* ▶

However, also during the Warring States Period, a new sect of Buddhism had already begun gaining in popularity, especially among the *Samurai* warrior class. This form of Buddhism had come to Japan not from India, but from China, and was called Zen (a Japanese transliteration of the Chinese word *Ch'an*). To allow an integration of the increasingly popular Zen religion and the native Japanese religion of Shinto, Buddhist monks and Shinto priests managed to find a way to coexist.

This integration was made rather simple by the introduction of the idea that the Japanese concept of the *Kami* was simply the Shinto equivalent of the Buddhist concept of a *bodhisattva*. Once this idea had been adopted, the two religions experienced a long and friendly coexistence that continues even now. During the Tokugawa Peace Period of Japanese history, it was not at all unusual to find clergy from both religions working side by side in the same temples and monasteries. To this day, most Japanese who are followers of Shinto are also practicing Buddhists. This resulted in the development of *Ryobu* or two-aspect Shinto. In this view, all things related to day-to-day living is the concern of Shinto and the afterlife is the concern of Buddhism.

The Meiji Restoration

In August of 1866 C.E., the final *Shogun*, Tokugawa Iemochi, died. The *Shogun* government had been progressively weakening in the face of numerous uprisings. *Shogun* Iemochi's heir, Hitotsubashi Keiki, resigned within a year. Seizing the opportunity, many *daimyo* and *Samurai* still loyal to the imperial family waged war against the Tokugawa-loyalists, called the **Bakufu.** Without a strong leader, the *Bakufu* were easily defeated and scattered. The rightful heirs to the Chrysanthemum Throne, the Meiji clan, were reinstated by the close of 1868. This began an era referred to as the Meiji restoration.

In an attempt to repair and solidify Japan's sense of national unity, as well as return to the ideals of imperial rule that had existed before the rise of the Tokugawa *Shogun*, the Meiji emperor proclaimed Shinto as the state religion of Japan. This marked a return of Shinto under the Meiji emperor. Shinto, now established as the official national religion of Japan, became increasingly separated from Buddhism. However, Buddhism was not outlawed or banned by the Meiji; it was simply separated from Shinto.

Hirohito's Proclamation

The most recent and extreme turning point in Shinto belief in modern times took place in 1946, when emperor Hirohito (under pressure from military officials) denounced his own divinity as a descendent of the goddess Amaterasu. The state religion of Shinto was disestablished shortly thereafter and replaced by what is referred to as **Jinja** Shinto. The religion continued to be practiced, but no longer in a state-endorsed manner.

Following the devastation of World War II, a number of new sects of Shinto began to spring up across Japan. These religions were very popular, as they offered followers peace and order in a time of extreme chaos. Such sects often stressed the Shinto aspects of faith healing, purification, and nature worship. Some even included ideas from Confucianism.

◀ *SEE ALSO 10.1, "Fundamental Tenets of Confucianism"* ▷

WORDS TO GO . . .WORDS TO GO . . .WORDS TO GO

The **Shogun** was the military lord of Japan. This word eventually came to be the title of a line of military rulers, beginning with Tokugawa Ieyasu.

The word **daimyo** referred to the provincial lords of feudal Japan. The *daimyo* served under higher-ranking lords, who, in turn, worked directly under either an emperor or *Shogun.* The *Shogun* were required to arm, pay, and maintain their own forces of elite warriors, called *Samurai,* who were expected to employ and maintain their own respective units of foot soldiers.

A **Samurai** (meaning "one who serves") was a member of the Japanese warrior class, trained from early childhood in the arts of combat, strategy, horsemanship, archery, and the use of the spear and sword.

The **Bakufu** were those Samurai and/or daimyo who remained loyal to the authority of the Tokugawa shogunate during the conflict with the forces of the returning imperial family, called the Meiji. Many *Bakufu* continued to remain loyal to the Tokugawa even after it fell.

The Japanese word **gaijin**, literally translated, means "barbarian." However, this word eventually came to be used to refer to *all* non-Japanese peoples.

The word **Jinja** refers to the unsanctioned, semiofficial practices and shrines of Shinto that existed both before and after the religion's period as the state-sponsored religion of Japan.

12.5

12.6 PRESENT-DAY FACTS

Shinto is still alive and well in Japan. In fact, before the start of any new construction project or other such undertaking, it is not unusual to see a Shinto priest present, giving blessings. In a world where technology seems to be overshadowing nature at times, Shinto has not been pushed aside. Today Shinto beliefs have spread and adapted to the ideas of modern technology. The idea is that, if human beings are a part of nature, and nature is the expression of the *Kami*, then the very things that human beings create are also expressions of the *Kami*. This belief has even begun to extend to computers and the World Wide Web.

Finding concrete estimates on the number of Shinto adherents in the world can be difficult, as reports often vary from one to the next. This is due to the fact that many Shinto followers also practice Buddhism. However, the majority of estimates put the number of Shinto adherents somewhere between two million and four million people. However, in Japan it is said that 85 to 90 percent of the population practices Shinto, and by this they claim that the number of adherents is closer to 100 million people.

13

HINDU DHARMA

13.1 FUNDAMENTAL TENETS

Basic Information on Hindu Dharma

The Core Beliefs of Hindu Dharma

The Godhead and *Trimurti*

The Four *Yugas*

The Caste Structure

Adherents of this ancient religion of India rarely use the term *Hindu*. The word is actually a Western transliteration of *Shindhu*, a Sanskrit term for the inhabitants of the regions near the Indus River (or a name for the region itself). *Hindu* actually means "Of the Indus." Many adherents of the religion refer to it as simply "Dharma," while others choose to call it "Hindu Dharma," especially when speaking to non-Hindus. In this chapter, the terms *Hindu Dharma, Hindu,* and *Hinduism* are used, to avoid confusion.

Basic Information on Hindu Dharma

▶ Origin Date: Prehistoric; therefore, the exact date of origin is unknown. However, the first Hindu texts are believed to have been written down between 2000 B.C.E. and 900 B.C.E.

▶ Founder/Originator: Believed to have come from the polytheistic religions of the now-extinct Aryans. However, no founding source can be 100 percent confirmed.

▶ View of God: Polytheistic view, with a unified monotheistic concept.

▶ Dietary restrictions: Vegetarian.

▶ View of Life/Death: Belief in *kharma, dharma,* and the wheel of reincarnation, called *samsara.*

▶ Lifestyle Foci: To transcend negative *kharma* and accumulate positive *kharma* by living a life in harmony with one's *dharma.* Also, although it is no longer part of India law, many Hindu Dharma adherents still live according to the ancient Hindu caste structure. Some of the more ascetic sects/castes, such as the **Brahman,** reject family life. However, the majority of Hindu Dharma sects encourage family life as a means of spiritual growth.

▶ Worship Restrictions: None; anyone may practice Hindu Dharma.

◀ SEE ALSO 11.1, *"Fundamental Tenets of Buddhism"* ▶

◀ SEE ALSO 14.1, *"Fundamental Tenets of Jainism"* ▶

The Core Beliefs of Hindu Dharma

The core beliefs of Hindu Dharma are as follows:

▶ Belief in the laws of *dharma* and *kharma*.

▶ Belief in the wheel of *samsara,* through which a person continues to reincarnate until liberation is achieved.

▶ Belief that the true God can and does take many different forms (often misunderstood by non-Hindus to be separate deities). However, the forms are but representations of the endless natures and layers that make up the one true God.

▶ Depending on sect, family, or personal beliefs, belief in strict adherence to the Hindu caste structure.

◀ SEE ALSO 11.1, *"Fundamental Tenets of Buddhism"* ▶

◀ SEE ALSO 14.1, *"Fundamental Tenets of Jainism"* ▶

The Godhead and *Trimurti*

Westerners and non-Hindus (and even some Hindus) have difficulty understanding why Hinduism is so difficult to classify. At first glance, Hinduism, with its thousands of deities, appears polytheistic. Even some Hindus view their religion in this way. In truth, however, Hinduism believes that there is a single, absolute entity. However, an entity so overwhelmingly universal in nature would be impossible for humans to grasp. Therefore, the many deities of Hinduism are representations of the many roles and natures encompassed by the absolute entity. This entity is sometimes referred to as the "Godhead."

13.1

The best illustration of how Hinduism's many divine entities are representations of one absolute entity is a concept called the *Trimurti.* The oneness of the *Trimurti* is often easier for Westerners to comprehend, as most are familiar with the concept of the Christian Trinity.

The *Trimurti* is itself a trinity and consists of three deities who are representations of the three primary natures of the absolute Godhead—creation, preservation, and destruction. Each nature is represented by one of three unique gods, which are Brahma, Vishnu, and Shiva, respectively. In addition to being a representation of the Godhead, the *Trimurti* is considered a symbol of the cycle of existence.

Hindus commonly believe that the existence in which humans currently live is not the first, and that hundreds to thousands of existences have taken place before this one. Each existence follows the same cycle of creation, preservation, and destruction. Hindus believe that every cycle of existence runs its course in four successive ages, called *Yugas.*

◀ SEE ALSO 3.1, *"Fundamental Tenets of Christianity"* ▶

Brahma

Brahma is the creator god, considered the most powerful and supreme god that interacts with the physical realm. Oddly, this deity is rarely worshipped directly. Some Hindus believe that humans cannot appropriately worship so great and powerful a god. Others claim a more mythological reason, citing a number of legends with varying explanations of how Brahma was once cursed to endure this existence without worshippers. In fact, Brahma is honored by only one temple, located in the city of Pushkar in the state of Rajasthan, in Northern India.

Unlike most other Hindu deities (including Vishnu and Shiva), Brahma was not created. This is because Brahma is said to be self-born, the **shvayambhu,** meaning "the creator who was not created." Hindu myths regarding the details of exactly how Brahma's self-birth transpired are numerous and varied. One myth claims that he spontaneously arose from the bud of the Lotus flower that grows from Vishnu's navel (see the next section). Another explains how the absolute Godhead, within the dark pre-creation void, created water and placed a seed in it. The seed eventually grew into a golden egg from which Brahma was born. This act allowed the Godhead, which is formless, to assume a form (though not necessarily a physical one).

In his few depictions, Brahma is usually portrayed with four heads. Each head faces a different direction, representing the numerological significance of four in Hinduism, which has four *Vedas* (the first Hindu texts), four *Yugas* (time periods in each cycle of existence), and four **varnas** (social castes). One Hindu myth explains that Brahma originally had five heads, but that Shiva, God of Destruction, cut one of them off in a fit of rage.

Vishnu

Vishnu is perhaps the most beloved figure of the *Trimurti.* He is also one of the most widely worshipped deities in the Hindu faith. Interestingly, Vishnu was originally written of in Hindu texts as a lesser god. However, his appearance as a prominent deity in Hindu myths/literature came rather late in the religion's development. In fact, both Vishnu and Shiva are believed to have continued gaining in popularity during a period before the *Trimurti* concept was established. Eventually, both gods collectively replaced the original primary deity of the *Vedas*, a thunder/storm god named Indra who encompassed the natures of both preservation (water/rain) and destruction (tempests and lightning).

Vishnu is called "the dreamer" and is often depicted in his true form as slumbering, with a lotus flower growing from his navel. As he sleeps, his wife, Lakshmi, tends to him. Vishnu's dream, according to Hindu belief, is what unenlightened humans mistakenly consider "reality." Since human existence is his dream, Vishnu is omniscient when it comes to the situation of the planet and humankind.

Vishnu, unlike Brahma, is always portrayed as interactive in the realm of humans. The God of Preservation is often depicted as very sympathetic and loving when it comes to humans, and often he intervenes on their behalf. This likely stems from the fact that Vishnu is also tasked with protecting the law of *dharma* as well as maintaining the cosmic balance of good and evil. Any time *dharma* (an individual's or the world's) is threatened or the cosmic balance is disrupted, it is Vishnu's responsibility to see that things are returned to normal. When Vishnu incarnates and comes to Earth, the forms he assumes are referred to as ***avatars***.

In Hindu lore, Vishnu has 10 avatars. However, only nine of these avatars have come to pass. His tenth and final avatar will appear in a white horse, delivering justice and ushering in the end times of this existence. The 10 avatars of Vishnu are as follows:

1. **Matsya or Matsyavatara:** Meaning "Fish Avatar," this first manifestation of Vishnu came to rescue a man named Vaivashwata, who was tasked with preserving civilization when the Earth was overcome by a massive deluge.

2. **Kurma:** As the "Tortoise Avatar," Vishnu allowed the mountain of Mandara to rest on his enormous shell until the waters receded following the flood.

3. **Varaha:** As the "Boar Avatar," Vishnu came to slay a demon that had stolen the sacred writings of the *Vedas*, and returned land to the flooded Earth in the process.

4. **Narasingha or Narashima:** As the "Lion-Man Avatar," this half-lion, half-man manifestation of Vishnu came to slay a demon who went to Mount Madara and practiced austerities until he was granted a boon of protection from any demigod, human, or animal. However, the demon failed to realize that avatars do not fall into such categories. He was torn apart by Narasingha.

13.1

5. **Vamana:** As the "Dwarf Avatar," Vishnu rescued the three realms of existence from Bali, leader of the *asuras*. By appearing as a dwarf, and wagering with Bali that he could keep whatever parts he could cover in three steps, Vishnu rescued existence by traversing each realm with a single step.

6. **Parasurama:** The "Rama of the Axe" and one of the most violent manifestations of Vishnu, this vengeful avatar waged a war of 21 crusades against the members of the Kshatriya caste. Though he was himself an avatar of Vishnu, Parasurama was killed by Rama, the seventh avatar.

7. **Rama:** This manifestation of Vishnu is the hero of the Hindu epic *Ramayana*. Rama came to rid the world of the demon King Ravana and is considered the Hindu example of the "perfect man."

8. **Krishna:** This avatar is often called the "Charioteer" because he was charioteer to the Kshatriya called Arjuna. Krishna is the hero of the Bhagavad-Gita, a section of the Hindu epic called the *Mahabharata*.

9. **Buddha:** The "Enlightened One." Hindus considered the Buddha to have been an avatar of Vishnu. However, it is important to note that Buddhists do not share this view.

10. **Kalki:** Sometimes referred to as the "Avatar of the Apocalypse," this tenth and final manifestation of Vishnu has yet to occur. The Kalki avatar is commonly described as a "mechanized man" riding on a pale horse and will appear near the end of the last age of existence, called the *Kali Yuga*.

Shiva

Shiva, the Hindu God of Destruction, is the third and final member of the *Trimurti*. Shiva's recklessly destructive nature is kept in balance by his consort, the goddess Shakti. This joining of Shiva with a feminine figure sustains a balance of life and death, fertility and destruction. The balance, however, is only temporary and is not meant to be thought of as eternal.

At the end of this existence cycle's final age, called the *Kali Yuga*, Shiva will separate from Shakti and assume the *Shiva Nataraja* form, often called the "dancing Shiva." In this form, Shiva will join in a dance with Kali, the goddess of death, sickness, and darkness. This dance will be preceded by the appearance of Vishnu's tenth avatar and will result in the destruction of existence. Before their dance is over, Kali will murder Shiva and stand upon his corpse. As a result, the cosmic balance will be disrupted beyond repair when Shiva dies. Kali, the Hindu representation of death, is all that will remain. At the end of this period of destruction, yet another cycle for a new existence will begin.

The Four *Yugas*

Each existence cycle, according to Hindu belief, lasts about 4,320,000 years. This cycle is called *Dhivya-Yuga* and is separated into four lesser *Yugas*. Each *Yuga* represents a stage in humankind's development and evolution (physical, mental, and spiritual), which slowly causes them to lose their divine qualities and separate further from the Godhead. The four *Yugas* of the *Dhivya-Yuga* cycle are as follows:

1. *Satya Yuga:* Also called the *Krita Yuga*, this age makes up the first 1,728,000 years of the cycle. This is an age of *dhyana*, meaning "meditation." During this age, people are said to live for tens of thousands of years, and meditate on realizing the existence of Vishnu (some sects say Brahma). This is an "Age of Truth, " in which humankind is able to communicate directly with the representations of the Godhead.

2. *Treta Yuga:* This age lasts for about 1,296,000 years after the *Satya Yuga*. This is the age of the mind. Humankind has become aware of the divine and begins to make sacrifices, called **yajnas,** to the Godhead. In this age, according to Hindu belief, people lived for many millennia, and the average lifespan is said to have been about 10,000 years. During this age, humans come to realize that they are separating from the Godhead and are introduced to the concept of *Dharma*.

3. *Dwapara Yuga:* This age lasts for about the next 864,000 years. Humans have traveled even further from the Godhead. Whereas in the first age humans communicated with the Godhead directly, they now worship in temples. The separation from the Godhead has caused humans to significantly lose their divine qualities, and the average lifespan of people living in this age is about 1,000 years.

4. *Kali Yuga:* The "Age of Darkness" or "Age of Oblivion," which lasts the next 432,000 years, begins with the death of Krishna. The *Kali Yuga* is marked by materialism, hypocrisy, technology, and terrible wars. Few humans now remember their divinity (most now believe in the divine only through faith), and even they are reduced to chanting the names of the Godhead. The average lifespan at *Kali Yuga*'s start is 100 years. Hindus believe humankind is now roughly between the first and second quarters of the *Kali Yuga*. In the last few millennia of *Kali Yuga*, few human beings will live to see adulthood, having almost completely lost their connection to the Godhead.

The Caste Structure

Over time, the concept of Dharma in Hindu practice developed into a rigid social class structure, commonly referred to as a caste system. Most Hindus who believe in the caste system cite the words of the Vishnu *avatar* known as Krishna in the Bhagavad-Gita. However, caste is not universally accepted in the Hindu faith and remains a matter of much debate.

The traditional Hindus of India often believe the caste structure to be almost a divine proclamation (especially those of the wealthier echelons), while many liberal Hindus believe that the caste system is a misinterpretation of Krishna's intended message, which they believe was meant to be a commentary on the duty of properly following one's Dharma. These Hindus often believe that Dharma is not set by one's birth, but revealed as one continues to walk the path of life.

Regardless, there are four primary castes in Hindu Dharma, and a fifth "noncaste," or outcast, class. The Dharma castes of traditional Hindu practice are as follows:

1. *Brahmin:* The priest, teacher, and/or ascetic caste. Brahmins are the scholars, spiritual leaders, and ascetic monks of the Hindu faith. They do not work for pay or produce any material goods; therefore, they are traditionally supposed to be poor. However, generous alms from members of the Kshatriya and Vaishya castes give them the means to live comfortably enough (in the past, this relationship sometimes led to corruption within the Brahmin caste).

2. *Kshatriya:* The warrior and ruler caste. Traditionally, Kshatriyas were meant to be the protectors of the Hindus. Over time, they came to be the warlords of India. In modern times, they are the businessmen and landowning class.

3. *Vaishya:* The merchant, artisan, and farmer caste. These are the producers. Traditionally, Vaishyas often worked in the service of (or in conjunction with) members from the ruling Kshatriya caste (who, with their wealth, came to own the means of production).

4. *Sudra:* The laborer caste. A Sudra is born into a lifetime of servitude. This is the lowest echelon considered a part of the recognized caste system. Sudras often work as servants or manual laborers for members of the Kshatriya and/or Vaishya castes.

5. *The Noncaste:* This caste does not even have a name in Sanskrit, and its members are not considered Hindus. Sadly, noncaste members were for centuries eligible only for jobs considered too dangerous, taboo, or unhealthy for Sudras, such as removing and disposing of dead bodies (animals and humans), cleaning up human waste, and tanning leather (cows are considered sacred to Hindus).

Noncaste members are often called "untouchables," though this term has come to be viewed as insulting and inappropriate by much of Hindu society. Commonly, members of the noncaste are called *dalit*, meaning "broken people." In the twentieth century, the newly formed government of India took deliberate measures to encourage the removal of the traditional political enforcement of caste-based practices. The first measure was the abolishment of the "untouchable" noncaste in 1950. In 1951, when the government of India drafted its official constitution, *dalit* members were written about under the title of "scheduled castes." The constitution also indirectly abolished the caste system by outlawing "caste-based discrimination." However, on social levels, the caste system is still an issue, and many of the older generations of India still adhere to it … sometimes violently.

WORDS TO GO . . .WORDS TO GO . . .WORDS TO GO

Brahman is the creator God of Hinduism, and the primary figure of the **Trimurti**.

The **Trimurti** is the three-member assembly of primary Hindu gods, making up three natures/roles of the divine—creator, sustainer, and destroyer. These three roles are represented by Brahman (creator), Vishnu (sustainer), and Shiva (destroyer).

Yugas are the ages that make up one cycle of existence in Hindu cosmology.

Shvayambhu, meaning "the creator who was not created," is a title for the god Brahman, who existed before existence.

Varnas is the word for the Hindu caste structure.

Avatars are physical incarnations of gods. In Hinduism, gods frequently choose to be born in human form. Usually, avatars come to accomplish a particular task, such as righting an injustice.

Yajnas are the sacrifices that humans begin making to the gods, beginning in the **Treta Yuga.**

13.1

13.2 SACRED TEXTS

The *Vedas*

The Upanishads

The Puranas

The Hindu Epics

Hinduism has a deep and ancient literary tradition. The texts of the Hindu religion are some of the oldest texts in existence. The basic Hindu canon is made up of three main texts—the Vedas, the Upanishads, and the Puranas. However, in addition to these texts are a number of Hindu epics, such as the Ramayana, Mahabharata, and Bhagavad-Gita. These epics offer tales of heroic and pious figures who are often used as examples of perfection in the Hindu tradition.

The *Vedas*

The oldest sacred texts of the Hindu Dharma faith are undoubtedly the *Vedas*. These texts, which are arranged into four parts, were composed over a period of time between 2000 B.C.E. and 200 B.C.E. The four *Vedas* are as follows:

1. *Rig-Veda:* This is the "Mantra *Veda*." It is believed to have been first written down in Sanskrit sometime between roughly 700 B.C.E. and 300 B.C.E. However, it is believed to have been orally composed many centuries before this, possibly as far back as 2000 B.C.E.

2. *Yajur-Veda:* This is the "Ritual *Veda*" or "*Veda* of Proper Sacrifice." It was likely first orally composed around 1400 B.C.E. and then written down sometime between 400 B.C.E. and 300 B.C.E. This *Veda* is a guide for priests/Brahmins in the performance of ceremonies, sacrifices, and rituals. Perhaps the most important element of the *Yajur-Veda* is the information it provides on the act of sacrifice. Most of the higher forms of sacrifice have to do with forms of self-denial. Please understand that the Hindu Dharma faith does not practice any form of animal or human sacrifice.

3. *Sama-Veda:* This is the "Holy Songs Veda," which is primarily a condensed version of information from the *Rig-Veda*, written in the form of hymns. While there are estimates about the date of its composition, no evidence exists to verify any specific date. All that can be said of this text's date of origin is that it was composed and written down sometime after the *Rig-Veda*.

4. *Atharva-Veda:* This is the "*Veda* of Spells" or the "Mystical *Veda.*" The *Atharva-Veda* was likely orally composed around 1000 B.C.E., but for reasons that are not quite clear, it was the last of the *Vedas* to be written down. This text was written in Sanskrit around 200 B.C.E. Some claim that writing down this *Veda* was forbidden for a long time because its mystical teachings were considered too powerful and thought to be dangerous if a written copy fell into the hands of the wrong person.

The Upanishads

The term *Upanishad* translates literally as "to sit down near." However, the term has come to mean "mystic/inner teachings." This text is a collection of Brahmin commentaries on and examinations of the teachings of the *Vedas*. In fact, the Upanishad writings are thought of as going hand-in-hand with the *Vedas*. Most of the Upanishads are believed to have been written down over a period of time between 800 B.C.E. and 400 B.C.E. However, unlike the *Vedas*, the Upanishads are not believed to have been orally composed at an earlier time.

The Puranas

The Puranas are basically a retelling of the cosmological myths of the Hindu Dharma faith. The text is divided into three main parts, each consisting of between five and seven *Puranas*. Traditionally, there are 18 total Puranas, each addressing the origins and stories for a particular time period, hero, and/or deity.

The Hindu Epics

Hindu Dharma has two main epics, the *Ramayana* and *Mahabharata*. These two stories are as much a part of India's culture as they are a part of the Hindu Dharma religion. Both are considered ancient in origin and offer a rich and colorful telling of the history of the Hindus as a people.

The *Ramayana*

The exact period in which the *Ramayana* was written is often debated, and a number of extremely contrasting theories exist. However, most estimates claim and 400 B.C.E. The story was likely composed and transferred via oral tradition long before Valmiki ever recorded it.

Ramayana means "Power of Rama" and is the story of the seventh avatar of Vishnu. Rama is considered one of the greatest heroes of Hindu culture and is viewed as an example of both the perfect man and the ideal Hindu. Despite being an avatar, Rama endures a number of hardships. However, he accepts his *dharma* with a calm understanding that surpasses the most serene of sages.

13.2

The *Mahabharata*

The *Mahabharata* is commonly believed to have been written down sometime between 540 B.C.E. and 300 B.C.E., although it was likely composed as much as a thousand years earlier. This epic tale portrays a long period of war between the Kshatriya clans of ancient India. Most of the tale follows the exploits of the five sons of King Pandu, who, in the epic, is recently deceased. King Pandu's five sons must now struggle to maintain their father's kingdom against the 100 sons of the evil King Dhritarashtra, called the *Dhartarashtras*.

Due to a curse, mortal sex was fatal to King Pandu. He was so favored by the gods, however, that five of them each fathered a son for him. On the other hand, King Dhritarashtra was a servant of evil, and the story claims that his sons are actually the incarnations of malignant demons. The stage is set for a battle between good and evil. Interestingly enough, the two clans are said to be related.

Much like Homer's Greek epic, the *Iliad*, the figures of the *Mahabharata* are often aided or hindered by the gods.

The Bhagavad-Gita

The Bhagavad-Gita is actually a part of the *Mahabharata* epic. In fact, it is probably the most well-known section of the text. The Bhagavad-Gita describes how Krishna, serving as charioteer to Arjuna, a descendent of King Pandu, revealed to the prince his true form as the god Vishnu. Krishna, eighth avatar of Vishnu, explained the truth of the universe to the young prince to ease his inner moral struggle about going into battle against his relatives.

13.3 RITUALS AND HOLIDAYS

The following is a list of rituals and holidays of Hindu Dharma:

- ▶ *Holi:* Festival of colors and spring (February/March)

- ▶ *Mahashivaratri (Shiva Ratri):* Night sacred to Shiva (February/March)

- ▶ *Rama Navami:* Birthday of Lord Rama (April)

- ▶ *Krishna Jayanti:* Birthday of Lord Krishna (July/August)

- ▶ *Raksabandhana:* Renewal of bonds between brothers and sisters (July/August)

- ▶ *Kumbh Mela:* Pilgrimage every 12 years to four cities in India (July/August; last one 2003)

- ▶ *Ganesha-Chaturthi (Ganesha Utsava):* Festival of Ganesh (August/September)

- ▶ *Dassera:* Victory of Rama over demon king Ravana (September/October)

- ▶ *Navaratri:* Festival of Shakti (in Bengal) or Rama's victory over Ravana (South India) (September/October)

- ▶ *Diwali:* Festival of lights and Laksmi (September/October)

13.3

13.4 ORIGINS AND FOUNDER

The religion of Hindu Dharma, as it exists today, evolved from events that took place thousands of years ago. When a now-extinct group of Indo-European tribes, called Aryans, left Iran and entered the regions along the Indus River Valley, they began to interact with the indigenous peoples there. The Aryans are believed to have first been a small group of valley-dwelling tribes, whose diet likely consisted of horse meat (which likely made them significantly taller than the indigenous peoples of the Indus River Valley). Over time, they discovered that the horses could be better used as an efficient means of conveyance. This is believed to have had a dramatic impact that forever changed the Aryan culture from sedentary valley dwellers into a warring, nomadic people.

Little is known about the details of the Aryans' interactions with the indigenous peoples of the Indus River regions. However, they left behind two large pieces of evidence with the Hindu people before they were either wiped out or absorbed over the centuries into other cultures. No one knows for certain. The first main contribution of the Indo-European Aryans to the people of the Indus Valley was a phonetic system of writing called Sanskrit, which they found could be adapted to their dialect. All of Hindu Dharma's sacred texts were originally written down in Sanskrit. Their second contribution was the introduction of their religious cosmology, which is believed to have been at least the original inspiration for the beginnings of Hindu cosmology as it survives today.

13.5 HISTORICAL DEVELOPMENT

For centuries, the practice of Hindu Dharma remained stable in India. However, the religion suffered a period of difficulty from the sixteenth to eighteenth centuries C.E. when the Turkish Mogul Empire invaded the country. At first, although the Moguls had declared Islam as their state religion, the first few Mogul rulers allowed the Hindus to practice their faith without fear of persecution. However, all of this changed in 1658, when the Mogul Emperor, Shah Jahan, died.

Shah Jahan's four sons quarreled over the division of the kingdom, eventually leading them to take up arms against one another. This period is called the War of Twenty-Seven Years, and it remains the longest-lasting open war to take place in India.

When the War of Twenty-Seven Years was over, Shah Jahan's most militantly Islamic son, Aurangzeb, arose victorious. His victory, however, was largely due to the support he'd received from wealthy Islamic nobles. Now ruler of India, Aurangzeb began enforcing the Islamic law of the Sharia and ended the period of religious tolerance for the Hindus. This sparked a period of forced conversions and religious persecution against Hindus. To this day, Aurangzeb remains one of the most hated figures in the entire history of India.

Aurangzeb died in 1707 C.E., and several of his subordinates immediately declared themselves the new ruler of India. This led to yet another period of violence in India. The Mogul Empire finally fell in 1857 C.E. when the elderly emperor, Bahadur Shah Zafar, was tried by the East India Company for inciting and organizing an 1857 mutiny and sowing seeds of rebellion in the region. Bahadur was found guilty of inciting treason and exiled to the island of Rangoon, where he lived out the rest of his days.

13.5

13.6 PRESENT-DAY FACTS

Hindu Dharma has more than 830 million practicing adherents in the world today. Most reside in India, which is home to well over 750 million of the world's Hindu adherents. However, the countries of Nepal and Bangladesh have significantly large Hindu populations as well, with over 18 million in Nepal (almost 90 percent of the country's population) and roughly 12 million in Bangladesh. The United States is home to less than a million Hindu Dharma adherents.

14

JAINISM

14.1 FUNDAMENTAL TENETS OF JAINISM

Basic Information on Jainism

The Core Beliefs of Jainism

The Nine Principles *(Tattvas)*

The Five Great Vows *(Maha-vratas)*

The Ten Ascetic Virtues

The Twelve Vows of the Layperson

Jainism is believed to be one of the world's most ancient religions, even predating Buddhism. Originating in India, Jainism is also one of the most difficult religions to practice, requiring adherents to follow a disciplined way of life that involves self-denial and restricted modes of living. Jainism at its foundation is dependent on Hindu Vedic thought, namely the doctrines of *samsara*, *kharma*, and *moksha*. Yet it also radically rejects Vedic teaching, adopting the vow of *ahimsa (non-injury of life)*. The vow of Ahimsa made a permanent impact on Indian culture and even helped alter the path of Hinduism as it evolved from the vedic animal sacrifices of its distant past to the non-violent rituals and lifestyle choices of the present.

Basic Information on Jainism

▶ Origin Date: Sixth century B.C.E.

▶ Founder: Commonly credited to Vardhamana (later called Mahavira, or "Great Hero"), but some historians claim that the origins of Jainism are, for the most part, unknown.

▶ View of God: An unspecified belief in the divine.

▶ Dietary Restrictions: Strictly vegetarian.

▶ View of Life/Death: Belief in *samsara*, the cycle of reincarnation caused by the accumulation of *kharma*, which can be broken only by extreme asceticism resulting in the *moksha* (release/liberation) of the soul.

▶ Lifestyle Foci: To do absolutely no harm or commit any unnecessary actions in life. Jain adherents often wear loose-fitting white robes (some sects wear no clothing at all, however) and walk with a broom to sweep clear the ground before they tread upon it. This is done to avoid treading on insects and other small organisms, as this is seen as "treading on souls." Some of the more disciplined adherents of Jainism even wear masks over their mouths and noses, to avoid "inhaling souls."

▶ Worship Restrictions: None; anyone may practice Jainism.

◀ SEE ALSO 13.1, *"Fundamental Tenets of Hindu Dharma"* ▶

◀ SEE ALSO 11.1, *"Fundamental Tenets of Buddhism"* ▶

The Core Beliefs of Jainism

The core beliefs of Jainism are as follows:

- ▶ Do no harm to any living organism.
- ▶ Adhere to the Five Great Vows.
- ▶ Practice the Ten Ascetic Virtues.
- ▶ If the Jain is not a monk, he or she is expected to adhere to the Twelve Vows of the Layperson.

The Nine Principles (*Tattvas*)

The Nine *Tattvas*, meaning "principles," are perhaps the single most crucial and debated subject of the Jain religion. These nine virtues laid the foundation of Jainism, from which all other tenets and vows arose. Though Jainism was influenced in part by ideas from the Hindu *Vedas*, the Jain *Tattvas* were, in turn, greatly influential on the ideas of Buddhism, as can be seen through that religion's "Three Jewels." The Nine *Tattvas* of Jainism are as follows:

1. *Jiva:* This means "soul" or "consciousness." This is a sentient yet formless entity, and Jains believe there are 563 different types.

2. *Ajiva:* This term means "absence of soul" or "without consciousness," and refers to entities that do not have and will never have souls. Jains believe that there are 560 types of *Ajiva* entities.

3. *Ashrava:* This word refers to the cause of *kharma* (both good and evil), which Jains believe is human action. *Ashravas* are described as holes through which the energy of *kharma* enters a human soul, making it impure. As a result, some take the concept literally, believing that *kharma* accumulates in physical orifices in the body, hence the practice of sweeping the ground or wearing masks over the face. Jain scripture claims there are 42 *Ashravas*.

4. *Bhandh:* This term means "bondage" and refers to the Jain concept that one's accumulation of *kharma* traps one's soul in the cycle of *samsara*. This is an idea that Jainism shares with Buddhism and Hinduism (religions that also originated in India).

14.1

5. *Punya:* This term means "merit" and refers to the soul's accumulation of good **kharma-pudgalas** (which means "kharmic matter"), which counters negative/evil *kharma*. Jains believe there are a number of specific ways to accumulate *Punya*: giving alms to ascetic monks, water to the thirsty, vessels (jars, pitchers, and so on) to those in need, clothes to the poor, and beds or shelter to those without; praising and honoring deserving people; being of service to righteous people; and thinking positively of others.

6. *Papa:* This term means "demerit" and refers to the soul's accumulation of negative *kharma-pudgalas*. The single most important factor regarding *Papa* is injury to and killing of living beings. *Papa* may also be caused by negative or evil thoughts, behaviors, or words. Jains believe that 18 sins cause this—violence, lying, jealousy, anger, stealing, adultery, greed, covetousness, pride, deception, attachments, needless arguing/quarreling, betrayal, speaking under oaths/swearing, excessive emotions (specifically joy or misery), the act of judging/criticizing, faith in false doctrines, and falsehoods committed by way of deception.

7. *Samvara:* This term means "to arrest, prevent, or stop," and refers to the intake and accumulation of *kharma*. It relates to the *Ashrava Tattva*, in that it refers to the closing of the holes through which *kharma* enters the soul. Conceptually, this means avoiding the accumulation of *kharma*.

8. *Nirjara:* This term means "to dry up" and refers to how, once the *Samvara Tattva* has been achieved, the accumulation of *kharma* will cease. Over time, as long as no more is accumulated, a soul's existing *kharma* will simply "dry up," allowing one to achieve Jainism understanding of **nirvana** and break free from *samsara*.

9. *Moksha:* This term means "liberation" and refers to the final principal of Jainism—liberation from the bondage (*Bhandh*) of *kharma* through the successful achievement of the *Nirjara Tattva*.

The Five Great Vows (*Maha-vratas*)

The following is a list of the Five Great Vows:

1. I vow to abstain from violence.

2. I vow to abstain from sexual pleasure.

3. I vow to abstain from lying.

4. I vow to abstain from stealing.

5. I vow to abstain from physical and emotional attachments.

The Ten Ascetic Virtues

The Ten Ascetic Virtues are also referred to as the Ten Virtues of Jain Monks. While the layperson is not expected to follow the Ten Virtues to the letter, Jain monks are required to do so. It is understood that only monks can be totally dedicated to the Ascetic Virtues.

1. *Tyaga:* Renunciation (of the world)

2. *Maardava:* Humility

3. *Kshamaa:* Forgiveness

4. *Aarjava:* Straightforwardness

5. *Akinchanya:* Nonattachment (both physically and emotionally, to both objects and people)

6. *Brahmacharya:* Celibacy

7. *Tapa:* Penance (self-inflicted punishments for impure actions and thoughts)

8. *Saucha:* Contentment

9. *Satya:* Honesty

10. *Samyam:* Self-control (meaning exercising control over both one's body and one's senses)

The Twelve Vows of the Layperson

Whereas the Ten Ascetic Virtues are not meant to be strictly followed by non-monks, an alternative set of vows exists for the Jain layperson. These vows are meant for those who want to remain in a family-centered life, which requires that they have sex, obviously, for the procreation of children. These 12 vows are separated into three parts by the theme of their vows *(vratas)*—Anuvratas, Gunavratas, and Sikshavratas. The Twelve Vows of the Layperson Jain are arranged as follows:

Part I: The Five Vows of Limited Nature *(Anuvratas)*

The following are the Five Vows of Limited Nature (*Anuvratas*):

1. *Ahimsa:* The vow of nonviolence. This is the most important doctrine in Jainism, and includes an emphasis on vegetarianism. Jains take great care to avoid injuring any living thing, even a gnat. This limits Jains from pursuing many professions (such as agriculture). For this reason, Jainism grew into an urban religion.

2. *Satya:* The vow of honesty.

3. *Achaurya:* The vow to abstain from stealing.

4. *Brahmacharya:* The vow of chastity (for the layperson, this vow primarily applies to abstinence from adultery and promiscuity).

5. *Aparigraha:* The vow of nonattachment (the layperson is compelled to keep this vow to a lesser degree than Jain monks and nuns).

Part II: The Three Vows of Merit (*Gunavratas*)

The following are the Three Vows of Merit (*Gunavratas*):

1. *Dik Vrata:* The vow to maintain a limited area of activity (primarily to minimize one's potential to accidentally inflict harm).

2. *Bhoga-Upbhoga Vrata:* The vow to limit one's use of consumable items (food, water, and so on). However, this vow also applies to nonconsumable items (money, lumber, tools, and so on).

3. *Anarthadanda Vrata:* The vow to avoid committing purposeless sins.

Part III: The Four Vows of Discipline (*Sikshavratas*)

The following are the Four Vows of Discipline (*Sikshavratas*):

1. *Samayik Vrata:* The vow to practice a certain amount of meditation (48 minutes daily is the standard minimum).

2. *Desavakasika Vrata:* The vow of limited duration of activity. This vow limits an adherent's activities (travel, business, and so on) to only certain days and times.

3. *Pausadha Vrata:* The vow of a limited ascetic life. This vow requires Jain laypersons to live the life of an ascetic monk for at least one full day in their lifetimes.

4. *Atithi Samvibhaga Vrata:* The vow of limited charity. This vow requires the layperson to give all charitable items (such as uneaten food or extra clothing) to monks, ascetics, or people of piety. The food should not be specially prepared, however, as monks are forbidden to accept such food.

WORDS TO GO . . .WORDS TO GO . . .WORDS TO GO

Samsara is the cycle of life, death, and rebirth that will continue until an individual achieves enlightenment through **nirvana.**

Kharma is the accumulation of either positive or negative energies in one's lifetime, which are the result of one's thoughts, words, and actions

Moksha is a release from the bonds that tie one's soul to the endless cycle of birth, death, rebirth.

Nirvana, in Jain thought, is the blissful state of enlightenment in which one is completely free from all desires and material attachments.

The term **kharma-pudgalas** means "kharmic matter," the accumulation of which causes one to become trapped in the cycle of **samsara.**

Maha-vratas are the Five Great Vows taken and strictly adhered to by all Jain ascetics or monks.

The Sanskrit word **vrata,** roughly translated, means "vow."

14.2 SACRED TEXTS

The Jain Sutras (*Agamas*)

Mahavira's teachings, along with many other early Jain ideas and concepts from teachers who preceded him, were originally taught via an oral tradition. For nearly a millennium, the Jain Sutras were passed down orally from teacher to disciple.

In Jainism, however, one of the strictest tenets is that of nonattachment. The early Jains were concerned that written texts could come to be treated as possessions, thus leading to attachments. Therefore, the original Jain scriptures were never written down. Most of what still exists in Jain texts consists of what could be recalled from the oral tradition, along with commentaries from Jain monks and ascetic teachers.

The Jain Sutras (*Agamas*)

The Jain Sutras, called the *Agamas* or *Jain Shrut*, did not exist in written form until roughly 500 C.E., approximately 1,000 years after the death of Mahavira, the first man to organize the beliefs of Jainism into a religious system. Eventually, Jain monks conceded that memorizing the increasingly large entirety of Jain scriptures was becoming more troublesome as time went on.

Also, a few layperson Jains, as well as some non-Jain scribes, had already attempted transcription with very unsatisfactory results. As a result of the gap between the origins and transcriptions of these texts, a large amount of the original knowledge had been lost to all but the most learned of Jain ascetic monks. Much of what had been transcribed up to this point had been altered, manipulated, misinterpreted, or inaccurately explained. To counter this, the Jain *sangha* (monastic community) decided that it was time to write down the Jain Sutras, as they understood them. This led to the compilation of the Jain Sutras as they now exist.

To this day, however, different sects of Jainism have their own beliefs on which of the *Agamas* are genuine and which are "lost," meaning texts either that could not be accurately reproduced or that the sect believes have been manipulated or altered.

Lord Tirthankar's Teachings

The Jain scriptures explain the origins of the Sutras as follows:

> Having climbed the tree of perfect knowledge, the omniscient being, Lord Tirthankar, showered flowers of knowledge to his most enlightened disciples, called **Ganadhars**.

The *Agamas* claim to be the teachings of the "omniscient" Lord Tirthankar to his most enlightened pupils, a small group of disciples called *Ganadhars*. The original text (handed down orally from Lord Tirthankar to his students) was composed in 14 sections called *Purvas*. The *Ganadhars* later created a collection of "Twelve Limbs," called **Ang-Pravishtha.**

The original 14 *Purvas* of Lord Tirthankar were still included in the final section, or "Twelfth Limb," of the *Ang-Pravishtha*, which is titled *Drastivad*. The *Drastivad* is no longer available and is only partially described in other sections of the *Agamas*. Unfortunately, the "twelfth limb" is the only section of the *Agamas* that every existing sect of Jainism agrees to being a "lost" *Agamas*, conceding that it had faded too greatly during the passage of so many centuries.

The Fate of the *Agamas*

In addition to the Twelve Limbs composed by the *Ganadhars*, other scriptures were later composed by elder Jain monks, called **Stathviras,** and are also included as part of the *Agamas*. This section of the *Agamas* is called *Ang-Bayha*.

In its entirety (meaning without the omission of any "lost" scriptures), which is considerably large, the *Agamas* is comprised of the following sections:

1. The Fourteen *Purvas* of Lord Tirthankar

2. The *Ang-Pravishtha*, or "Twelve Limbs," written by the *Ganadhar* disciples

3. The *Ang-Bayha*, which varies in number from one sect of Jainism to another—the *Murtipujak* sect accepts 34 sutras, the *Sthanakvasi* sect regards the validity of 21 sutras, and the *Digambar* sect believes there are only 14 genuine or acceptable sutras in the *Ang-Bayha* section of the *Agamas*

14.2

14.3 RITUALS AND HOLIDAYS

Mahavira Jayanthi

The Diwali of Jainism

Paryushana Parva

Many of the holidays observed in Jainism are also observed in Hinduism, though sometimes in different ways. One example of this is the festival of Diwali in India. However, Jainism does have its own set of unique holidays such as the Mahavira Jayanthi (the birth of the "Great Hero") and Paryushana Parva (the tradition of "staying in one place).

Mahavira Jayanthi

Mahavira Jayanthi celebrates the birth of Jainism's founder, Vardhamana, who was later called Mahavira, or "Great Hero." On this day, Jain adherents make offerings of rice and milk, and are encouraged to give alms. In India, a grand parade takes place on this day, during which images of Mahavira are carried through the streets. Much as is done with the tale of Christ's birth around the holiday of Christmas, during this festival, one often sees dramatic reenactments of Mahavira's birth, as well as the events and divine visions Mahavira's mother experienced during her pregnancy.

The date on which this festival is observed changes from year to year because it is based on the solar calendar. The next Mahavira Jayanthi will be celebrated on April 7, 2009.

The Diwali of Jainism

Diwali is a festival celebrated throughout the country of India. This festival is observed by nearly every faith of India, including Hindus, Buddhists, Sikhs, and Jains. However, each faith has its own unique significance for this auspicious day. For Jains, this day celebrates the *mosksha* (liberation) of Mahavira (in more basic language, it's the day Mahavira died). Diwali is a festival of lights. Its symbolism revolves around reminding Jains to light up their internal lamps by following the path of the Mahavira and the other 23 **Tirthankaras.**

Since Diwali is so widely celebrated in India, the dates are often decided upon years in advance. From 2009 to 2014, the dates for the Diwali Festival are as follows:

▶ October 28, 2009

▶ November 10, 2010

▶ October 26, 2011

▶ November 13, 2012

▶ November 3, 2013

▶ October 23, 2014

Paryushana Parva

The term *Paryushana* means "to stay in one place," and it originates from the ancient practice of ascetic monks of not traveling during the monsoon season. This allowed them a time for deep meditation and reflection. Today this practice is observed as an eight-day-long festival during a period between August and September, depending on the year and the sect of Jainism to which one subscribes.

The most difficult issue of Paryushana Parva is that nearly every sect of Jainism believes that it takes place on a different day. This is unfortunate, since it is considered one of the most sacred days in Jainism. In recent years, attempts have been made to unify the date of Paryushana Parva. None have met with much success.

In the most densely populated regions of India, Paryushana Parva will begin (for 2009 only) on August 28, 2009, and end on September 5, 2009.

The most important practice of Jains during Paryushana Parva is called the Pratikramana meditation. *Pratikramana* means "to turn back." This is a meditative practice during which a Jain takes some time to reflect on the progress of his or her spiritual journey and ends with a renewal of faith. For ascetic monks, this is done more frequently, but the annual Pratikramana during Paryushana Parva is a minimum requirement for any Jain, whether an ascetic, monk, or layperson. The basic and most common elements of the Pratikramana meditation (though certain sects may require more or less) are as follows:

14.3

▶ Prayers to the 24 Tirthankaras (ascetic masters), which began with Lord Tirthankar and ended with Mahavira

▶ Prayers to the Supreme Being (sometimes referred to in English as the "Godhead")

▶ Reflections on one's Jain Vows (the *vratas*)

▶ Consideration of the sins, mistakes, and other transgressions one has committed in the last year

▶ *Kayotsarga*—an attempt to use one's control of mind, body, and spirit to separate the soul from the body

▶ *Pratyhakyhan*—making spiritual resolutions and reaffirmations of faith to be pursued over the next year, until the time for Paryushana Parva returns

WORDS TO GO . . .WORDS TO GO . . .WORDS TO GO

The 24 **Tirthankaras** (literally meaning 24 "bridgebuilders" or "pathfinders") are "pure" human beings who have shown the way to the liberation of the soul from *samsara* (reincarnation). These have purified their souls of kharmic impurities. Mahavira was the final and greatest Tirthankara. Since Jainism is focused on humans gaining release from the endless cycle of reincarnation, it is humans that Jains emulate in their own personal journeys for release. Jains venerate the 24 Tirhankaras and have erected 40,000 temples in India to worship these figures. The Jain temple on Mount Abu is considered one of the seven wonders of India.

14.4 ORIGINS AND FOUNDER

Jainism was developed into a religion by a man named Vardhamana, who later came to be called Mahavira, which means the "Great Hero." The Jains consider Mahavira to have been the last in a line of 24 divinely wise beings known as *Tirthankaras.*

Mahavira was born in 599 B.C.E. in Bihar, India. He was born a prince of a royal household. However, at the age of 30, he left his family and renounced his royal birthright. He also gave up all of his possessions and turned to the life of an ascetic.

Mahavira spent 12 years in meditation, conquering the desires, emotions, and attachments that he believed were hindering his spiritual development. During these years, he fasted frequently and for long periods. He took diligent care not to harm any living organism—animals, insects, birds, and even certain plants. When 12 years had passed, Mahavira experienced a moment of spiritual awakening, called *keval-janan.*

For 30 years after his meditations had ended, he traveled barefoot across India, preaching his realizations to all who had ears to listen. In contrast to the caste system of Hinduism, Mahavira preached to all people, regardless of their financial situations, social status, class, or gender.

Seeing so many followers at so many different levels of enlightenment led Mahavira to organize them into four categories. This is sometimes referred to as the "Fourfold Order" and is as follows:

1. *Sadhu:* Monk
2. *Sadhvi:* Nun
3. *Shravak:* Layman
4. *Shravika:* Laywoman

14.4

The primary concept Mahavira taught consisted of three elements that would eventually lead one to liberation through enlightenment in *nirvana.* These three tenets, according to Mahavira's teachings, were the keys to unlocking the bondage of *kharma:*

1. *Samyak-darshana:* Right faith

2. *Samyak-janan:* Right knowledge

3. *Samyak-charitra:* Right conduct

In 527 B.C.E., Mahavira died at the age of 72. Jains do not refer to him as having "died," but instead say that he "gained *nirvana.*" Jains believe that, upon dying, Mahavira became what is called a *Siddha,* meaning "pure energy" or "pure consciousness."

14.5 HISTORICAL DEVELOPMENT

A few centuries after Mahavira's death, the various groups that made up the Jain religion reached a point at which some groups began to disagree on certain details of their beliefs. This resulted in a schism that created two main sects of Jainism, Shvetambara, and Digambara, from which branched a number of other subsects.

Shvetambara means "clad in white" and refers to the sect's mode of dress. Shvetambara adherents commonly wear loose-fitting white robes. In 1500 B.C.E., the Shvetambara sect divided into three primary subsects—Shvetambara Murtipujak, Shthanakvashi, and Terapanthi. These sects, however, do not disagree on doctrine. Instead, the main point of contention between them is which of the Jain Sutras and texts are genuine and valid.

Digambara means "clad in air" and refers to the fact that the monks of the sect often wore little or no clothing at all, preferring instead to walk naked. While adherents of the Digambara sect may still be found today, they are rare. The *Digambara* also believe that women have no chance of liberation in this life but must wait until they are born as males in another life. In contrast, the *Shvetambara* believe that men and women may achieve *moksha* and include both monks and nuns in their sect. Of the two main sects of Jainism, Shvetambara remains the most common.

Jains view total detachment as essential to achieving *nirvana* and ultimately *moksha*. This detachment from people and things is extreme. This is why the monastic life and asceticism are viewed so positively in this religious perspective. At the layperson level this kind of detachment is impossible, and therefore the ultimate liberation of the soul may only be achieved in another life. A radical expression of the Jain's attempt at detachment is *sallekhana* (holy death). This is death by self-starvation. Though not required of adherents, it certainly is viewed favorably and is interesting since it demonstrates the Jain's desire for ultimate detachment from the world.

14.5

14.6 PRESENT-DAY FACTS

Today Jainism is still practiced by millions of Jains all over the world, especially in India. Unlike Buddhism, however, it never spread to other countries with much success. In fact, only over the last century has Jainism been found in any country outside of India. Today there are still roughly 4.2 million practicing Jains in India.

In the United States, estimates vary among polls. Estimates range between 5,000 and 90,000 practicing Jains.

Worldwide estimates of Jain adherents range from between 9 million and 10 million.

15

SIKHISM

15.1 FUNDAMENTAL TENETS

Basic Information on Sikhism

The Core Beliefs of Sikhism

Five Thieves vs. Five Weapons

Sikh Codes of Behavior

The Five K's of Sikhism

Understanding Sikh Names

Despite the fact that Sikhism is the world's fifth-largest religion, many people in the west are unaware of its existence. Chances are that you have seen a Sikh and did not realize it. Since male adherents of Sikhism wear turbans and often have long beards, many westerners automatically (though mistakenly) assume that they are Muslims. In truth, Sikhism is unique, and stands alone as the youngest of the world's major religions.

Basic Information on Sikhism

▶ Origin Date: Approximately 1496 C.E.

▶ Founder: Guru Nanak Dev Ji.

▶ View of God: Monotheistic.

▶ Dietary Restrictions: Nearly all Sikhs are strict vegetarians, and most abstain from consuming that which contains alcohol, caffeine, or other mind-altering substances.

▶ View of Life/Death: Belief in reincarnation until spiritual liberation is achieved.

▶ Lifestyle Foci: Extremely disciplined, with very specific codes of behavior and appearance.

▶ Worship Restrictions: Anyone may worship in a Sikh temple. However, certain rites and codes must be adopted before a person may be baptized as a Sikh and given the name of Singh or the title of *Khalsa*.

The Core Beliefs of Sikhism

The core beliefs of Sikhism are as follows:

▶ Belief in *Ek Onkar*. There is only one god, who is both the creator and sustainer of all things, and is the same one worshipped by all religions. This god has neither beginning nor end, and is the only entity that has always and will always exist. The Sikhs refer to this concept of monotheism as *Ek Onkar,* meaning "One."

▶ Belief that all human beings are equal under God, regardless of sex, class, or religion.

▶ Belief in reincarnation, *kharma,* and salvation. Humans have souls, which pass from one body to another after death (reincarnation) until one transcends *kharma* and is liberated through salvation.

▶ Belief in the defense of morality. All living things have the right to exist. Every Sikh has a duty to defend the rights of living creatures—most importantly, human beings.

▶ Preparation for martyrdom. A Sikh must be prepared to give his or her life, if necessary, for the sake of moral principles.

▶ No observation of holy days. Every day is a gift and should be treated as holy. No particular day should be thought of as more sacred than another. However, Sikhs believe there are many paths to spiritual salvation.

▶ Belief that all paths lead to *Ek Onkar.* Sikhs are not the chosen people of God. Being a Sikh does not deliver one to salvation. All people of all faiths have the right to be liberated from *kharma.*

▶ Adherence to discipline. Once a person has been baptized, he or she must live a disciplined life, frequently reciting the **Bani** prayers, always wearing the Five K's, and strictly adhering to Sikh codes of conduct.

◀ SEE ALSO 11.4, *"Origins and Founder of Buddhism"* ▶

◀ SEE ALSO 11.2, *"Sacred Texts of Buddhism"* ▶

Five Thieves vs. Five Weapons

Every Sikh strives to conquer the temptations referred to as the Five Thieves, which are as follows:

1. *a'Hankar:* Pride

2. *Mo'h:* Attachments, as they easily lead to pride, greed, jealousy/anger, and/or lust (the other four Thieves)

3. *Lob'h:* Greed

4. *Kr'odh:* Anger

5. *K'haam:* Lust

Many English-speaking Sikhs refer to these Five Thieves using the abbreviation P.A.G.A.L.

15.1

Each Sikh must battle the Five Thieves with five specific virtues. These virtues are referred to as the Five Weapons and are as follows:

1. *Santokh:* Contentment, by keeping one's heart absent of greed

2. *Dan:* Charity and generosity

3. *Nimarta:* Humility/modesty

4. *Daya:* Kindness, mercy, and compassion

5. *Chardi Kala:* Positive energy created by having an optimistic outlook on life and finding joy in the knowledge that God is everywhere, in all things

Sikh Codes of Behavior

A number of practices are considered strictly forbidden by those of the Sikh faith. These forbidden practices are believed to be detrimental to achieving spiritual liberation from the cycle of life, death, and rebirth or reincarnation.

▶ *No mind-altering substances:* A Sikh is not to consume drugs, alcohol, tobacco, or any other mind-altering substance.

▶ *No needless or harmful speech:* A Sikh should not speak needless words by lying, boasting, speaking ill of others, or gossiping.

▶ *No maya (material attachments):* Material attachments are useless and should be strictly avoided. Sikhs should desire not material wealth such as gold or property, but the wealth of the spirit.

▶ *No priests:* Sikhs are to have no priestly class. Priests and clergy are to be neither appointed nor consulted in the Sikh faith. Though some Sikhs may assume roles of leadership, such as managing **gurdwaras** or organizing assemblies, no Sikh is to be treated or considered as more holy than another.

▶ *No illogical rituals or behaviors:* A Sikh should not perform superstitious actions (such as "knocking on wood"), pray to dead ancestors, or worship idols, figures, or graven images. This rule of behavior also prohibits Sikh women from covering themselves with veils (as is sometimes required of Muslim women).

▶ *No sacrifices of living beings:* This rule forbids the sacrifice of both humans and animals. For example, it forbids such actions as the ancient practice of a wife throwing her body onto the funeral pyre of her dead husband (called *suttee*). It also forbids religious animal sacrifices.

▶ *No religious seclusion:* Sikhs are encouraged to live a family-oriented life-style. They are not supposed to adopt religious practices that are counter to this, such as living in monasteries, taking vows of celibacy, viewing marriage as "impure," living alone in reclusive locations, and so on.

▶ *No consumption of meat from ritualistically killed animals:* Many Sikhs are vegetarians by choice. However, this rule does not forbid the consumption of meat. Many Sikhs just choose not to consume meat at all. Regardless of whether a Sikh is vegetarian, none is to consume any meat from an animal that was killed in a religious or ritualistic fashion. For example, they won't eat kosher meat.

◀ SEE ALSO 2.1, *"Fundamental Tenets of Judaism"* ▶

The Five K's of Sikhism

The code of appearance, called the Five K's, is perhaps one of the most sacred aspects of the Sikh lifestyle. These five articles of faith are observed by most Sikhs at all times, but are strictly followed by those of the Khalsa Order.

The Five K's of Sikhism are as follows:

1. *Kesa:* Sikhs rarely, if ever, cut their hair, whether on the head, face, or any other part of the body. As a result of this, Sikhs wear turbans (which is often mentioned alongside the Five K's) to keep their extremely long hair clean and out of the way. This is also why adult male Sikhs have rather long beards.

2. *Kanga:* A wooden comb, used to maintain a Sikh's long hair. Also acts as a symbol of cleanliness. Some Sikhs carry a Kanga comb under their turbans.

3. *Kaccha:* A special garment that is worn underneath the clothing. This undergarment serves as a symbolic reminder of virgin chastity and sexual abstinence until marriage, as well as of practicing marital fidelity, controlling sexual desire, and avoiding adultery.

4. *Kirpan:* A ceremonial dagger that represents the vow of the order of Khalsa to be warriors for justice and defenders of the innocent, weak, and/or helpless.

5. *Kara:* A steel bracelet that encircles the entire wrist and symbolizes the unity of the Sikh community, as well as their devotion to seeking out eternal/absolute truth and abstinence from evil actions.

In recent times, the Five K's have become a matter of much debate. Unfortunately, since the tragedy of 9/11, this code of appearance has caused many Sikhs to become targets of misguided anti-Muslim violence.

15.1

◀ SEE ALSO 11.6, *"Present-Day Facts of Buddhism"* ▶

Understanding Sikh Names

Whether one is born a Sikh or converts, it matters not. Sikhs do not have traditional family names. Their shared names act as a symbol of unity, equality, and the brotherhood/sisterhood of humankind. Upon being baptized into the faith, all Sikhs share one of two surnames:

▶ Singh: Meaning "lion," this last name is given to all male Sikhs.

▶ Kaur: Meaning "princess," this last name is given to all female Sikhs.

That these names are different depending on sex is somewhat because of the fact that Sikh first names are often gender neutral, and therefore could belong to either a man or a woman. So the use of gender-specific last names simply prevents any confusion over whether a Sikh is male or female.

Often non-Sikh Westerners misunderstand the significance of these Sikh names and that of the title *Khalsa,* which means "Pure" or "The Pure Ones." Often people who are unfamiliar with Sikh names mistakenly assume that Khalsa is a last name. In actuality, Khalsa is a title that follows the given surname of any Sikh who has been baptized into the Khalsa Order. One can become a Sikh without becoming a member of the Khalsa. However, one cannot become one of the Khalsa without first becoming a Sikh. Below are some examples of Sikh names.

The following names would belong to male Sikhs who have been initiated into the Khalsa:

▶ Gurusimran Singh Khalsa

▶ Dharma Singh Khalsa

The following names would belong to a female Sikh who has also been initiated into the Khalsa:

▶ Kirti Kaur Khalsa

▶ Gurpreet Kaur Khalsa

These names would belong to Sikhs who have *not* been initiated into the Khalsa Order:

▶ Ram Das Singh (male)

▶ Charankawal Kaur (female)

The word **Bani** means something like "vibration" or "frequency." In Sikhism, this word refers to prayers that are recitations of the words of the **Gurus.** Khalsa and devout Sikhs recite five specific **Bani** prayers daily, often in the morning—**Japji Sahib, Anand Sahib, Jaap Sahib, Benti Chaupai,** and **Tav-Prasad Savaiye.** However, these five **Banis** are not the only such prayers. Everything written in the **Guru Granth Sahib** is considered a Bani.

A **Gurdwara** is a Sikh holy place where Sikhs go to conduct worship. The word can be translated as either "Home of the **Guru**" or "Door/Gate to the **Guru.**" Sikhs also share communal meals in a Gurdwara. The doors of any Gurdwara are open to all people of all faiths.

15.2 SACRED TEXTS

Languages of the *Guru Granth Sahib*
The Arrangement of the *Guru Granth Sahib*

The *Guru Granth Sahib* is a holy text containing the teachings of Guru Nanak Dev Ji, as well as other **Gurus,** and teachings from other sacred texts such as the Koran, Bible, and Bhaghavad Gita. As dictated by the final orders of the Tenth Sikh Guru, Gobind Singh, this text is considered the final and eternal successor to the line of the Sikh *Gurus.*

Languages of the *Guru Granth Sahib*

Although most of the *Guru Granth Sahib* is written in common Punjabi dialect used at the time in which it was written, it also employs a number of other languages, such as Hindi, Sanskrit, and Arabic. Regardless of the language, however, all hymns in the texts are written in the script known as Gurmukhi, which was created and developed by Sikh Guru Angad. Every version of the *Guru Granth Sahib* is precisely 1,430 pages long.

The Arrangement of the *Guru Granth Sahib*

The hymns of the *Guru Granth Sahib* were laid out in a very specific arrangement that was devised by Sikh Guru Arjun Dev, according first to the melody in which they are sung. The secondary element of the arrangement is based on the nature or poetic meter of the hymns. Lastly, they are arranged according to author.

The *Guru Granth Sahib* is divided into 33 sections. The first section is the epic poem called *Japji,* which was written by Guru Nanak. However, Sikhs believe that this hymn should never be sung. The next section contains a number of assorted Sikh verses. The last 31 sections are called the *Ragas,* which are *Sri Rag, Majh, Gauri, Asa, Gujari, Devgandhari, Bihagra, Wadhans, Sorath, Dhanasari, Jaitsari, Todi, Bairari, Tilang, Suhi, Bilawal, Gaund, Ramkali, Nat, Maligaura, Maru, Tukhari, Kedara, Bhairo, Basant, Sarang, Malar, Kanara, Kalian, Prabhati,* and *Jaijawanti.*

The *Ragas* are further divided into a number of specific meters:

▶ *Chaupadas:* Four-line verses
▶ *Chhants:* Six-line verses

▶ *Ashtpadis:* Eight-line verses

▶ Long poems

▶ Short poems

▶ *Vars:* A minimum of two paragraphs followed by a single concluding stanza

▶ *Bhagatas:* The assorted poems of saints

WORDS TO GO . . .WORDS TO GO . . .WORDS TO GO

Guru literally means "teacher." In the Sikh faith, it refers to a line of 10 spiritual men who were leaders of the Sikh people from 1469 to 1708. The tenth *Guru,* Gobind Singh, brought an end to the appointment of *Gurus* by declaring that the *Guru Granth Sahib* text would be his successor, and therefore the last Sikh *Guru* for the rest of eternity.

15.2

15.3 RITUALS AND HOLIDAYS

The New Sikh Calendar
The Order of Khalsa

Sikhs do not observe many rituals, aside from baptisms and inductions into the Khalsa Order. Technically, they also do not observe holy days, which stems from their belief that no certain day should be considered any more or less holy than another. They do, however, celebrate a number of festivals throughout the year. Sikhs follow their own calendar.

The New Sikh Calendar

As of 1999, they began using a new system, the *Nanakshahi* Calendar, the years of which begin with Guru Nanak's birth in 1469 C.E. This calendar is based on a solar cycle, as opposed to the previous Sikh calendar, which was based on a lunar one and therefore caused the dates of each festival to change from one year to the next. With the new solar-based *Nanakshahi* calendar, the dates remain the same. The annual Sikh festivals and other dates of interest, in chronological order, are as follows:

- ▶ *January 5:* Guru Gobind Singh's birthday.

- ▶ *January 13:* Lohri Festival, an honor to the symbolic and purifying nature of fire. This festival is a special moment for newlywed couples, even more so for those who have given birth to their first child. People congregate around bonfires, and children sing songs door to door in praise of the folk hero Dulha Bhatti, who (like the European Robin Hood) stole from the rich and gave to the poor. The children are often given treats at each home they visit.

- ▶ *March 13:* New Year's Eve of the *Nanakshi* Calendar.

- ▶ *March 22–24: Holla Mohalla*, the Punjab Festival, a three-day-long celebration that, for Sikhs, is a day to remember the many Sikh warriors who gave their lives in battle to protect the land from foreign invaders. On this day, the *Nihang* warrior Sikhs, a nomadic people who descend from the armies created by Guru Gobind Singh, give demonstrations of *Shastar Vidyaa* (Punjabi forms of martial arts).

- ▶ *April 14: Baisakhi*, a festival commemorating the formation of the Khalsa Order.

- ▶ *May 2:* Guru Arjan Dev's birthday.

▶ *June 16:* Commemoration of the martyrdom of Guru Arjan Dev.

▶ *September 1:* Remembrance of the First *Parkash* (installation) of the "living guru," the text of the *Guru Granth Sahib.*

▶ *November 24:* Commemoration of the martyrdom of Guru Tegh Bahadur.

◀ SEE ALSO 9.3, *"Rituals and Holidays of Taoism"* ▷

The Order of Khalsa

In Sikhism, there is a basic spiritual progression that all human beings have the capacity to complete. However, many human beings have neither the discipline nor the understanding to reach the higher levels of this progression. This progression is divided into four stages:

1. *Manmukh:* A common person, unenlightened, uncaring, and self-centered. This person thinks only of the material and neglects the spiritual.

2. *Sikh:* One who has started on the path to education, enlightenment, salvation, and spiritual liberation. The word *Sikh* means "disciple" or "student." More specifically, this refers to one who follows the Sikh codes of conduct and behavior.

3. *Khalsa:* One who displays absolute devotion to the Sikh faith. A Khalsa is supposed to behave as an example to other Sikhs and must strictly maintain the Five K's at all times. While a Sikh has the choice not to wear all of them, a Khalsa does not.

4. *Gurmukh:* One who has achieved spiritual liberation and salvation, and returns to become one with *Ek Onkar.*

Of these, most Sikhs reach the stage of Khalsa. The word *Khalsa* means "Pure" or "The Pure Ones." Sikhs who bear this title have undergone a special initiation ceremony called the Amrit Ceremony. This ceremony was begun by the tenth Sikh *Guru,* Gobind Singh, on March 30, 1699, a day referred to by Sikhs as *Baisakhi.* On that day, Guru Gobind Singh baptized five Sikhs into the Khalsa Order. The Amrit ceremony of Khalsa initiation first has the initiate drink sugar water (called *Amrit*) that has been stirred with a dagger (called a *Kirpan*).

Initiation as a Khalsa is nothing to be taken lightly, as it requires one to be totally devoted to the disciplined lifestyle that the order demands. The Five K's are no longer a suggestion, but a requirement. Codes of conduct must be strictly adhered to and transgressions are a serious issue. As the initiate drinks, five Khalsa Sikhs must be present, along with a copy of the *Guru Granth Sahib.* Once the Amrit has been swallowed, the initiate is told the following:

15.3

"You shall never remove any hair from any part of your body. You shall never use tobacco, alcohol, or other intoxicants. You shall not eat meat killed in the Muslim way. You shall not commit adultery."

Meat killed in the "Muslim way" refers to the fact that most butchers in India were Muslims (since killing is forbidden in Hinduism). Often these animals were slaughtered in ritualistic fashions, or they were slaughtered kosher for Jewish clients.

Lastly, Khalsa (as well as some noninitiate Sikhs) will greet another Khalsa with the following statement:

Wahe Guru ji ka Khalsa. Wahe Guru ji ki fateh.

"The Khalsa belong to the Guru. Victory belongs to the Guru."

15.4 ORIGINS AND FOUNDER

The Path of the Guru

Nanak Fights the System

Sri Guru Nanak Dev Ji, more commonly referred to by the short name Guru Nanak, is the man credited with founding the Sikh faith. He was born in 1469 in the farming region of Talwandi, which was then a part of northern India but is now in Pakistan.

Guru Nanak's father, Mehta Kalu, was the village accountant and a member of the ruling Kshatriya class of the Hindu caste system. This allowed Nanak to become well educated in the years of his youth, mastering the written and verbal languages of Sanskrit, Arabic, and Persian, and the regional dialects of Hindi and Punjabi. From an early age, young Nanak displayed an enthusiastic interest in religious philosophy and other spiritual matters. He also proved to have a natural tendency for religious tolerance, making friends with people of both the Hindu and Muslim faiths. In fact, he even assumed a manner of unusual dress that integrated clothing from a number of religious faiths. These early friendships had a great influence upon Nanak's revolutionary religious philosophies, now known as Sikhism.

◀ *SEE ALSO 13.3, "The Sacred Texts of Hindu Dharma"* ▶

One story tells of how, when Nanak was 12 years old, his father gave him 20 rupees and told him to use it for a business venture. Nanak took the money to the local grocery market and bought food with it, which he then distributed (without charge) among the poor, the homeless, and the wandering holy men of the area (Muslim and Hindu alike). When Nanak later returned home, he arrived empty-handed. His father asked him, "What happened to your business?" Nanak told his father that he had used the money to conduct "true business." According to Sikh texts, the *Gurdwara* of Sacha Sauda was built on the spot where the young Guru Nanak first fed the poor.

In 1485, Nanak was appointed the position of Accountant of Provisions for the local Muslim ruler of Sultanpur, Daulat Khan Lodhi. Nanak received the position and soon proved to be a competent employee. He remained in Sultanpur for the next 14 years. Two years after Nanak received this position, at age 18, his sister Nanaki arranged for him to be married to Mata Sulakhni of Batala, with whom he had two sons.

15.4

The Path of the Guru

While there is some debate surrounding the events of Guru Nanak's life in Sultanpur, nearly all historical and religious accounts agree that his enlightenment took place in 1496. He departed on his first mission with one simple yet bold statement: "There is no Hindu, nor any Mussalman (Muslim)." This statement, which proclaimed that all men were brothers under God, regardless of what doctrine they practiced or religious path they followed, became the founding idea of the Sikh faith. In a time and place when Muslims and Hindus were often at violent odds with one another, this statement called upon all men of all faiths to love one another as brothers under God. Such an idea was both unprecedented and controversial.

In his life, Guru Nanak continued making spiritual missions throughout parts of Pakistan, Punjab, and India. He made five such missions before his death, during which he spoke out against the caste structure, religious rituals, and holy pilgrimages. Nanak preached to, befriended, lived among, and dined with people of all castes, classes, religions, and races. Such cross-caste interaction was a social taboo in a region where strict caste segregation had been common practice for over a thousand years.

◀ SEE ALSO 13.1, *"Fundamental Tenets of Hindu Dharma"* ▶

Nanak Fights the System

While on one of his spiritual missions, Guru Nanak received two dinner invitations in the same day. One invitation was from a carpenter of a lower caste, and the other was from a rich landowner of a higher caste. Guru Nanak refused the invitation of the landowner and chose instead to dine with the carpenter. Nanak's choice was based on the knowledge that the food in the poor carpenter's home was earned by hard work, while the food in the rich landowner's home was not earned, but gained by exploiting the poor.

During this incident, Guru Nanak verbalized yet another primary concept of the Sikh faith: "Riches can only be amassed through sinful and evil means." By this, Guru Nanak meant that excessive wealth often comes from or leads to the evil of greed, is gained sinfully, and yet can never be carried along after one's death. Only "spiritual wealth" could follow one into the next world, making it far superior in value when compared to material wealth.

15.5 HISTORICAL DEVELOPMENT

The Line of Sikh *Gurus*

Accomplishments of the *Gurus*

Guru Nanak died at the age of 69, in the year 1539. Some accounts claim he died in 1538, though this dating conflict may be due to the fact that Nanak died in 1539 *before* his seventieth birthday. This misunderstanding may have resulted in a mathematical error in regard to the year of his death.

Though Nanak had two sons, he found neither worthy of succeeding him in spreading the ideas of Sikhism. Nanak appointed a disciple named Angad as his successor, making Guru Angad the second Sikh *Guru*. After Nanak's death, there were nine more Sikh *Gurus*. The tenth *Guru*, Guru Gobind Singh, declared that the line of *Gurus* would end with him, and he appointed as his successors the teachings of the Sikh holy text, called the *Guru Granth Sahib*, and the Sikh Order of the Khalsa.

◀ SEE ALSO 15.2, *"Sikh Names"* ▶

The Line of Sikh *Gurus*

The Sikh *Gurus*, in chronological order, followed by their years of service as *Gurus* of the faith, are as follows:

1. Guru Nanak Dev Ji, 1469–1539
2. Guru Angad Dev Ji, 1539–1552
3. Guru Amar Das, 1552–1574
4. Guru Ram Das, 1574–1581
5. Guru Arjan Dev, 1581–1606
6. Guru Hargobind, 1606–1644
7. Guru Har Rai, 1644–1661
8. Guru Har Krishan, 1661–1664
9. Guru Tegh Bahadur, 1665–1675
10. Guru Gobind Singh, 1675–1708
11. *Guru Granth Sahib*, 1708–on

15.5

Accomplishments of the Gurus

Aside from Guru Nanak, many others in the Sikh line of *Gurus* made significant contributions to the religion's development. The Sikh *Gurus* who are of special note, in chronological order, are mentioned in the sections that follow.

Guru Angad

Guru Angad developed the written language called Gurumukhi script, in which the *Guru Granth Sahib* is written. This alphabet became the official written form of the Punjabi language. This allowed Sikhs to further separate themselves from Hindus, who wrote solely in Sanskrit.

Guru Amar Das

Guru Amar Das (sometimes spelled as Amardas ji) appointed a large number of disciples throughout many regions of the country to preach the ideas of Sikhism to the people. He also created a system of Sikh assembly, whereby all of his preaching disciples, as well as all Sikhs, could gather biannually.

Guru Ram Das

Guru Ram Das founded and developed the town of Ramdaspur, which later was called Amritsar, and is now the home of the main Sikh Gurdwara, called "The Golden Temple." He also constructed the first main center of Sikhism, called the Goindwal Sahib.

Guru Arjan

Guru Arjan commissioned and oversaw the construction of the Sri Harimander Sahib (Golden Temple) in Amritsar. Construction of Sri Harimander Sahib was completed in 1604. Guru Arjan was executed by the Moguls at Lahore in 1606.

Guru Hargobind

Guru Hargobind was very much a warrior saint, creating a force of skilled warriors to protect Amritsar and all Sikhs from the ever-present threats of violence from other religions and neighboring lands. In Punjab, he led the Sikhs to victory in six great battles against the Mogul invaders, often against overwhelming odds. He was so skilled in battle that many Punjabis of many faiths came to fight alongside him. Hargobind always wore two scimitar swords, called Meeri (temporal power) and Peeri (spiritual power). This inspired the creation of the Sikh emblem called the Khanda, which has two scimitars, crossed at the hilts, with a single double-edged sword between them. In the center of the emblem is a circle, called a Chakram, which was a throwing weapon. To this day, many Sikhs practice the stick- and sword-fighting art of Gatka.

Guru Har Rai

Guru Har Rai was the oldest of Guru Hargobind's five sons. Unlike most of the *Gurus*, he never composed any verses for inclusion in the *Guru Granth Sahib*. However, he emphasized the importance of learning the *Gurus'* teachings which are written within its pages. He appointed Guru Har Krishan as successor, who, in turn, appointed Tegh Bahadur as his successor with his dying breath.

Guru Tegh Bahadur

Guru Tegh Bahadur proved to be another strong warrior leader for the Sikhs. This is no surprise, considering that he was the youngest (and, most agree, the most beloved) of Guru Hargobind's five sons. At the age of only 14, he fought alongside his father in his sixth and final battle against Mogul invaders. Though he found himself surrounded and was under orders to retreat, the young Tegh Bahadur (as well as his four older brothers) refused to turn his back and flee.

Guru Gobind Singh

Guru Gobind Singh was the last of the Sikh *Gurus*. He declared that the text of the *Guru Granth Sahib* would be treated from then on as a living *Guru*, and that no Sikh would again assume that position. Guru Gobind was both a warrior and a poet. He founded the Sikh Order of the Khalsa, personally initiating the first five members. He also established the Five K's. In the end, Guru Gobind Singh was betrayed by a jealous officer (because of how well the emperor treated him), who sent two assassins to murder the Sikh leader. Though he defeated his would-be assassins, Guru Gobind received a deep wound. Despite being attended to by the emperor's own skilled English surgeon, the wound never fully healed and was prone to reopening and bleeding terribly. The wound slowly began to drain his life. Just before the end, on October 7, 1708, Guru Gobind had the *Guru Granth Sahib* brought before him. He then declared, "This is my commandment: Utilize Sri Granth ji in my place. Whosoever acknowledges it will gain its reward. The Guru will rescue him. Know that this is the truth." With these words, Guru Gobind Singh passed from this life, and with him the tradition of the Sikh *Gurus*.

15.5

15.6 PRESENT-DAY FACTS

Sikhism remains the youngest of the world's major religions, having existed for just over 500 years (the year 2008 C.E. will mark 512 years since the foundation of the Sikh faith, if dated from Guru Nanak's first spiritual mission in 1496 C.E.). While estimates vary, the Sikh faith is currently said to be the world's fifth-largest religion and is practiced by between 23 million and 26 million people worldwide. The majority of Sikhs, roughly 75 percent, live in Punjab or other regions of India.

16

ZOROASTRIANISM

16.1 FUNDAMENTAL TENETS

Basic Information on Zoroastrianism

The Core Beliefs of Zoroastrianism

The Three Tenets of Moral Conduct

Though many people in the West are aware of the historical existence, if not the teachings, of Zoroaster, few are aware that the religion of Zoroastrianism is still being practiced. Adherents of Zoroastrianism worship the god Ahura Mazda, and the religion was founded upon the teachings of the prophet Zarathustra (whose name was later Latinized to Zoroaster. For roughly 1,000 years, from 560 B.C.E. to 650 C.E., Zoroastrianism was one of the most dominant of the world's religions.

Basic Information on Zoroastrianism

▶ Origin Date: there is currently a debate between scholars who place the religion's origins between 1000 B.C.E. and 600 B.C.E. and those who date it earlier between 1400 B.C.E. and 1000 B.C.E.

▶ Founder: Zoroaster (originally called Zarathustra).

▶ View of God: monotheistic, integrated with a dualistic ("good" god vs. "evil" god) perception of the divine.

▶ Dietary Restrictions: None; nearly all things are permitted, if consumed with moderation.

▶ View of Life/Death: One's place in the afterlife, in Heaven or Hell, is determined by the balance of good vs. evil actions, thoughts, and/or words in one's life. If an individual has done more good deeds than evil, the bridge that leads to paradise is broad and the journey easy. If the individual has done more evil than good, then the bridge to paradise becomes as sharp as a razor blade and that individual falls into the depths of hell.

▶ Lifestyle Foci: Maintaining a pure and righteous life and a reverence for the sacredness of the four elements of earth, air, water, and fire. Adherents age 7 or older in India, or age 10 or older in Persia, must make five daily prayers and wear two sacred garments—the *sudreh* (a special shirt) and a *kusti* (prayer cord). These serve to remind believers to pray and maintain virtue and purity.

▶ Worship Restrictions: Contrary to some mistaken assumptions, Zoroastrianism allows for converts. Adherents must undergo regular purification rituals and strictly maintain practice of daily prayers. However, some of the more traditional sects believe that only Iranians or ethnic **Parsis** (as they are called in India) may legitimately practice Zoroastrianism.

◄ SEE ALSO 4.1, *"Fundamental Tenets of Catholicism"* ▶

The Core Beliefs of Zoroastrianism

The core beliefs of Zoroastrianism are as follows:

▶ Belief in the divinity and omnipotence of the benevolent god Ahura Mazda (literally, "the Wise Lord") and the evil nature of the malevolent entity called Angra Mainyu. Both have spiritual entities who serve them, similar to angels and demons.

▶ Belief in the constant struggle between good and evil; between Ahura Mazda and Angra Mainyu. In the end times, Ahura Mazda will defeat Angra Mainyu (the destructive spirit) also known as Shaitin/Satan. At this time there will be a final judgment through fire and every trace of evil will be eliminated.

▶ Belief in the truth and divinity of the teachings of the prophet Zoroaster/ Zarathustra.

▶ Belief that people are free to choose between good and evil in this life.

▶ Belief that the actions and phenomena of the natural world, both creative and destructive, are manifestations of Ahura Mazda.

The Three Tenets of Moral Conduct

In Zoroastrianism, true morality is defined by far more than one's deeds or physical actions. Purity of mind, speech, and actions must all exist within an individual in order for true morality to be achieved. Simply "doing the right thing" is not enough in the Zoroastrian belief. For example, Zoroastrians believe that to perform a seemingly moral action while harboring the desire to do that which is immoral is unacceptable and immoral in itself. Such problems are avoided by the practice of the following three tenets:

▶ *Humata:* Proper thought; purity and morality of thought. To think morally but fail to speak out against immorality is not moral.

▶ *Hukhta:* Moral speech; purity and morality in one's speech. To speak morally and fail to act as such is not moral, but hypocritical.

▶ *Huvarastha:* Right action; purity and morality in one's actions. To perform moral actions while thinking obscene thoughts or speaking obscene words is not moral.

16.1

A **sudreh** is a special shirt Zoroastrians wear once they have come of age and/or undergone the appropriate rituals of purification.

A **kusti** is a prayer cord Zoroastrians wear. Each time a Zoroastrian performs one of the five required daily prayers, he or she wraps this cord once around his or her body. The cord is comprised of 72 threads representing the 72 chapters of the *Yasna,* a Zorastrian sacred text.

The word **Parsi** is used to refer to ethnic Iranians practicing Zoroastrianism in India. The majority of *Parsis* (literally "those who came from Persia") fled to India from Iran during or shortly after the time of the Muslim Arabic invasion and occupation of Iran in the mid-seventh century C.E.

16.2 SACRED TEXTS

The *Avesta*

The *Yasna*

The *Khorda Avesta*

The primary sacred text of the Zoroastrian religion is called the *Avesta*. This text is named for the language in which it is written, Avestan. However, the dialects differ, primarily depending on the time in which they were written. For example, the sections believed to have been written by Zarathustra himself are written in the Old Avestan dialect.

The *Avesta*

The core text of Zoroastrianism, the *Avesta*, is separated into four main parts, followed by a fragmentary section. The four main parts of the *Avesta* are as follows:

▶ *Yasna:* This section is considered the most sacred, as it contains the *Gathas,* or Hymns spoken by Zarathustra.

▶ *Khorda Avesta:* The Book of Common Prayer. This is a section of Zoroastrian prayers.

▶ *Visperad:* This section extends, explains, and/or elaborates upon the sacred rites and rituals of Zoroastrianism.

▶ *Vendidad:* Broken up into 22 sections called **fargards,** this part discusses the sacred laws, offering definitions of offenses and the proper punishments for each. The *Vendidad* covers everything from broken contracts to the unlawful killing of someone's livestock. Offenders often had to make reparations to the victim as well as Ahura Mazda (commonly through prayers and/or fire sacrifices).

The *Yasna*

The *Yasna*, or "sacred liturgy," consists of 72 chapters and is the first book of the *Avesta*. These chapters may be grouped by themes as follows:

▶ *Chapters 1–8:* Mainly praises of Zarathustra and Ahura Mazda, as well as announcements made by any Zoroastrian who has assumed the faith.

▶ *Chapters 9–11:* The *Hom Yasht,* a collection of eulogies to the sacred plant called *Hoama,* which was considered divine.

16.2

- ▶ *Chapter 12:* The creed of the Zoroastrian faith, which declares the divinity of Ahura Mazda and denounces the pre-existing polytheistic religions.

- ▶ *Chapters 13–27:* Invocations, prayers, and dedications to Ahura Mazda.

- ▶ *Chapters 28–34:* The *Ahunavaiti Gatha*, a 100-stanza hymn meant to be sung as a prayer to Ahura Mazda. In fact, it contains the prayer for which it is named, Ahuna Vairya.

- ▶ *Chapters 35–41:* The *Yasna Haptanghaiti*, or "Seven Chapters of Worship." Each chapter is a hymn. Yasna 42 is a supplement to this section.

- ▶ *Chapters 43–46:* The *Ushtavaiti Gatha*, or "To Have Happiness." This is a 66-stanza hymn.

- ▶ *Chapters 47–50:* The *Spentamainyush Gatha*, or "For the Bountiful Spirit." This is a 41-stanza hymn.

- ▶ *Chapter 51:* The *Vohukhshathra Gatha*, or "The Precious Dominion." This is a 22-stanza hymn.

- ▶ *Chapter 52:* An eight-verse hymn to *ashi*, which is the Zoroastrian concept of both spiritual and material reward.

- ▶ *Chapter 53:* The *Vahishtoishiti Gatha*, or "The Most Beloved Possession." This is a nine-stanza hymn.

- ▶ *Chapters 54–72:* A collection of invocations, dedications, and prayers, some of which repeat those written in Chapters 13–27.

The *Khorda Avesta*

The *Khorda Avesta*, which means "small or little *Avesta*," is the second book of the *Avesta* text. This book is a collection of prayers and can be split up into four primary sections:

- ▶ A section of 11 commonly used short prayers.

- ▶ The *Gahs*, the prayers for each of the five periods of the day, which are to be recited daily by Zoroastrians—*Hawan* between sunrise and midmorning, *Rapithwin* at midday, *Uzerin* in the afternoon, *Aiwisruthrem* between sunset and midnight, and *Ushahin* between midnight and dawn.

- ▶ The *Niyayeshes*, eight litanies to the elements and directions of nature. For example, there are litanies to the sun (*Kwarshed*), the moon (*Mah*), water (*Aban*), the four directions, and fire (*Atash*, which is considered the most sacred element of nature and is considered a manifestation of Ahura Mazda's power).

- ▶ The *Yashts*, hymns to Ahura Mazda, as well as to his angels and archangels (often represented by natural forces).

▶ The *Sirozas*, a two-part section containing dedications to each of the 30 days of each month.

▶ The *Afrinagans*, prayers meant for the purpose of bestowing blessings.

WORDS TO GO . . .WORDS TO GO . . .WORDS TO GO

A **Fargard** is a section of the *Vendidad,* a book of the *Avesta* that deals with sacred law and addresses crimes and punishments.

16.2

16.3 RITUALS AND HOLIDAYS

No Ruz

Fravardigan

Khordad Sal

Funeral Rites

Zoroastrianism is a faith with a multitude of ritualistic practices, as well as a rich calendar of holidays and festivals. Most festivals and holidays in Zoroastrianism are meant to pay respects to the Seven Creations, as well as to the holy immortal beings (a concept similar to that of angels) created by Ahura Mazda. The Seven Creations, sometimes called the Seven Bounties, are considered seven gifts given to this world by the Great God on High, the all-powerful entity who created even Ahura Mazda and his evil counterpart, Angra Mainyu. The Seven Creations of Zoroastrianism are celebrated with festivals called *Gahambars,* "festivals of obligation," and are as follows (in no particular order):

1. Sky/Heavens
2. Earth
3. Water
4. Plants
5. Animals
6. Humans
7. Fire

The frequent veneration of fire has led to the common mistaken assumption that Zoroastrianism is a fire-worshipping religion, but this is not the case. Fire is considered sacred, but it is not worshipped by Zoroastrians. Fire is the visible symbol of righteousness in Zoroastrianism. Just as physical impurities are removed by fire, spiritual impurities will one day be removed by fire. Fire is the symbol of Ahura Mazda. It serves as a reminder of the eschatological future judgment. It is also a symbol of the duty of Zoroastrians to cleanse their inner impurities and seek to eradicate evil in the world.

No Ruz

No Ruz, or "The New Day," has been celebrated in the Middle East, by people of all faiths, for well over 5,000 years. In Zoroastrianism, it is considered the most sacred of the seven festivals honoring the Seven Creations. For those who are not adherents of the Zoroastrian faith, this day is simply celebrated as the New Year. This festival begins with the spring equinox, usually on or near March 20.

The date of *No Ruz* changes somewhat from one year to the next, since it is based upon the solar cycle. Therefore, the celebration of this festival may begin as early as March 20 or as late as the first few days of April. For the years 2009 and 2010, the spring equinox (for the Northern Hemisphere) will take place on March 20.

In Zoroastrianism, *No Ruz* is celebrated in honor of the symbolic victory of Ahura Mazda over Angra Mainyu. This belief has a cosmological origin. Ahura Mazda is represented by the sun, whereas Angra Mainyu is represented by darkness. In Zoroastrian mythology, when the sun disappears over the horizon, Ahura Mazda descends into the dark realm and must battle Angra Mainyu and his evil minions in order to rise victoriously on the following morning. After the vernal equinox, Ahura Mazda is at his most vulnerable, as this is the time when the forces of Angra Mainyu are at their most powerful—hence the reason why night (the symbol of Angra Mainyu) begins to become longer than day (which is illuminated by the fire of the sun, the symbol of Ahura Mazda).

No Ruz is celebrated for roughly two weeks, beginning at the time of the spring equinox, when day and night are once again equal in length, showing that Ahura Mazda has triumphed over the evil of Angra Mainyu for yet another year. This change in the seasons shows that Ahura Mazda is regaining his strength and overcoming the powers of darkness. Soon the tables will again turn and so begin the period of summer, when day becomes longer than night and Ahura Mazda is at his most powerful. This flux of day and night is a symbol of good versus evil, in a constant yet shifting balance.

No Ruz is traditionally celebrated by first arranging seven objects on a beautifully ornamented table. The objects must all begin with the Persian letter S. For example, wheat, apples, and garlic are commonly used, as they are all symbolic of life and begin with the letter S in the Persian alphabet. In modern times, families in Iran often assemble around the television or radio and wait for the announcement of the New Year (much as is done in Western culture with the "countdown" to midnight on New Year's Eve). This announcement is met

16.3

with immediate celebration. The family members wish each other a happy *No Ruz*, and the children of the family kiss the hands of their elders. Often gifts are exchanged, such as flowers and small mirrors. In traditional Zoroastrian families, the patriarch or father of the family and his firstborn son bless the home by walking around the house with a lighted candle.

The family is of extreme importance at the time of *No Ruz*. Distant family members often pay visits to one another. Men and women often spend time with their closest friends. Children are given gifts, and sweet meats are prepared for the holiday.

Fravardigan

The festival of *Fravardigan* (sometimes called *Mukhtad*) is often referred to in English as The Feast of All Souls or The Ten Days of the Dead. This festival is celebrated during the 10 days that precede *No Ruz*, when darkness/night is being progressively overtaken by light/day. The name of the festival comes from the root word *Fravashi*, which is the immortal part of the human soul/spirit. According to the *Avesta*, one's *Fravashi* experiences three stages:

▶ *Fravashayo Zatanam:* Soul/spirit of an unborn human being

▶ *Fravashayo Zavantam:* Soul/spirit of the living human being

▶ *Fravashayo Irirathusham:* Soul/spirit of the dead human being

After death, one's body may decay and pass, but one's *Fravashi* does not. During the time of this festival, it is believed that the dead return to and remain present in this world for 10 days. During the *Fravardigan*, food that has been specially blessed is laid out to feed the *Fravashayo Irirathusham*, or souls of the dead.

Aside from these practices, the *Fravardigan* is also seen as a time for personal reflection and consideration of life and death. This time allows adherents to consider their lives and the concept of death, to take stock of their accomplishments and transgressions. This is the time for adherents to examine the wrongdoings of the past and to repent and/or make amends for them.

Khordad Sal

The festival of *Khordad Sal* commemorates the birth of Zarathustra/Zoroaster. The date of this holiday varies depending on which of the religious calendars an adherent is using. Since the groups of Zoroastrians became geographically separated over time, adherents of the faith eventually came to use three different religious calendars, each with its own date for *Khordad Sal*. Since the exact historical birth date of Zarathustra cannot be concretely verified, any of the three could be seen as valid:

▶ *Fasli*: According to this calendar, *Khordad Sal* should be celebrated on March 26.

▶ *Shenshai*: According to this calendar, *Khordad Sal* is on August 24.

▶ *Kadimi*: According to this calendar, *Khordad Sal* is on July 26.

Funeral Rites

The death ritual of Zoroastrians is unique and has purpose. Upon death, adherents are placed into a low circular tower called a *dakhma*. These towers expose the body of the deceased to the elements of nature and birds of prey. Zoroastrians believe that a corpse contaminates the air if cremated and the earth and water if buried. Disposing of the corpse in this way is thought to least contaminate the elements. These towers are still in use in India and Iran but contemporary adherents living in places without *dakhmas* in other parts of the world are allowed to make use of burial or cremation.

WORDS TO GO . . . WORDS TO GO . . . WORDS TO GO

Gahambars are "festivals of obligation," meaning the seven festivals observed in veneration of the seven elements of Ahura Mazda's creation of physical existence, which are sky/heaven, earth, water, plants, animals, humans, and fire (which is considered the most sacred element in Zoroastrianism).

16.3

16.4 ORIGINS AND FOUNDER

The prophet Zoroaster was born between 1200 B.C.E. and 1000 B.C.E. somewhere near the region of either northeast Iran or southwest Afghanistan. Aside from this, very little historical data exists on the early life of Zoroaster. What few details are available come from the *Gathas*, which are said to have been composed by Zoroaster himself. The facts of Zoroaster's life, prior to the age of 30, are as follows:

▶ He was a son of the warrior Spitama clan.

▶ For many years, Zoroaster was a priest by occupation.

▶ He had a wife and six children, three sons and three daughters.

Though Zoroaster was a priest, he disliked polytheism, pantheism, and caste structures, all of which were prevalent in the religions of his time. He also felt that animal sacrifices were both unnecessary and vulgar. Lastly, he was opposed to the ritualistic use of hallucinogenic drugs, a common practice of the time.

At the age of 30, Zoroaster experienced a divine revelation while undergoing a purification ritual. In this revelation, it is written that Zoroaster was shown the truth of God and existence. He claimed that there was only one god and that only this god should be worshipped. He also claimed that many deities from the pre-existing religions were, in fact, demons in service to the evil god Angra Mainyu. Specifically, he claimed that the **daevas** (*devas* of Hinduism) were not gods, but evil spirits.

Needless to say, the religious establishment of the time did not take kindly to Zoroaster's teachings. He was now preaching against almost every preconceived religious idea that secured their power and authority. As a result, Zoroastrianism was not very popular in the first years following Zoroaster's revelation. In fact, he is said to have had only one convert—his cousin.

Twelve years passed, and Zoroaster became increasingly disenchanted with the opposition he experienced. As a result, he abandoned his home, hoping to find another place that might be more tolerant of new religious ideas. His journey ended in Bactria, which was ruled by King Vishtaspa and Queen Hutosa.

One day, Zoroaster was engaged in a religious debate with some of the clergy of the region. Upon hearing him speak, Vishtaspa and Hutosa were greatly impressed with his ideas. They immediately adopted his ideas and beliefs as their own, and from that day, Zoroastrianism became the official state religion of Bactria. The religion began gaining in popularity, spreading all across Persia. According to one legend, Vishtaspa converted to Zoroastrianism after Zarathustra miraculously healed the king's most prized horse.

Little factual information exists regarding the nature or exact date of Zoroaster's death. However, it is known that he died sometime during his late 70s.

WORDS TO GO . . .WORDS TO GO . . .WORDS TO GO

Daevas, in Zoroastrianism, refer to demonic spirits who serve the evil Angra Mainyu. Such spirits seek to deceive and harm human beings, especially those who serve Ahura Mazda. It is thought that this word was likely a transliteration of the Hindu term for a race of deities called *devas*, in order to ensure that Zoroastrianism remained separate.

16.4

16.5 HISTORICAL DEVELOPMENT

In the middle of the sixth century B.C.E., Cyrus the Great conquered Iran and established the first unified Persian Empire. Cyrus's clan, the Archaemenians, being devout Zoroastrians themselves, ruled the land under Zoroastrian laws. However, Cyrus was also rather tolerant, both socially and religiously, and other religions were allowed to continue being practiced. No attempts were made to force a state religion of Zoroastrianism upon the people of the newly formed Persian Empire.

Roughly 300 years later, in 331 B.C.E., Alexander the Great conquered Persia, having defeated Darius III (a descendent of Cyrus). Though Alexander imposed no extreme changes to the governmental arrangement of Persia, he detested the religion of Zoroastrianism. He believed it threatened the divinity that he claimed as the son of the polytheistic thunder god, Zues-Ammon. Priests of the Zoroastrian faith were executed, and many Zoroastrian texts and temples were destroyed. The *Gathas,* however, somehow escaped destruction.

After Alexander's death in 323 B.C.E., a group of Greek rulers, called the Seleucids, took over the land of Persia. Under their reign, Zoroastrians ceased to be persecuted. The Seleucids were defeated in less than a century by the Parthian Arcasids, thus returning the land to the governance of Iranian rulers. As a result, Zoroastrianism experienced a revival of sorts. Zoroastrians began gathering long hidden texts, and the *Verdidad* was assembled during this time.

The religion of Zoroastrianism continued to thrive in Iranian Persia until the seventh century C.E., when Islamic Arabs invaded and conquered all of Persia. This sparked the beginning of a long and difficult period for Zoroastrians, one that has continued to this day.

At first, Zoroastrians were considered *Dhimmis,* or "People of the Book," and were viewed as being the same as Jews or Christians. Though considered infidels, they were allowed to continue practicing their faith as long as they paid the appropriate extra taxes. As the years passed, however, a large number of Zoroastrians converted to Islam. Though the rulers often changed, Iran remained under the rule of Islamic dynasties for nearly 500 years.

In the year 1218 C.E., however, a war began between Persia and Mongolia. This was sparked when Genghis Khan learned that a group of envoys he had sent to the city of Otrar had been executed under order of the local governor. The Khans immediately attacked Otrar and began a campaign to invade Persia. Not long after, Persia found itself under Mongolian rule. No longer under the threat of death, Zoroastrians once again began openly practicing their religion. In 1295 C.E., Ghazan Khan, also known as Mahmud Ghazan, converted to Islam. This led to yet another period of Zoroastrian persecution.

By the tenth century C.E., a large exodus of Zoroastrians fled Iran in search of a place where they could practice their religion without fear of persecution. They soon settled in Gujarat, India. This was the beginning of the Indian *Parsi* (meaning "Persian") community. To this day, the majority of Zoroastrian adherents live in either Iran or India.

16.6 PRESENT-DAY FACTS

Though the practice of Zoroastrianism has fallen into obscurity over the last millennium, the number of adherents who still practice this religion are somewhere between 125,000 and 250,000. Most Zoroastrians currently live in the Middle East (primarily Iran) and India. However, this ancient religious practice has experienced a rebirth of sorts, with an increasing number of adherents surfacing in parts of Europe and the United States. Approximately 5,000 people in the United States currently practice Zoroastrianism.

17

SCIENTOLOGY

17.1 FUNDAMENTAL TENETS

Basic Information on Scientology

The Core Beliefs of Scientology

The States of Human Existence

The Tone Scale

The Eight Dynamics of Survival

The Truth About Xenu

In recent years, the religion of Scientology has come into the public eye. Until a number of Hollywood celebrities began claiming Scientology as their religion of choice, many people were not even aware that it existed.

Scientology consistently affirms the belief that by increasing the ability and intelligence of the individual through practical training in interpersonal relationships, dealing with the past, and other life issues that individuals can overcome the factors that hold them back from success in life. It doesn't try to solve people's problems, but tries to give them the tools to solve their own problems. In this religious perspective, life change is entirely self-driven.

Basic Information on Scientology

▶ Origin Date: Developed in 1952, but officially established as a religion in December 1953.

▶ Founder/Originator: Lafayette Ron Hubbard; he is usually referred to by only his first initial, L. Ron Hubbard. When spoken of indirectly, he is sometimes referred to by initials alone—LRH.

▶ View of God: A basically monotheistic belief in an unspecified Divine Entity.

▶ Dietary Restrictions: None.

▶ View of Life/Death: Belief similar to that of reincarnation, in that humans are spiritual beings trapped in physical reality until they are liberated, a state which Scientology calls becoming "clear."

▶ Lifestyle Foci: Scientologists may take only prescribed drugs to treat physical ailments. Recreational drugs and psycho-pharmaceuticals (drugs used for psychological disorders such as depression, dementia, or Schizophrenia) are expressly forbidden. Some Scientologists, however, choose to abstain from the use of any foreign substances, even to treat physical ailments.

▶ Worship Restrictions: Becoming a recognized Scientologist begins with a free personality test, followed by a Communication Course (which costs $50–$100). This is followed by years of educational/philosophical courses and *audits.*

The Core Beliefs of Scientology

The basic beliefs of Scientology are explained in the Creed of the Church of Scientology, which may be summarized as follows:

▶ Humans are immortal, spiritual beings trapped in physical bodies.

▶ Human beings exist, as spiritual beings, for many lifetimes.

▶ The abilities of human beings are unlimited, though few have yet to realize these abilities.

▶ Humans are basically good.

▶ Humans are seeking to survive.

▶ A human's survival is dependent upon the individual human being, his or her fellow humans, and an individual's ability to attain oneness with the universe.

▶ Belief that the laws of God forbid humans from destroying their "own kind."

▶ Belief that the laws of God forbid humans from harming the sanity of others.

▶ Belief that the laws of God forbid the destruction or enslavement of another human soul.

▶ Belief that God forbids humans from inhibiting the survival of their companions and/or religious, familial, or social groups.

▶ All human beings have equal, inalienable rights to life, sanity, defense of safety, opinions, free religious practice, and "the creation of their own kind."

▶ Belief that human souls have the previously mentioned human rights.

▶ Belief that only God may suspend these human rights

▶ Belief that the study of the human mind and mental illnesses "should not be alienated from religion or condoned in nonreligious fields."

▶ Belief that the "spirit alone may save or heal the human body."

17.1

The States of Human Existence

In Scientology, differing States of Human Existence classify a person's distance from the higher spiritual states. The first five of these states should not be thought of in any particular order, aside from the fact that they are below the states of a trained Scientologist. Persons in Scientology who have not achieved the state of "clear" are referred to as "pre-clears" or by the lowercase abbreviation of "pc."

▶ *Communication:* Though the individuals in this state of existence are viewed as higher on the chain than most people, they are still considered pre-clears. These are people such as painters, musicians, writers, and poets, able to communicate on a higher level of consciousness by creating great works that speak to people.

▶ *Relief:* This is also considered a higher level of pre-clear. These people are born with the natural skill to bring relief to those who are suffering.

▶ *Problems:* Many pre-clears are classified at this level, where one's life is hindered by both minor and significant problems. This is because Scientology considers the inability to shed one's "problems" to be the primary handicap of most human beings.

▶ *Non-Freedom:* This is the state in which humans are chained by the grief of the past, present, and anticipated future.

▶ *Hindered Ability:* In this state, the individual is prone to act even though he or she lacks the wisdom of a "clear" to do so.

▶ *Overwhelming Power:* In this state, a person either avoids responsibility/authority or seeks out power to abuse it. Scientology claims that only through their training can such people gain the ability to appropriately and responsibly manage power.

▶ *Clear:* This is the first significant stage of a Scientologist's training. Through audits, a person at this stage is said to have shed the hindering thoughts and confusions of his or her physical mind, or become a "Clear." Scientologists who reach this stage are no longer considered "pre-clears."

▶ *Operating Thetan:* This is the highest state of Scientology. *Thetan* is a term for the "spiritual beings" that have always made up the trapped spirit of the basic human self. This term originates from the Greek term *theta,* meaning "life," "consciousness," or "spirit." An Operating *Thetan,* according to Scientology, is an individual who has mastered his or her spiritual self. At this stage, Scientologists believe that they will begin to exhibit special powers, such as immunity to illness, ability to travel outside the body, and even abilities of levitation or flight.

The Tone Scale

The tone scale is a scale which shows the successive emotional tones a person can experience. The scale contains both a habitual/chronic aspect and a temporary/acute aspect. You go up or down on the tone scale based on your personal successes or failures. It is the goal of scientology to raise a person's chronic position on the tone scale. The full tone scale is very detailed and rather long, with levels ranging from –40.0 to +40.0. Scientology claims that most people fall into the level between +.05 and +4.0.

▶ *+.05/Apathy:* Has almost completely lost the will to live, resulting in an extreme state of apathy.

▶ *+.5/Grief:* This range of the scale includes individuals who are endlessly grieving about the "terrible hand" they've been dealt in life.

▶ *+1.0/Fear:* Constantly experiences anxiety from or thinks about past losses and/or the possibility of future losses.

▶ *+1.5/Anger:* Constantly fighting against threatened losses. Such people have hostile personalities and often exhibit violent tendencies.

▶ *+2.0/Antagonism:* Suspicious that loss may take place. Such people are resentful in nature.

▶ *+2.5/Boredom:* Exists in a situation that is not good enough to result in enthusiasm, but not bad enough to result in resentment. This person has lost some goals and cannot immediately locate others.

▶ *+2.8/Contentment:* The midrange, in which most people are okay with the state of their lives.

▶ *+3.0/Conservative:* Still wary of loss, but does not allow it to hinder him or her from pursuing the goals of his or her life.

▶ *+4.0/Enthusiastic:* Loving, helpful, frequently happy, friendly in almost any sort of company, and usually contributes to society selflessly.

The Eight Dynamics of Survival

According to the beliefs of Scientology, as explained by L. Ron Hubbard, all living beings follow at least one simple urge—to survive. However, an individual's ability to successfully obey this order has a lot to do with how he or she interacts with the universe. The order of humankind's relational existence is divided into eight parts. Scientology refers to this as the Eight Dynamics of Survival, which are as follows:

17.1

1. *Self:* This dynamic addresses the most basic human urge and the ultimate expression of individuality. This is the survival of the individual, concerned with only the state of his or her own body, mind, and material possessions, and only in the present moment. Someone who exists solely on this level does not even acknowledge the future and spiritual matters. This dynamic also excludes any efforts to aid other people in survival.

2. *Creativity:* In this dynamic, the person begins thinking ahead of the present moment. He or she also begins to consider the survival needs of a family—spouse, children, parents, and so on. Sexual activity is also included in this dynamic, as it is a means by which to secure the future survival of the family unit.

3. *Group Survival:* This dynamic includes the urge to survive as a member of a larger group and contribute to the perpetuation of said group—a tribe, political affiliation, church, fraternity, community, and so on.

4. *Species:* This is the urge to survive as part of the human species, regardless of race. In this dynamic, the individual acknowledges the need to aid in the survival of the human race.

5. *Life Forms:* In this dynamic, an individual seeks to protect and ensure the survival of all forms of life, having recognized that their survival is linked to his or hers.

6. *Physical Universe:* In this dynamic, the individual works to become one with and thus contribute to the survival of physical existence, of which he or she is a part. In Scientology, the combined whole of physical existence is referred to by the acronym MEST, which stands for Matter, Energy, Space, and Time.

7. *Spiritual:* In this dynamic, the individual experiences an urge to understand his or her spiritual existence.

8. *Infinity/God:* This is the urge that motivates humans to understand the path by which to obtain an infinite existence or spiritual immortality. In Scientology, the concept of Infinity is thought of as synonymous with God, since God is the only being that is and has always been undoubtedly infinite.

The eight dynamics are concentric circles starting with number one as the outer circle. As you progress as an individual, you are able to expand into the other dynamics. Only when one reaches the seventh dynamic will he or she be able to attain the eighth dynamic. A person is at his best and happiest when he is surviving well in every area of his life.

The Truth About Xenu

Probably the most controversial, misunderstood, and frequently misrepresented part of the Scientology religion has to do with a Scientology myth commonly referred to as the Legend of Xenu. While this story has now been undoubtedly proven a part of the religion (despite the fact that church representatives often deny its existence), the story's true role in Scientology is often misrepresented by its critics as proof that they "believe in alien parasites." While the story may indeed seem odd, this is simply not the case.

While the issue is still being debated, a number of former Scientologists have stated that the story of Xenu is supposed to be a metaphor and was never meant to be taken as factual truth. However, the church feared that if it were revealed to nonmembers, they would not understand. The story is actually meant to be a working myth, illustrating the Scientology belief that humans were at one time spiritual beings, existing on infinite levels of intergalactic and interdimensional realities. At some point, the beings that we once were became trapped in physical reality (where we remain to this day). This is supposed to be the underlying message of the Xenu story, not that humans are "possessed by aliens." Such harsh statements are the reason many Scientologists now become passionately offended at even the mention of Xenu by nonmembers.

The Xenu story tells of how, 75 million years ago, a race of spiritual beings called *Thetans* had elected an entity named Xenu as their governing authority. Xenu proved to be terrible at his job, and the 90 planets inhabited by this race of beings began to experience serious problems with overcrowding. The story states that an average of 178 billion beings inhabited each planet. Xenu eventually came up with a rather sinister solution.

Using methods ranging from forceful coercion to psychological manipulation, Xenu rounded up *Thetans* he viewed as undesirable from the populations of all the planets, placed them into a state similar to suspended animation, and transported them to a new planet. This planet soon became a holding cell for 250 billion exiled *Thetans* and was called *Teegeeack* (pronounced with a hard G, *Tee-Gee-Ack*), now called the planet of Earth. Xenu then detonated hydrogen bombs at the crowns of the planet's most active volcanoes. The explosion made it temporarily impossible for the *Thetans* to use their abilities due to a device built by Xenu that imprisoned their now weakened spirits. The result of Xenu's plan was a civil war between the *Thetans*.

17.1

Xenu now had the *Thetans* mentally conditioned with a holographic three-dimensional device that basically fooled them into believing that they belonged in physical reality. The *Thetans* were tricked into believing in a number of false ideas about the nature of the universe. Eventually, the *Thetans* were forced to assume physical forms in order to survive. This further trapped the *Thetans* in physical reality, which was Xenu's plan, and caused them to lose what remaining memories they had of their spiritual origins. Eventually, Xenu was imprisoned for all eternity. However, the story states that the exiled *Thetans* could not be freed after Xenu was defeated. Until humans come into harmony with their inner *Thetans*, they will remain trapped in physical reality.

WORDS TO GO . . . WORDS TO GO . . . WORDS TO GO

Audits, in Scientology, are regularly conducted interviews meant to rid one of past emotional baggage by asking questions while one is attached to a special machine called an E-Meter, which reads emotional responses. The goal is to pass though rounds of questions until one is able to do so without the machine reading a response. When this has been done, each "item" of emotional baggage is said to be part of one's "bank."

17.2 SACRED TEXTS

The Canon of Scientology

Perhaps it should not be surprising that Scientology has a large amount of written works, seeing as how it was founded by a man who had a reputation as a prolific writer. Scientologists are expected to immerse themselves in Scientology literature. For every step of the faith, Scientologists are provided with numerous manuals, guidebooks, and other such literature.

The Canon of Scientology

While the following list does not encompass every text in Scientology, it does cover the basic canon of the religion's texts. Almost all authorized Scientology texts have both Hubbard's name and the Church of Scientology logo on the cover. For the most part, every Scientologist will eventually read the following 16 texts:

1. *Dianetics: Modern Science of Mental Health*
2. *Advanced Procedure and Axioms*
3. *The Creation of Human Ability*
4. *Handbook for Scientologists*
5. *Dianetics: Original Thesis*
6. *Dianetics: 55*
7. *Handbook for Pre-Clears*
8. *Introduction to Scientology Ethics*
9. *Science of Survival*
10. *Scientology: A History of Man*
11. *Scientology Basics: 0–8*
12. *Scientology: 8–80, Discovery and Increase of Life Energy in the Genus Homo sapiens*
13. *Scientology: 80–8008*
14. *Scientology: A New Slant on Life*
15. *Self-Analysis*
16. *The Way to Happiness: A Common Sense Guide to Better Living*

17.2

17.3 RITUALS AND HOLIDAYS

Scientology does not celebrate any of its own specific religious holidays. The primary ritual of Scientology, however, is the practice of audits.

Audits, in Scientology, are regularly conducted interviews meant to rid one of past emotional baggage by asking questions while one is attached to a special machine called an E-Meter, which reads emotional responses. The goal is to pass though rounds of questions until one is able to do so without the machine reading a response. Each "item" of emotional baggage is said to be part of one's "bank."

The E-Meter was designed by the religion's founder, L. Ron Hubbard. This machine registers emotional responses, in much the same way that a polygraph (lie detector) registers physiological reactions of stress. The E-Meter, however, is designed only to register emotional reactions to questions asked by the conductor of the interview, called an auditor. An auditor is not one who offers solutions or advice. They are trained to listen and help the adherent locate those experiences of the past that need to be addressed. These experiences can be issues of this life or even prior lives.

Two wires reach out from the device, at the ends of which are cylindrical electrodes. These are held by the person being audited. An extremely weak current of electricity passes through the person and is disrupted by emotional response, which then causes the machine's needle to move. The amount of electricity emitted by the machine is so weak that the person being audited cannot even sense it.

The theory behind the E-Meter's use in Scientology audits is that the human mind is hindered by "images" of painful past memories. Many of these images are, in Scientology belief, illusions created by the brain. As they accumulate, these images become increasingly harmful to the human being, resulting in sickness, pain, and even death. The energy emitted by emotional responses into an E-Meter is believed to be the result of the negative energy these images create. This energy is referred to as "charge." The wider the needle moves, the greater the amount of charge.

17.4 ORIGINS AND FOUNDER

The Church of Scientology has openly published its own authorized biography of L. Ron Hubbard's life and the origins of Scientology. However, it is important to note that a number of sources either challenge or contradict some of the information published by the Church of Scientology. The information provided here comes from the Church of Scientology's authorized history.

L. Ron Hubbard was born on March 13, 1911, in Tilden, Nebraska. He was the son of Harry Hubbard, a naval officer, and his wife, Ledora May Hubbard. Six months after his birth, the family relocated to Durant, Oklahoma. Shortly thereafter, they moved again, this time to Kalispell, Montana. They remained in Montana for about five years. Ron and his mother later settled in Helena, Montana, when his father was called away by the Navy. As a child, Hubbard became close to the local Blackfoot Indians, particularly a man called Old Tom, a Blackfoot Medicine Man. At the age of 6, Hubbard was made an honorary blood brother of the Blackfoot tribe.

From 1918 to 1921, the Hubbard family moved from Montana to California, first living in San Diego and later Oakland. In 1922, they moved to Puget Sound, Washington. Within a year, Hubbard had become greatly involved with the Boy Scouts of America. He is said to have advanced to the rank of First Class Scout in only a few months.

In October 1923, Hubbard's father received orders to Washington, D.C. The family traveled there via the Panama Canal, aboard the USS *Ulysses S. Grant*. During this trip, Hubbard is said to have been tutored in Freudian psychology by a naval intelligence officer named Comm. Joseph "Snake" Thompson, who had just returned from personally studying with Freud on a naval assignment.

Once in Washington, D.C., Hubbard resumed his involvement with the Boy Scouts, earning a record number of merit badges over the next year. On March 20, 1924, he represented his Boy Scout troop on a visit to U.S. President Calvin Coolidge. Five days later, Hubbard was awarded the rank of Eagle Scout. He was now the youngest Eagle Scout in the country. The day after, Hubbard returned alone to Montana to participate as an Assistant Scoutmaster. A year later, he moved to Seattle, Washington, to pursue his high school education at Queen Anne High School. He left Queen Anne High School in June 1927, boarding a ship bound for Guam. His journey is said to have taken him all over Asia, through countries such as Japan, China, the Philippines, and Hong Kong. As he traveled, he wrote furiously about his experiences, filling many journals. He is said to have carried a journal with him at all times.

Hubbard returned to Helena, Montana, in September 1927 to continue his education. Not long after, he left again and boarded a ship bound for the Far East. He traveled for over a year, visiting western China, Japan, the Philippines, and Java. He studied the religious philosophies of Buddhism and Hindu Dharma during this time. He was temporarily employed as a commercial sailor during some of this trip.

Hubbard returned to his family in Washington, D.C., in September 1929 and finally completed his high school education at the Woodward School for Boys. He graduated high school in 1930 and enrolled at George Washington University, where he studied engineering and physics. He was one of the first university students in the country to take classes in atomic and molecular physics. At this time, he began to consider the possibility that these sciences could provide answers to the problems of the human condition, a task at which he felt psychology had failed. Hubbard later left the university and had a short career in the U.S. Marines. He also became a fairly accomplished glider pilot during this time.

From 1932 to April 1933, Hubbard participated in the West Indies Mineralogical Expedition, which completed the first mineral survey of Puerto Rico. Here Hubbard was fascinated by the faith-based mystical practices of **Santeria, Voodoo,** and **Espiritismo.**

In 1933, Hubbard began pursuing his career as a fiction writer. By February 1934, he had published his first adventure story, *The Green God.* Hubbard continued to experience success as a writer for a number of years and soon gained a reputation as one of the most prolific writers in the world. It is said that he normally produced his stories at an average rate of 100,000 words a month (putting him well over one million words a year). He also succeeded across the lines of genre, writing adventures, suspense, Westerns, mysteries, and romance stories. Concerned that publishers might start to avoid him if his name dominated too many magazine covers, Hubbard began writing under pen names, adopting as many as 15 that are known.

In 1941, Hubbard began a career in the U.S. Navy. However, the details of his career are too widely disputed to be included here.

Hubbard was officially discharged from the Navy in 1946. After a year of writing and publishing, he moved to La Brea, California, and began to test the theories that made up the foundations of his new work, which he later called *Dianetics.*

The manuscript was compiled and passed around through private channels only for a number of years. In 1950, Hermitage House contracted Hubbard to write a complete manuscript on the concept of *Dianetics*. He finished the book in only a couple of months, and it was released to the public on May 9, 1950, as *Dianetics: The Modern Science of Mental Health*.

WORDS TO GO . . .WORDS TO GO . . .WORDS TO GO

Santeria, Voodoo, and **Espiritismo** are three similar but unique systems of faith-based mystical practice. All three practices integrate the faith of Catholicism with various cultural superstitions and indigenous magical rites.

Voodoo (though the correct term is **Vodun**), is primarily practiced today in Haiti and the Southern United States, and integrates Catholic-based icons with the indigenous rites of West and Central Africa.

Santeria, or "Way of the Saints," integrates Catholic icons with Latin superstitions and magic rites that are believed to originate from the Nigerian Yoruba tribe. Today, Santeria is primarily practiced in Cuba, the Caribbean, and in certain parts of the Southern United States (mainly in Florida).

Espiritismo shares some beliefs with Voodoo and Santeria. However, this practice focuses on manipulating spirits for beneficial results. In **Espiritismo**, or "Spiritism," it is believed that good and evil spirits hold influence over the physical realm. Good spirits can bring prosperity, while evil spirits are said to inflict sickness and/or bring misfortune. One who believes they are being attacked by evil spirits will consult with an **Espiritista**, who will exorcise the evil spirit(s) with charms, sacrifices, or magic rituals. Today, it is practiced mainly in Cuba and Puerto Rico.

17.4

17.5 HISTORICAL DEVELOPMENT

Over the next year, Hubbard published a total of six books on the subject of *Dianetics*. He also traveled extensively on lecture tours. He spent a brief time in Havana, Cuba, writing the follow-up to *Dianetics*, called *Science of Survival*. Upon his return, he purchased a modest property in Wichita, Kansas, which became Hubbard College. Here Hubbard taught courses and offered lectures on the concepts of *Dianetics*. By fall of that year, Hubbard's research had taken a drastically spiritual turn. By the year's end, he had begun to refer to *Dianetics* as Scientology.

In 1952, Hubbard established a new location in Phoenix, Arizona, which he dubbed the Hubbard Association of Scientologists International (HASI). In September 1952, he purchased property in London, England, and traveled there to establish yet another Scientology chapter called HASI in London. After this, Hubbard spent a year traveling and lecturing from the United States across the span of Europe. In Europe, he traveled along World War II routes in an attempt to study the effects of that war's devastation on human beings.

In 1954, a number of Hubbard's Scientologist followers established the first Church of Scientology in Los Angeles, California. In 1955, Hubbard left the HASI of Phoenix and returned to Washington, D.C. There he established The Founding Church of Washington, D.C., and wrote out the first rules, regulations, and guidelines by which the Church of Scientology would be conducted.

By 1959, the headquarters of Scientology was relocated to a 55-acre estate in Saint Hill, Sussex, England. Also in 1959, the first E-Meter, manufactured via Hubbard's instructions, was put into use at the Saint Hill facility. By October 1959, Hubbard again began traveling the world.

In 1965, Hubbard completed and released the Scientology *Classification and Gradation Chart*. This publication, printed on a single page, outlined the exact steps that Scientologists were to follow as they progressed in their spiritual evolutions.

In 1967, Hubbard established the Sea Organization of Scientology. After purchasing his own sea vessel, the *Enchanter*, Hubbard assembled his most dedicated followers and trained them to crew the ship. Most of them had never been to sea. He then did the same with another vessel, the *Athena*. Once training was complete, the two vessels set sail for the Mediterranean. This was called the Hubbard Geological Survey Expedition of the Mediterranean. By November 1967, Hubbard had purchased a third, larger vessel, the *Royal Scotsman,* which he soon renamed *Apollo.* To this day, the Sea Organization is considered one of the most elite groups in the Church of Scientology.

In the mid-1970s, Hubbard began to dedicate much of his time and energy to developing drug-rehabilitation programs for new Scientology members. The techniques he developed later came to be used by Narco-Non, a nonprofit drug-rehabilitation organization.

On January 24 1986, L. Ron Hubbard died at the age of 74. The Church of Scientology prefers to say that Hubbard "departed his body."

17.6 PRESENT-DAY FACTS

There are currently no precise figures on the number of Scientology adherents in the United States, and most of the available estimates range greatly, from as few as 30,000 to as many as 4.5 million. Global estimates of Scientology adherents also vary similarly. The Church of Scientology officially claims an estimated eight million adherents worldwide. Other global estimates range from anywhere between one million and five million Scientology adherents worldwide.

In recent years, the Church of Scientology was officially recognized by the U.S. Internal Revenue Service as a nonprofit religious organization. As a result, this may cause the religion to become included more commonly in census results. Therefore, more accurate census estimates may become available within a few years.

18

RASTAFARIANISM

18.1 FUNDAMENTAL TENETS

Basic Information on Rastafarianism
The Core Beliefs of Rastafarianism

The Rastafarian faith is the single youngest religion in the world. While not among the world's major religions, it is perhaps one of the most misunderstood and misrepresented religions in existence. Though often inaccurately portrayed as a faith of marijuana-smoking slackers, the Rastafarian religion is, in fact, one of strong national pride and unity, as well as one that encourages its adherents to maintain a strong work ethic and to follow a strict moral code.

Basic Information on Rastafarianism

► Origin Date: 1930 C.E.

► Founder/Originator: Ras Tafari Makonnen, later known by the title Haile Selassie, meaning "Power of the Trinity." Sometimes he is referred to by the abbreviation H.I.M. an abbreviation for "His Imperial Majesty" and emphasizing his kingship.

► View of God: Monotheistic.

► Dietary restrictions: Rastafarians follow all Old Testament biblical dietary laws, a practice that Rastafarians call *ital.* More than anything, they do not eat pork or shellfish.

► View of Life/Death: Belief in an eternal life with God after death. They believe that a chosen few may become physically immortal, being given the gift of immortality by God.

► Lifestyle Foci: Rastafarians style their hair in dreadlocks (however, the faith requires only that one not use chemicals, combs, or scissors on one's hair) and wear clothes that are the colors of the *Bandera* flag of Africa—red, green, and black.

► Worship Restrictions: Originally, all Rastafarians were of African descent. However, contemporary Rastafarianism has abandoned such worship restrictions in favor of racial equality.

The Core Beliefs of Rastafarianism

Please note that the beliefs listed below are those of contemporary Rastafarianism, some of which differ greatly in a number of ways from some of the original beliefs of the religion.

The core beliefs of Rastafarianism are as follows:

▶ Belief that the Prince of Ethiopia, Ras Tafari Makonnen, was the messiah of the African nation

▶ Belief that the African people are the true chosen people of God that are written of in the biblical Old Testament

▶ Belief in the one supreme god, **Jah**

▶ Belief in the rejection of hatred

▶ Abstinence from indulgent vices such as sex, alcohol, and drugs (however, the smoking of **ganja,** or "marijuana," is often done as a form of sacrament)

▶ Rejection of all bodily desecrations, such as tattoos, piercings, and the shaving of body hair

▶ Belief in the equality of all human beings, regardless of race, class, or gender

---

WORDS TO GO . . .WORDS TO GO . . .WORDS TO GO

Ital, in Rastafarianism, refers to the dietary laws of the biblical Old Testament. Rastafarians, believing they are the true chosen people spoken of in the Old Testament, follow the same dietary rules as Orthodox Jews.

The **Bandera** is the red, green, and black flag of Africa, as designed by Marcus Garvey. This term is also used to refer to the colors of Rastafarian dress.

Jah is short for *Jehovah,* and is used in Rastafarianism to refer to God. Many people have come to the mistaken conclusion that Rastafarians believe Ras Tafari Makonnen is *Jah.* However, this is inaccurate. Rastafarians view Ras Tafari Makonnen as a Messiah, the son of *Jah,* similar to how Christians consider Christ the son of God.

Ganja is a sacramental herb that is commonly smoked by Rastafarians. More commonly, it is known as cannabis or marijuana, which is an illegal controlled substance in most of the Western world. In the United States, it is frequently argued that Rasta adherents should be allowed to smoke *ganja,* as forbidding it violates their freedom to practice religion.

18.1

18.2 SACRED TEXTS

The *Kebra Nagast*

The Holy *Piby*

While Rastafarianism bases its beliefs on the text of the Judaic Old Testament, neither the Judaic *Torah* nor Christian *Old Testament* are considered Rastafarian texts. The primary texts that make up the canon of Rastafarianism are the *Kebra Nagast* and the Holy *Piby*. The first text is considered genealogical history, while the second was adopted by Rastafarians from a pre-existing, Afro-centric religious movement that held many of the same beliefs.

The *Kebra Nagast*

The title *Kebra Nagast* means "The Glory of Kings." This 117-chapter text is considered one of the most important writings in the Rastafarian canon. In the Rastafarian faith, the *Kebra Nagast* is believed to be the true account of the origins and lineage of the House of Solomon (meaning the bloodline of King Solomon from the biblical Old Testament). The text also explains that a line of Ethiopian emperors, into which Ras Tafari Makonnen was born, are descendents of the House of Solomon. The book also tells the stories of Solomon and the Queen of Sheba, and of how the biblical Ark of the Covenant was brought to Ethiopia.

Kebra Nagast was originally thought to have been written in Coptic Egyptian script, and later translated into Arabic in 1225 C.E. by a team of Ethiopian linguists. This belief stemmed from a claim in the Arabic text that stated it had been translated from Coptic. However, recent historical investigations have been unable to uncover any evidence of the original Coptic version of the text, leading some historians to question whether such a version ever existed. Others believe it is far more likely that the original Coptic text was simply destroyed or lost.

Eventually, by the order of a political official named Yaibika Igzi, the text was translated into the Ethiopian Ge'ez language from 1314 to 1322. When this translation took place, the linguists did not translate the biblical quotes of the text directly from Arabic. Instead, they simply inserted the passages from their own Ge'ez language version of the Bible. Some speculate that a number of Judaic texts may also have been borrowed from. However, this cannot be substantiated.

The importance of the *Kebra Nagast* comes not from its value as a literary work. Especially to Rastafarians and the Ethiopian people, the true value of the text comes from the fact that it is viewed as a record of the country's noble ancient past. For Ethiopians, the *Kebra Nagast* is a beacon of national pride. For Rastafarians, it is of great religious importance, as it offers a record of Ras Tafari Makonnen's noble biblical ancestry.

The Holy *Piby*

The Holy *Piby*, referred to by some as the "Black Man's Bible," was compiled from 1913 to 1917 by Robert Athlyi Rogers (often called by the title of Shepherd by Rastafarians). Rogers was originally from the Caribbean region of Anguilla. The text was published in 1924 as part of Rogers's own Afro-centric religious movement, called Athilicanism. His organization came to be known as the Afro-Athlican Constructive Gaathly (or Church). Tragically, the organization disintegrated not long after Rogers took his own life on August 24, 1931.

Rastafarians disagree with the view that Rogers committed suicide and do not speak of his death in such a way. Instead, they prefer to say that he voluntarily "took himself away from this life." The concept states that Rogers took his own life in order to send his soul to be with *Jah*.

Rogers did not intend the Holy *Piby* to be a text for the Rastafarian faith. However, Rastafarians soon adopted the work as one of their main sacred texts. Many of the ideas in the Holy *Piby* either validated or supported Rastafarian beliefs.

The Holy *Piby* consists of the following four books:

1. *Athlyi:* Two chapters long.

2. *Aggregation:* The largest book of the text, consisting of 15 chapters. In the seventh chapter of this book, Rogers names Marcus Garvey as one of God's three apostles.

3. *The Facts of the Apostles:* Book that names two other individuals, Henrietta Davis and Robert Poston, as the other two of God's "Holy Trinity" of apostles.

4. *Precaution:* A series of dialogues, in which Rogers asks questions of Garvey, Davis, and Poston, and receives their answers as prophets of the religion. It is in this book that Marcus Garvey predicts that a "Black King" will soon be crowned in Africa and that he will be the savior of the people.

It should come as no surprise that many people were violently opposed to the content of the Holy *Piby*. Many believe that members of such oppositional parties destroyed most of the original copies. Oddly enough, to this day, the Library of Congress does not have any copies of the book in their archives. The text was also banned in a number of Caribbean Islands, including Jamaica, in the 1920s. When Ras Tafari was made King of Ethiopia, however, such bans were lifted rather quickly.

18.3 RITUALS AND HOLIDAYS

The *Nyah Binghi* Chants

Rasta Holidays

Rastafarians have a multitude of unique holidays and practices. While the religion bears Judeo-Christian parallels, it does not share any holidays with neither the Judaic or Christian religions. In their rituals and holidays, Rastafarians stand apart as adherents of their own unique faith.

The *Nyah Binghi* Chants

A multitude of *Nyah Binghi* chants exist. The term is believed to have originally been the name of a group of African warriors who gave their lives defending the country from invasion and occupation. These chants, which heavily influenced the musical style of reggae, are often recited on Rastafarian holidays. However, such recitations are not limited only to holidays and may be performed at any time by a Rasta adherent.

Rasta Holidays

The Rastafarian faith celebrates a number of holidays, most of which commemorates the births, lives, and/or deaths of the movement's key figures. The following are the most commonly observed holidays of the Rastafarian faith:

▶ *Rasta Christmas:* January 7. In Ethiopia, most of the non-Rastafarian population is Orthodox Christian. Therefore, the country celebrates Christmas by the Eastern Orthodox calendar. Rastafarians observe this date as Christmas because they view Ethiopia as the God-given homeland, to which they one day hope to return.

▶ *February 6:* Bob Marley's Birthday. Born on February 6, 1945, Bob Marley was both a talented musician (one of the founding fathers of reggae) and a political activist in the 1960s. After hearing the teachings of Emperor Haile Selassie (Ras Tafari), both he and his wife converted to Rastafarianism. Marley is credited with bringing the religion to the attention of the world through his music.

▶ *April 21:* Grounation Day. This holiday commemorates the day in 1966 when Haile Selassie (Ras Tafari) first visited Jamaica. Jamaica later became one of the primary centers of Rastafarianism.

▶ *July 23:* Haile Selassie's birthday. This day celebrates Ethiopian Emperor Haile Selassie's birth on July 23, 1891.

▶ *August 17*: Marcus Garvey's birthday. This date commemorates the birthday of Marcus Garvey, a Jamaican politician who, in the writings of Rogers's Holy *Piby*, predicted the crowning of a king in Africa and was the head of the "Back to Africa" movement, which encouraged all people of African descent to return to the country of their ancestors.

▶ *November 2*: Coronation Day. This holiday celebrates the anniversary of Haile Selassie's 1930 coronation as the Emperor of Ethiopia.

18.4 ORIGINS AND FOUNDER

Marcus Garvey is viewed by Rastafarians as a prophet, much like John the Baptist from the Christian tradition. Oddly enough, he was not very interested in religion and cared little for the Rastafarian movement. Far from being a saint, he spent a period of time in prison for illegal business practices. Despite the fact that Garvey never considered himself a figure of the religion, his prediction of a messianic King of Africa later became the catalyst that spawned the Rastafarian faith.

Ras Tafari Makonnen, whom Rastafarians view as their Messiah, was crowned on November 2, 1930. He was given the name of Haile Selassie, meaning "Holy Trinity," as a sign that he was fulfilling the prophecy of Marcus Garvey (considered one of the three apostles in the "Holy Trinity" of Rogers's Holy *Piby*). Rastafarians also often refer to him by the titles of the King of Kings, the Son of Solomon, and the Lion of Judah. He is also sometimes referred to by the abbreviation H.I.M. Despite the religious significance of Selassie's coronation, the event was also of great global significance. In fact, the prestige of his coronation resulted in his being the first black person to appear on the covers of both *National Geographic* and *Time* magazine.

18.5 HISTORICAL DEVELOPMENT

In 1934, a Rastafarian by the name of Leonard Howell was charged with sedition by the British authorities (the occupational rulers of what was then the British colony of Jamaica) for refusing to swear his loyalty to King George V. The British government chose to make an example of Howell, fearing that an uprising might occur if too many Jamaicans became loyal Rasta followers of Haile Selassie. Howell was convicted (after a very short trial) and sentenced to two years in prison. Upon his release, Howell founded a very successful Rastafarian commune, which he called The Pinnacle.

In 1954, Howell again came under attack. This time, his Pinnacle commune was completely destroyed, its community members beaten and structures burned to the ground. This time it was not the British authorities, but middle- and upper-class Jamaicans who were responsible for the persecution of Rastafarians. The Rastafarian belief in social equality was not well received by members of the ruling upper classes of Jamaica. The tensions increased, eventually leading to open mob attacks on Rastafarians by members of the upper classes. The majority of Rastafarians belonged to the poor lower classes. Many now became targets of violence. A large number of Rastafarians were savagely beaten on the streets by mobs. Some did not survive their attacks. Sometimes the mobs simply desecrated their beliefs or publicly humiliated them by cutting off their dreadlocks.

Haile Selassie first visited the island of Jamaica on April 21, 1966. Somewhere between 100,000 and 200,000 Rastafarians from all over Jamaica descended on Kingston airport, having heard that the man whom they considered to be the Messiah was coming to visit them. During this visit, Haile Selassie informed the leaders of the Jamaican Rastafarian community that they first needed to liberate the people of Jamaica before they could "return" to *Jah*'s promised land of Ethiopia, explaining that they must have "liberation before repatriation."

Haile Selassie died on August 27, 1975, at the age of 83. The circumstances surrounding his death became a matter of much controversy. The government officially announced that he had died from complications due to a recent surgery. The surgeon who performed the operation, however, refused to support their claim, stating that there had been no such complications. Many of Haile Selassie's loyal supporters, as well as many Rastafarians, believed that the emperor had been assassinated.

18.5

In 1992, the alleged remains of Haile Selassie were discovered beneath a concrete slab on the grounds of the imperial palace. However, whether the remains are actually those of Haile Selassie has yet to be confirmed.

Since Rastafarians believe that physical immortality is possible through the power of *Jah*, there is some debate between certain sects of the religion over whether Haile Selassie ever actually died at all.

18.6 PRESENT-DAY FACTS

Because of the loose manner in which Rastafarian adherents are organized, it is difficult to pinpoint an exact number of followers the faith currently has. Conservative estimates claim the number is as low as 10,000 adherents. The most generous of estimates claims well over one million Rastafarian adherents. Based on the populations of the regions in which Rastafarianism is most widely practiced, however, it is highly unlikely that either of these estimates is even close to being accurate.

Today there are most likely between 600,000 and 800,000 Rastafarian adherents practicing worldwide. Most of today's Rastafarians are not spread out across the globe, and the majority of them can still be found in Ethiopia and the Caribbean Islands. However, a number of Rastafarian communities and/or sects have arisen in the United States and the United Kingdom.

18.6

19

WICCA

19.1 FUNDAMENTAL TENETS

Basic Information on Wicca
The Core Beliefs of Wicca
The Rule of Three

The nature-based religion of Wicca is often misunderstood or misrepresented as "devil worship" or "black magic." In actuality, Wicca is a revival of the ancient religions that were forced into obscurity during the spread of the Roman Empire and Christianity. Wiccans are not cackling witches riding around on broomsticks. Today, one may find Wiccans in every facet of civilizations—some are officers and firefighters, some teachers. Chances are that you have met a Wiccan at least once in your life and were not even aware of it.

Basic Information on Wicca

▶ Origin Date: The origins of Wicca are prehistoric, and therefore unknown.

▶ Founder/Originator: Unknown.

▶ View of God: Pantheistic and/or polytheistic. (Wicca is a very individualistic religion, so this view may change from one practitioner/sect/**coven** to the next.)

▶ Dietary Restrictions: Commonly, it is left to the individual Wiccan to decide what dietary practices are best for his or her mental, physical, and/or spiritual health and well-being. However, a significant number of Wiccans are either vegetarians or vegans.

▶ View of Life/Death: Belief in the cycle of life, death, and rebirth (however, this cycle is not viewed by Wiccans in the same way as is the concept of *samsara* in Buddhism, Hindu Dharma, and/or Jainism).

▶ Lifestyle Foci: To live in harmony with the natural forces of the universe, with a practical acknowledgment of the Rule of Three.

▶ Worship Restrictions: This varies, since some sects claim that Wiccans are passed the ability to conduct magic through heredity, while others claim that anyone may practice Wicca.

The Core Beliefs of Wicca

The core beliefs of Wicca are as follows:

▶ Belief in the divinity of nature

▶ Belief in the forces of the **magic arts**

▶ Belief in the Rule of Three

The Rule of Three

Wiccans believe in what is popularly referred to as the Rule of Three, which works somewhat like the Eastern concept of *kharma*. The Rule of Three states that whatever a person does in life, whether good or bad, it will eventually be returned to that person threefold.

In Wiccan belief, the Rule of Three is believed to apply strictly to the use of magic and/or spells. For example, beneficial or nonharmful spells, which are popularly referred to as White Magic, will result in a threefold return of good energy. This good return might manifest in a number of ways, such as good fortune, prosperity, or good health. However, malicious uses of magic or spells, such as curses and hexes, popularly referred to as Black Magic or Dark Magic, will result in a threefold bad return. This return may also manifest in a number of possible ways, such as ill luck, financial loss, and/or deteriorating health.

WORDS TO GO . . .WORDS TO GO . . .WORDS TO GO

Covens are groups of Wiccans with common religious goals and purposes, which meet regularly for the purpose of holding Esbats, Sabbats, teachings, or for any other activity having a direct connection with Wicca.

The **magic arts** refers to causing change through the systematic use of the will and other natural forces. Some common goals in magic are healing, guidance, protection, and insight.

19.2 SACRED TEXTS

Technically, Wiccans do not have any established sacred texts. The closest thing Wiccans have to a sacred book is called a *grimoire*, popularly referred to as The Book of Shadows. However, no two *grimoires* are alike. Nearly every Wiccan keeps his or her own *grimoire*.

These books are often part journal and part spell book, and are sometimes passed from teacher to student. However, each owner of a *grimoire* makes the book his or her own by adding new spells, improving upon or adding to the spells within, recording his or her uses of spells, and/or removing spells that prove fruitless or dangerous.

The contents of a *grimoire* may also be influenced by the tradition that a Wiccan follows. Four primary Wiccan traditions currently are being practiced:

1. *Celtic:* This tradition comes from the polytheistic and somewhat pantheistic beliefs and practices of the ancient Celts (mainly peoples of Ireland and Scotland).

2. *Norse/Germanic:* This tradition comes from the polytheistic and pantheistic beliefs and practices of the Norse and/or the indigenous Germanic tribes.

3. *Anglican:* This tradition comes from the pantheistic beliefs and practices of the pre-Christian clans of Old England.

4. *Greek:* This tradition comes from the polytheistic beliefs and practices of the ancient Greeks. This tradition is often popular since it has the most textual resources. The Roman church viewed the Greek mythical texts of writers such as Homer as "classics." Therefore, they were spared destruction at a time when the church was destroying the "old ways" of many other cultures.

19.3 RITUALS AND HOLIDAYS

Wiccan holidays are often dated in conjunction with the cycles of the moon and sun. When Christianity spread across Europe, the Church dated many holidays in an attempt to counter those celebrated by the pre-existing pagan religions. The most universally observed holidays in the Wiccan tradition are as follows:

▶ *October 31:* November Eve, or *Samhain.* Many believe this practice probably originated with the religion of the ancient Celts, and thus consider this night to be the eve of the Wiccan New Year. Some Wiccan sects believe that on this night the boundary that separates the land of the living from the realm of the dead becomes blurred or unstable. Such sects of Wicca believe that the spirits of ancestors walk among the living on this night and can even give them blessings from the spirit realm. Many Wiccans also believe this to be an auspicious night for the practice of certain spells, especially those for the purpose of divination.

▶ *December 21:* Winter solstice, or *Yule* (which comes from the Norse word for "wheel," referring to the annual solar cycle). This is the longest night of the year. Some Wiccan **covens** celebrate what is called the Festival of Light, in honor of the Mother Goddess giving birth to the male Sun God. Some sects celebrate this holiday in commemoration of a benevolent Sun God, the Lord of Light, triumphing over a malevolent deity, called the Lord of Darkness. This observance is done because the days that follow will become increasingly longer.

▶ *January 31:* February Eve, also called *Oimelc* or *Brigid.* Candles are lit on this holiday to both acknowledge and quicken the warming of Earth as the days begin to become noticeably longer. *Oimelc* is an Old Celtic word, believed to mean "lamb's milk." This likely comes from the fact that lambs began to breed around this time. For Wiccan sects that follow the more Celtic-based tradition, this day is observed in honor of Brigid, Goddess of Fire.

▶ *March 21:* Vernal equinox, or *Ostara.* On this day, both day and night are of equal length, marking the coming of spring. This holiday is very much a fertility ritual that celebrates nature's rebirth from the winter season. Wiccan sects that follow the Norse tradition observe this day in honor of Ostara, the Goddess of Dawn. Sects of the Anglican tradition refer to this goddess as Eostre (from whose name the title of the Christian holiday of *Easter* comes). Wiccans of the Celtic tradition celebrate this as the day when the cosmic egg called Olwen is laid, often by a regenerating snake or divine bird, a symbol of life emerging out of death. Wiccan sects that follow the Greek (sometimes called Pagan) tradition celebrate this day in honor of the Earth Goddess Demeter's daughter, Persephone, being returned from Hades for half the year.

▶ *April 30:* May Eve, or *Beltaine.* The temperature rises and vegetation thrives with the coming of spring. Wiccan sects of the Anglican and Celtic traditions may celebrate by dancing around a Maypole, originally a fertility symbol. To Wiccan sects of the Greek tradition, May 1 is the midpoint of a five-day festival to Chloris, Nymph of Flowers (the Romans, who called her Flora, later promoted her to goddess status). The word *Beltaine* derives from the Celts and means "the Fires of Bel." This name originates from a time when the Celts would drive their cattle between two fires as a form of purification. Some Wiccans of the Celtic tradition still observe the ancient practice of jumping over small fires.

▶ *June 21:* Summer solstice. This is the longest day of the year. In some Wiccan sects, especially those of the Greek tradition, this day is observed in celebration of the divine union between Mother Goddess and Sun God (sometimes just the Goddess and God). However, most sects celebrate such things during May Eve. Wiccans of the Greek tradition observe this time in honor of the goddess Rhea, who is said to have breathed all things into existence.

▶ *July 31:* August Eve, *Lughnasadh,* or *Lammas.* Wiccans of Celtic tradition hold fire festivals on this day in honor of the Sun God Lugh. For those of the Anglican tradition, this is called the Feast of Bread. Originally, this day marked the first grain harvest. Today this is symbolized by the ritual consumption of small loaves of bread. For those of the Greek tradition, this day is observed in honor of Artemis, Goddess of the Hunt and Hearth.

▶ *September 21:* Autumnal equinox, *Mabon,* or Home of the Harvest. This is the second day of the year during which night and day are of equal length. To Wiccans, this signifies the turn of the annual cycle and the coming return of winter. Most Wiccans observe this day with feasts and parties, and often offer up sacrifices of grain or prayers of thanks to the Mother Goddess for the bounty of the earth. Traditionally, this bounty had to feed people during the barren months of winter. Some sects call this day the Home of the Harvest and hold festivals in celebration. Often Wiccans with strong ties to farming or agriculture celebrate in this way.

19.4 ORIGINS AND FOUNDER

A Religion Lost ... Then Found

Pinpointing any exact origin for Wicca is difficult, as the practice can be based on a number of different ancient, indigenous, and polytheistic/pantheistic religions from various cultures, such as the Celtic, Anglican, Germanic/Norse, and/or Greek. Aside from that of the Greek tradition, most Wiccan practices are prehistoric in origin. Few things about Wicca can be said absolutely or concretely, especially when it comes to the origination of the religion's beliefs and practices.

A Religion Lost ... Then Found

Many of the original Wiccan practices were lost when the indigenous religions of Europe were persecuted during the spread of Christianity. Many adherents either abandoned their beliefs rather than brave danger or simply hid them out of fear. The indigenous religions of Europe were proclaimed by the Christian church to be "devil worship" or "witchcraft." It is for this reason that many of the original practices and pagan rites of Europe's ancient religions, from which Wicca descends, were lost. Sometimes even speaking of the "old ways" was a punishable offense, causing the oral traditions of such religions to fade into oblivion. Some still continued to transmit the traditions (usually from parents to children, and in the relative safety/privacy of their homes). Unfortunately, as often happens with oral traditions, pieces began to be lost or new pieces were added from generation to generation. It is from this tradition that Wicca survives.

19.5 HISTORICAL DEVELOPMENT

The Rosicrucian Order
Gerald Gardner

Over time, Wicca as it is now practiced came to be divided into four main traditions, each with various sects, organizations, brotherhoods/sisterhoods, covens, and other such groups. The four main traditions of Wiccan practice (Celtic, Anglican, Germanic, and Greek) were revived into the modern world during the last two centuries by a number of unique Wiccan orders.

The Rosicrucian Order

When one researches the Rosicrucian Order, as is often the case with mystical or secretive organizations, it soon becomes very difficult to discern between fact and fantasy, truth and rumor. When it comes to the background of the Rosicrucian Order, the line between history and conspiracy is almost impossibly blurred.

What came to be called the Rosicrucian Order began as the Ancient Mystical Order of the *Rosae Crucis,* or Rosy Cross. The true order was likely a secret alchemical and/or mystical society that was located in Germany sometime between the sixteenth and eighteenth centuries C.E. Likely a European organization of Christian mystics, little, if anything, can be concretely verified about who or what the Rosicrucian Order truly was. Today many organizations claim the name of Rosicrucian, though none of them is able to offer proof of lineage.

In truth, the Rosicrucian Order may never have actually existed, except in the mind of Lutheran scholar Johann Valentin Andrea. Andrea wrote several works, such as the *Fama Fraternis R.C.,* in which he told of a man named Christian Rosencreutz, a world-educated master of secret arts who he claimed had lived during the fourteenth century and founded an order of elite alchemists—the Roscicrucian. Andrea's books claimed to tell of the rites, practices, and secrets of the Rosicrucian Order. Around the time that his works were being published, anonymous pamphlets began popping up throughout Europe, especially in Paris. They told of an "invisible school" of talented mystics who had discovered the secrets of alchemy, such as turning lead into gold. These pamphlets made Andrea's books bestsellers, and a surge of Rosicrucian enthusiasm swept the continent. Soon groups began to pop up all over Europe claiming to be the true Rosicrucian Order, but nearly all of them were, at best, frauds and, at worst, creative con artists intent on separating people from their money with promises of wealth and power.

Later, Andrea admitted that the Rosicrucian Order was a hoax. However, to this day, some claim that his admission was a ruse in order to protect the secret of the Rosicrucian Order.

Whether or not the Rosicrucian Order ever truly existed, it spurred a renewed surge of interest in magic, mysticism, and even witchcraft. Therefore, the questionably real Rosicrucian Order may have paved the way, though somewhat indirectly, for the rise of modern Wicca. Many who sought out the knowledge of the fictional Rosicrucian Order, as well as those not fooled by the frauds, later found their way to the true underground practitioners of secret and ancient ways in Europe at the time—the Wiccans.

Gerald Gardner

Gerald Brousseau Gardner was born in England on June 13, 1884. The Gardner family was from a Scottish background, and over 200 years before Gerald's birth, one of his family's female ancestors, Grissell Gardner, had been burned at the stake for practicing witchcraft. Many other stories tell of Wiccans in Gardner's family tree. However, few others can be concretely verified.

Gardner suffered from asthma as a child. Josephine McCombie, Gardner's nanny and attending nurse, was given permission by his parents to take the boy with her on a winter trip through Europe, under the pretense that the weather would be less aggravating to his condition. However, Gardner spent the majority of the trip sitting alone in hotel rooms while his nanny traveled. Eventually, Josephine met and married a man from Ceylon, India. She moved to the Far East and took the boy with her.

In India, Gardner was fascinated by the ideas of Hinduism and other religious ideas that he had not known of until now. He remained in India for much of his adulthood and is known to have become somewhat of a connoisseur of exotic knives. This inspired Gardner to write his first publication, *The Kris and Other Malay Weapons,* in 1939. The man turned out to be an extremely talented writer and thorough researcher. His first book is still viewed as the standard by which all later texts on the subject of edged weaponry are measured.

In 1923, Gardner took a job as a high-ranking civil servant in Malaysia, with the role of customs officer and opium inspector. During this time, Gardner became very successful and began to make great financial gains as a result of his position. The money he earned now allowed him to pursue a new interest—archaeology. Though it was never found again, Gardner claimed to have located a lost ancient (though very real) city known as *Singhapura,* or "City of Lions."

In 1936, Gardner retired from his position as a customs official and returned west to England, the land of his birth. However, he did not stay long. He immediately began planning new archaeological expeditions to Asia and parts of Europe. One such expedition took him to the island of Cyprus. While there, Gardner experienced an odd sense of familiarity and felt as though he had dreamed about the places on Cyprus even though he'd never seen them before. This experience brought Gardner to the conclusion that he'd been a resident of Cyprus during a past life.

The trip to Cyprus inspired Gardner to write his second book, A Goddess Arrives, published in 1939, which used Cyprus as a backdrop. The fictional novel dealt with the custom of ancient Goddess Worship in the form of a cult of Aphrodite that (in the novel) existed in the year 1450 B.C.E.

Gardner returned to England shortly before the outbreak of World War II. At this time, he became acquainted with a local Wiccan coven, into which he was initiated and began to study the arts of magic. He also is known to have joined a group called the Fellowship of Crotona, a rather extreme mystical offshoot of the Masonic Fraternal Order (also called the Free Masons). While he was a member of the Fellowship of Crotona, they founded a rather unique place they called The First Rosicrucian Theatre. The purpose of the theater was to perform theatrical productions having to do with magical subjects.

Also while a member of the Fellowship of Crotona, he encountered within their ranks another mystical group. This group was actually a coven, and the members explained to Gardner that they were all "hereditary Witches." In 1939, Gardner was officially initiated into the coven.

Gardner met the self-proclaimed yet renowned spiritualist Aleister Crowley in 1946. Crowley initiated Gardner as an honorary member of his own mystical order, called the Ordo Templi Orientis. Later the group excommunicated Crowley.

Gardner wanted to write a book on Wicca, as it was in his nature to write about his passions. However, he was forced to refrain from doing so, as "witchcraft" was still illegal in England in the mid-twentieth century. As a compromise, he chose to write and publish a "fictional" novel, called High Magic's Aid, in 1949. Just to be safe, he did so under the penname of Scire. This novel actually portrayed the true rituals as practiced by his coven.

When England's laws against "witchcraft" were finally declared obsolete in 1951, Gardner left his coven and formed one of his own. In 1953, Gardner initiated a woman named Doreen Valiente into his coven. From 1954 to 1957, Gardner and Valiente began writing a comprehensive text on Wiccan practice, which they gave the title *Book of Shadows*. This text is still considered an authoritative resource on the subject of Wiccan practices and is the primary text for a part of Contemporary Wicca (which claims no specific cultural source, as do the four main traditions) known as "Gardnerian."

In 1954, Gardner was finally able to write and publish a truly nonfiction Wiccan text, titled *Witchcraft Today*. His book supported the belief that Wicca was not actually "witchcraft," but the surviving remnants of ancient, or at least pre-Christian, Pagan religions.

In 1960, Gardner was recognized for his years of civil service in the Far East, with a party held in his honor at Buckingham Palace. Shortly thereafter, Gardner's wife died. Then his childhood asthma aggressively returned, something which Gardner attributed to his first coven's attempt to cast a spell that would hold back the German army (five members of his coven are known to have died shortly after the attempted spell, and Gardner had long claimed that his health had suffered ever since).

In 1963, Gardner met an Englishman named Raymond Buckland shortly before Gardner left on an expedition to Lebanon. Before leaving, Gardner felt compelled to initiate Buckland into his coven. The initiation process was to be completed in his absence by the coven's high priestess, Monique Wilson, also commonly referred to as Lady Olwen. Raymond Buckland later brought the teachings of the Gardnerian Wiccan tradition to the United States in the 1970s.

On February 12, 1964, Gerald Gardner died while aboard a ship bound for Lebanon. He was laid to rest the very next day in the seaside Tunisian capital city of Tunis.

19.6 PRESENT-DAY FACTS

Since Wicca can be practiced privately or publicly, and at times in conjunction with other religions, it is difficult to find accurate estimates of the number of modern Wiccan adherents. Statistical estimates often clump religions such as Wicca in one category, "Neo-Pagans," not all of whom can be classified as Wiccans.

In the United States, the estimated number of "Neo-Pagans" is believed to be somewhere around roughly 800,000 adherents. However, this is the closest thing to an estimate currently available.

A

WORDS TO GO GLOSSARY

anapanasati   A Buddhist term meaning "mindfulness of one's breathing," and the title of a Mahayana Sutra regarding the same subject.

absolution   Forgiveness granted by a priest with the condition that an act or acts of contrition are performed by the penitent depending on the seriousness of the sin.

Akeidah   A Hebrew term that means "the binding," used in reference to the tenth and final trial of Abraham, in which he was ordered to bind his son Isaac to an altar so that he might be sacrificed. However, God stopped Abraham at the last moment.

Ang-Pravishtha   A Jain term meaning the "Twelve Limbs" and is the title of the text that the *Ganadhars* compiled of Lord Tirthankar's lessons.

apocrypha   A designation that is sometimes assigned to a group of deutero-canonical texts in the Catholic Bible. These texts were adopted into the Catholic canon from the Greek *Septuagint* (a Greek translation of the Hebrew Scriptures that included some apocryphal works). The controversy surrounding the *apocrypha* is that these texts are believed by some to have a questionable origin, thus explaining why they were not accepted into the Hebrew canon as Scripture.

Ark of the Covenant   A container in which the ancient Jews kept the writings God gave to Moses, such as the Ten Commandments. The Ark is considered one of the most sacred objects in the history of Judaism.

audits   In Scientology, regularly conducted interviews meant to rid one of past emotional baggage by asking questions while one is attached to a special machine called an E-Meter, which reads emotional responses. The goal is to pass through rounds of questions until one is able to do so without the machine reading a response. When this has been done, each "item" of emotional baggage is said to be part of one's "bank."

avatars   Physical incarnations of gods. In Hinduism, gods frequently choose to be born in human form. Usually, avatars come to accomplish a particular task, such as righting an injustice.

Bab   Literally means "Gate," and it is the title assumed by Siyyid Ali-Muhammad, Prophet-Founder of the Bab movement and forerunner of Baha'u'llah.

Bakufu   Samurai and/or daimyo who remained loyal to the authority of the Tokugawa Shogunate during the conflict with the forces of the returning imperial family, called the Meiji. Many *Bakufu* continued to remain loyal to the Tokugawa even after it fell.

Bandera   The red, green, and black flag of Africa, designed by Marcus Garvey. This term is also used to refer to the colors of Rastafarian dress.

Bani   A Sikh/Gurmukhi term that roughly translates to "vibration" or "frequency." In Sikhism, this word refers to special prayers that are actually recitations of the words of the Gurus. Khalsa and devout Sikhs recite five specific Bani prayers daily, often in the morning—Japji Sahib, Anand Sahib, Jaap Sahib, Benti Chaupai, and Tav-Prasad Savaiye. However, these five Banis are not the only such prayers. Everything written in the *Guru Granth Sahib* is considered a Bani.

Bedouin   Warlike, nomadic tribes of the Arabic world. These tribes often traveled a constant but annually cyclical migratory route. The Bedouin existed all over the Arabic world, and their routes expanded along with the expansion of the Islamic territories. At one point, Bedouin tribes could be found from the Arab regions to Syria to as far west as North Africa.

bodhisattvas   Reincarnations of the Buddha, or "Those who have arrived at the Bodhi." When the Buddha died, it is said that he chose not to remain in the heavenly realm. Instead, the Buddha returns to Earth from time to time, often reincarnating as more than one person at a time, to guide others to the Middle Way that leads to enlightenment. This term is used differently within Theravada and Mahayana Buddhism. The Lord Buddha refers to himself as a bodhisattva or someone "bound for enlightenment." This is seen in some of the stories of his previous lives found in the *Jataka Tales*. It simply means "someone on the path to liberation." In the Mahayana tradition there are many bodhisattvas. These are individuals who during their lives made vows to become bodhisattvas, postponing their achievement of nirvana in order to aid other human beings to enlightenment and release.

Brahman   The creator God of Hinduism, and the primary figure of the *Trimurti*.

canon   Literally means "measuring rod" and "standard." It is a group of sacred writings that a religious group accepts as authoritative in the life of that community.

Christ   A title, not indicative of a last name. It is derived from the Greek term *christos*, meaning the "anointed one." There have been, in fact, many who have claimed to be the Christ or Hebrew equivalent meaning "messiah" throughout the ages.

Christian faith and practice   The beliefs, doctrines, and practices that are supported by a given Christian community. Protestants claim to be restoring the original first-century doctrines and practices of Christianity that have been corrupted over time.

Chrysanthemum Throne   The title for the seat of the Emperor of Japan. This term comes from the fact that the royal family's crest is a *kiku,* or "chrysanthemum."

Church Fathers   In Catholicism, Bishops of the early Church who wrote and taught the content of the apostolic message in the successive generations after the apostles died. There are a number of early Fathers who identify apostolic writings as "inspired" that would later be included in the New Testament canon. These include but are not limited to: St. Clement of Rome, Polycarp, Irenaeus of Lyons, Origen, Tertullian, Ambrose, Augustine, and so forth.

covenant   A contractual relationship between human partners or between God and humans. A covenant is a legally binding agreement between two parties with duties and responsibilities to be fulfilled by both. In Hebrew history, God commits himself in covenant relationship to Abraham and his descendents through the Abrahamic covenant. He also later commits himself to the people of Israel in the Mosaic covenant.

covens   In Wicca, groups of Wiccans with common religious goals and purposes, which meet regularly for the purpose of holding Esbats, Sabbats, teachings, or for any other activity having a direct connection with Wicca.

daevas   In Zoroastrianism, this term refers to demonic spirits who serve the evil Angra Mainyu. Such spirits seek to deceive and harm human beings, especially those who serve Ahura Mazda. It is thought that this word was likely a transliteration of the Hindu term for a race of deities called *devas,* in order to ensure that Zoroastrianism remained separate.

Daimyo   A Japanese word for provincial lords in feudal Japan. The *daimyo* served under higher-ranking lords, who, in turn, worked directly under either an emperor or *Shogun* and were required to arm, pay, and maintain their own forces of elite warriors, called *Samurai.* These *Samurai* then were expected to employ and maintain their own respective units of lower-ranking foot soldiers.

Dharma   In Buddhism, this word refers to "the law," meaning the cosmic law, which is dictated by the accumulation of *kharma,* the wheel of *samsara,* and freedom through *nirvana.* In Hinduism, *Dharma* originally referred to an individual's purpose or destiny in a lifetime. It was later used as the basis for the creation of a strict caste system in India.

Dharmachakra   A Sanskrit term that translates to "Wheel of Law" (*Dharma* = law, *Chakra* = wheel/circle). In Buddhism, it refers to the very first teaching of the Buddha to his original five disciples.

domestic Shinto   The maintenance of a personal altar or *kami-dana* (god-shelf) where daily offerings (for example, incense, food, drink, salt, and so forth) and prayers are made to ancestral *kami* and other *kami* that may be beneficial to the family. In Shinto, salt is thought to be a purifying agent and is often present at the doorway of adherents' homes or perhaps on their *kami-dana* as an offering.

Dukkha   A term in Buddhism that refers to the pain and suffering resulting from desire and ignorance.

Espiritismo   A practice that shares some beliefs with Voodoo and Santeria. However, this practice focuses on manipulating spirits for beneficial results. In *Espiritismo*, or "Spiritism," it is believed that good and evil spirits hold influence over the physical realm. Good spirits can bring prosperity, while evil spirits are said to inflict sickness and/or bring misfortune. One who believes they are being attacked by evil spirits will consult with an *Espiritista*, who will exorcise the evil spirit(s) with charms, sacrifices, or magic rituals. Today, it is practiced mainly in Cuba and Puerto Rico.

Espiritista   See *Espiritismo*.

ethnic Jew   A term used to identify a person of Jewish parentage or background, meaning one who is not practicing religious Judaism but who is Jewish by birth.

Eucharist   In Catholicism, the centerpiece of one of seven sacraments celebrated by Roman Catholics as an action of thanksgiving to God for the sacrifice of Christ for sin and the promise of resurrection. Catholics also believe that the weekly celebration of Eucharist is indicative of the literal presence of Christ in the visible expression of the assembled Church. The transformation of the two Eucharistic elements of bread and wine into the body and blood of Christ (transubstantiation) has long been a controversial doctrine in Christian history.

ex cathedra   Literally means "from the throne." In Catholicism, the throne symbolizes the pope's authority to teach the entire Church. When a pope speaks *ex cathedra*, his teaching is, according to church doctrine, "infallible."

Fargard   A term for the individual sections of the Zoroastrian text *Vendidad*, one of the books of the *Avesta*. The *Vendidad* is a book explaining the sacred law of Zoroastrianism, addressing the issues of crimes and punishments.

Furukotofumi   See *Kojiki*.

Gahambars   "Festivals of obligation," meaning the seven festivals observed in veneration of the seven elements of Ahura Mazda's creation of physical existence, which are sky/heaven, earth, water, plants, animals, humans, and fire (which is considered the most sacred element in Zoroastrianism).

gaijin   A Japanese term that translates as "barbarian." However, this word eventually came to be used in the Japanese language to refer to *all* non-Japanese peoples. The English equivalent, therefore, would be "foreigner."

Ganadhars   In Jainism, the most enlightened pupils of Lord Tirthankar, upon whom he bestowed many sacred and valuable lessons of wisdom. They later compiled these lessons into a text called the *Ang-Pravishtha*.

ganja   In Rastafarianism, a sacramental herb commonly smoked by adherents. The herb is more commonly known as *cannabis*, or marijuana, an illegal drug or controlled substance in most of the Western world. In the United States, it is frequently argued that Rasta adherents should be allowed to smoke *ganja*, as forbidding it violates their freedom to practice religion.

Girondists   A political group of the French National Assembly whose members shared certain political and social opinions and principles. The name was first given to them because most members among them were initially deputies from Gironde, a region in Southwest France. Thomas Paine, one of the primary figures of the Deist movement, wrote his text *The Age of Reason* while serving a short prison sentence for his association with the *Girondists*.

Golden Rule   In Confucianism, this specifically refers to the belief "What one does not want done to one's self, one should not do to others." This idea of treating others as one would want to be treated is common to many religions, but Confucianism is unique, in that it gives the concept a specific title.

Gurdwara   A Sikh holy place for conducting worship. The word can be translated as either "Home of the Guru" or "Door/Gate to the Guru." Sikhs also share communal meals in a Gurdwara. The doors of any Gurdwara are open to all people of all faiths.

Guru   In the Sikh faith, means "teacher" and refers to a line of 10 spiritual men who were leaders of the Sikh people from 1469 to 1708. The tenth Guru, Gobind Singh, brought an end to the appointment of Gurus by declaring that the *Guru Granth Sahib* text would be his successor, and therefore the last Sikh Guru for the rest of eternity.

hadith   An Arabic term that translates to "news report." However, in the context of Islam, it refers to stories about the life of the prophet Muhammad (meaning stories that are not in the *Qur'an*). These stories are very informative, telling much about who Muhammad was as a man or offering practical life lessons. These *hadith* tales, some of which were more folklore than historic fact, became the basis for the *Sunnah*.

Halal   An Arabic term meaning "permitted" or "acceptable" in Islam. It is often used to identify permissible foods according to Islamic law. For example, animals that are not *haram* (forbidden) must still be slaughtered according to an Islamic prescription. Some sects of Islam allow a substitution of kosher meats when halal meats cannot be found. In some parts of the United States it is becoming more common to see meat packaged as "100% Halal."

haram   Pronounced "hah-rom" (not to be confused with *harem*, a different word that shares the same root), this Arabic term refers to "forbidden" or "unclean" items that are not consumed by adherents of the Islamic faith. Such items are often forbidden for reasons of physical and mental health. For example, the *haram* law that forbids alcohol is often extended to apply to any substance that confuses one's mind or might cause a Muslim to stray from pious behavior due to impaired judgment, such as drugs (many of which were not yet available at the time the law was written).

heresy   A term used to designate adopted beliefs that contradict or alter the orthodox (which literally means "right belief") position of a given community. The measurement of what is orthodox is determined by a given community (Roman Catholic, Eastern Orthodox, Protestants, etc.). Heresy occurs when adherents step outside the boundaries of acceptable belief as defined by that community.

ibn   An Arabic term/identifier that is frequently used in male names, especially those of noble descent. *Ibn* identifies the name of a man's father. Technically, the English equivalent is "son of." One should understand that while *ibn* is *part* of a name, it is not itself an Arabic name. For example, in English terms, Uthman ibn Affan would be said "Uthman, son of Affan." However, the word is sometimes used to extend a name further to trace a male's lineage. For example, Hakim ibn Muhammed ibn Rashad ibn Kareem would translate as "Hakim, son Muhammed, who was the son of Rashad, who was the son of Kareem."

Imam   The Islamic leader of a mosque or community. Sunni Muslims give this title to any recognized leader or teacher of Islam. Imams typically lead prayers at the mosque. The title Imam, however, has been given a technical usage by the Shi'a to identify individuals chosen by God to be special examples. Twelvers are the most common sect (80 percent). According to Twelvers, there are "Twelve Imams" that have been identified as appointed by God and have a status parallel to the Prophet Muhammad. Many Twelvers are awaiting the "Twelfth Imam" or the "*Mahdi*," who will one day return and establish Islam worldwide.

indulgence   Comes from the Latin *indulgeo,* meaning "to be kind or tender." In Roman Catholicism, indulgences are partial remissions of punishment for sins. In the past, indulgences could replace severe penance and the church practiced the sale of indulgences in return for monetary donations.

inspired   The biblical notion as presented in 2 Timothy 3:16 is that all Scripture is "God-breathed." This still needs clarification. "Inspiration" or "God-breathed" Scripture simply means that God the Holy Spirit worked together with the minds and hearts of the authors (apostles, prophets, etc.) to produce a trustworthy and reliable revelation of God's salvation story in the world. This is done through a complementary interworking between God and the human writer so that Scripture can truly be said to have dual authorship: Divine Author/human author.

ital   In Rastafarianism, *ital* refers to the dietary laws of the biblical Old Testament. Rastafarians believe they are the true "chosen people" of God who are written of in the Old Testament. Therefore, they follow the same dietary rules as Orthodox Jews.

Jah   Short for "Jehovah," this is a Rastafarian term that refers to God. Many people have come to the mistaken conclusion that Rastafarians believe Ras Tafari Makonnen is *Jah.* However, this is inaccurate. Rastafarians view Ras Tafari Makonnen as a messianic figure, or the son of *Jah,* similar to how Christians consider Christ the son of God.

Jewish   This term is complicated to define because of several different categories of Jew that can be identified. Not all Jews are religious, thus there is a distinction between cultural/ethnic Jews and religious Jews. For example, one can be a cultural/ethnic Jew and be an atheist. This simply means one remains within the Jewish way of life without religion. One can also be a cultural/ethnic Jew and a religious Jew. Finally, one can convert and become a religious Jew regardless of cultural or ethnic background.

Jewish mystical texts   These are texts only accepted by some within the Jewish religious community. For example, the classic *Zohar* text that acknowledges the possibility of reincarnation for Jews.

Jinja   A Japanese term that refers to the unsanctioned, semiofficial practices and shrines of Shinto, which existed both before and after that religion's period as the official state-sponsored religion of imperial Japan.

Ju-chia   A Chinese term that is the actual name of the religion that Westerners often refer to as Confucianism. *Ju-chia* translates as "Scholarly Tradition" or "School of Scholars."

Junzi   Literally means "nobleman" but the term was morphed by Confucius into the idea of the "superior/perfect man." A Junzi is much like Aristotle's "magnanimous man" concerned with living virtuously and cultivating benevolence throughout society. His is a standard not just for the nobility but for all of society.

Ka'bah   A cube-shaped structure that has a black stone on its eastern corner that is about twelve inches in diameter and surrounded by a metal frame. It is the holiest place in Islam and also the place that all Muslims face during prayer throughout the world (*quibla*). Islamic tradition says that the black stone fell from heaven during the time of Adam and Eve and that Adam built the first Ka'bah. According to the Qur'an, Abraham and Ishmael rebuilt the Ka'bah and it reflects a house in heaven. The *hajj* pilgrimage (fifth pillar of Islam) is to be taken to Mecca, the home of the Ka'bah during the last month of the Islamic year. This place also later became part of the *umrah* (Lesser Pilgrimage). Pilgrims traditionally circle the structure seven times and kiss the stone. If the crowds are too large, the adherent may walk around the Ka'bah and point to the stone on each cicuit. One story claims that when Muhammad first saw the Ka'bah stone, tears fell from his eyes and he touched and kissed its surface. It has stood as a powerful symbol of the Muslim faith ever since.

Kami   A Japanese/Shinto term, often misunderstood as an equivalent to English words such as *deity* and God. However, *Kami* is not as restricted in definition as such terms, and can also be used to refer to a nature spirit, demon, demigod, or even high-ranking and/or revered human being.

Kami-no-Michi   A Japanese/Shinto term that is most easily translated into English as "Way of the *Kami*." However, this is not the literal meaning, and, in certain contexts, it can also mean something more along the lines of "The Will of the *Kami*" or "The Standards of the *Kami*." The term *Kami-no-Michi* is also used as an alternate word for Shinto, the title by which the religion is more commonly known.

kashrut   A Hebrew term that refers to the proper method by which animals must be slaughtered before they can be considered kosher. However, the meat of some animals, no matter how they are slaughtered, is still forbidden in Judaism (such as pork).

Kesshi Hachidai   The title for the fourth chapter of the Shinto text, called *Nihongi*. In English, it is sometimes called "The Chronicle of the Eight Undocumented Emperors." This chapter of the *Nihongi* lists factual information for the second through ninth rulers of the Chrysanthemum Throne of Imperial Japan.

kharma   This is a Sanskrit term used in Hinduism, Buddhism, Jainism, and Sikhism. It refers to the positive or negative energies that humans accumulate over lifetimes (past and present). Kharma, whether good or bad, is the result of a human being's thoughts, words, and actions.

kharma-pudgalas   A Sanskrit term that translates roughly as "kharmic matter." *Kharma-pudgalas* specifically refers to a human being's accumulation of *kharma*, which is the reason the individual remains trapped in the wheel/cycle of *samsara*.

kiku   See Chrysanthemum Throne.

Kitab-I-Aqdas   The title of the "Most Holy Book" in the Baha'i faith, which is the book of laws. This book was revealed by Baha'u'llah in 1873.

Kojiki   The oldest existing Shinto, although it is used less frequently than its descendent text, the *Nihongi*. The *Kojiki* is also known by the title *Furukotofumi*, which means "Record of Ancient Matters."

kosher   A Hebrew term that refers to the dietary restrictions of Judaism.

kusti   A prayer cord worn by adherents of Zoroastrianism. The *kusti* cord is primarily used during a Zoroastrian's daily prayers. Each time a Zoroastrian completes one of the five daily prayers required by the faith, he wraps this cord once around his body. The cord is comprised of 72 threads representing the 72 chapters of the *Yasna*, a Zoroastrian sacred text.

Li   In reference to the writings of Xun Zi, refers to certain purifying rites which he claimed a person had to undergo before they could understand the true natures of goodness and righteousness.

Macabees   A band of Hebrew warrior rebels who rose up against the Seleucid Emperor Antiochus IV Epiphanes for his persecution of the Jewish people.

magic arts   In Wicca, refers to causing change through the systematic use of the will and other natural forces. Some common goals in magic are healing, guidance, protection, and insight.

Maha-vratas   A Sanskrit term that, in Jainism, refers to the "Five Great Vows" that all Jain ascetics or monks swear to and strictly adhere to.

Mandate of Heaven (t'ien-ming)   In Confucianism, refers to a concept that is similar to the Western ideas of Divine Right or Divine Principle, in which a ruler is believed to have been chosen by some divine entity. However, unlike the Western concepts of divinely chosen rulers, the *Mandate of Heaven* could and would be changed if the Jade Emperor deemed a ruler unworthy to rule the people.

Mass   A term originally used to mean "Sacrifice," referring to the act of taking Communion. Today, the term is used to refer more broadly to Catholic chapel services.

mosque   An Islamic place of worship. It is primarily a place of prayer, but many activities within the life of the community are fulfilled there as well (for example, education, certain community holy day celebrations, and so forth). On Friday, in lieu of the midday prayer time, Muslims are required to attend a prayer service and there will often be a message.

Nihon Shoki   See *Nihongi*.

Nihongi   Also called the *Nihon Shoki*, the title of this Shinto text means "Chronicle of Japan." It is a compilation of the works of the *Kojiki*. However, the *Nihongi* also includes as many existing versions of each story and myth as could be found in Japan at the time it was written. More important, the stories of the *Nihongi* seek to show how the Japanese royal family's lineage is connected to Amaterasu, the female *Kami* of the Sun.

Nikayas   The five *Nikayas* are subsections of a larger text, the *Sutta Pitaka*, which, in turn, is the second of the three main *Pitaka* sections that make up the Buddhist Canon, or *Tripitaka* (sometimes *Tipitaka*).

nirvana   A Sanskrit term used in Buddhism to refer to the blissful state of enlightenment, in which one is freed from the cycle of *samsara*. *Nirvana*, roughly translated, is a state in which a human being is freed from all desires and material attachments. In Jain thought, it is the state of enlightenment in which one is also completely freed from all desires and material attachments.

Norito   A Japanese term for spiritual rituals, mainly used to refer specifically to the rituals of Shinto. The existing record of Shinto rituals was compiled in a text called the *Yengishiki* sometime during the early years of the tenth century C.E., a time period referred to as the Yengi Era.

Pali   The language in which the original Theravada texts of Buddhism were written and for which they are named.

Parsi   A Hindi term used to refer to ethnic Iranians who migrated to India so they could practice the religion of Zoroastrianism without threat of harm. The majority of *Parsis* (literally "those who came from Persia") fled to India from Iran during or shortly after the time of the Muslim Arabic invasion/occupation of Iran during the mid-seventh century C.E.

Patimokkha   A Sanskrit/Buddhist term for the code of ethics and behavior that members of the *Sangha* monastic community must follow. The *Patimokkha* is said to have been given in a sermon to 1250 monks by the Lord Buddha himself.

pitaka   Means "basket." In Buddhism, refers to a main section of the Pali Canon.

Posek   A title in Judaism used to refer to a religious/spiritual scholar who is not necessarily considered a *rabbi*.

Purgatory   Purgatory, Heaven, and Hell are the three possible destinations for a soul upon death, according to Roman Catholic doctrine. Purgatory is a third place for those who are not ready for Heaven but not condemned to Hell. It is a place of purification, often associated with fire, and includes painful punishment for a period of time.

Qibla   Arabic term for the direction a Muslim faces when praying. All Muslims pray toward Mecca and the Ka'bah during the various times of prayer throughout the day. Mosques quite often contain a niche (also called a *mihrab*) that indicates the direction of Mecca.

Qiblih   In Baha'i, means "The Point of Adoration." This is the direction in which Baha'i adherents turn during prayer. Geographically speaking, it is in the direction of a shrine to Baha'u'llah in Bahji.

Rabbi   Hebrew for "teacher." However, this term is almost exclusively used to refer to the spiritual leaders/advisors of Judaism.

repentance   A term from the Christian New Testament that simply means a change of mind about living in disobedience to God and a turning to obedience and living according to God's will.

Sabbath   In all Judaic religions, including Christianity, the *Sabbath* refers to the Holy Seventh Day when YHVH/God/Allah rested after having completed creation. In Judaism, this is Saturday. In Christianity, it was eventually changed to Sunday (however, some Christian sects/denominations still observe the Sabbath on Saturday).

Sacraments   In general, simply outward signs or rites that convey an unseen reality within the adherent. In Christianity, the two most common sacraments are baptism and the Eucharist. Within Roman Catholicism, there are seven sacraments.

Sacred Tradition   A technical term within Roman Catholicism given to the Christian tradition taught by Jesus to his first followers and passed down to the Church. According to Catholic teaching, this tradition is part of the "deposit of faith" given to Christians, and this combined with Sacred Scripture is the entirety of Jesus Christ's divine revelation. Sacred Tradition includes but is not limited to creedal statements like the "Apostles Creed" and the "Nicene Creed."

Sahabah   An Arabic term meaning "Companions." In Islam, this term usually refers to the early followers of Muhammad who followed him to Madina from Mecca. *Sahabah*, in a certain context, can also refer to four specific members of the Caliphate electoral body who supported the election of Ali as first Caliph. Today this term is sometimes used loosely to refer to the Muslim religious community as a whole.

samsara   A Sanskrit term used in Buddhism, Hinduism, and Jainism. *Samsara* is the cycle of life, death, and rebirth. This cycle will continue repeating over until an individual achieves enlightenment through nirvana.

Samurai   A Japanese term which, literally translated, means "one who serves." Samurai were members of feudal Japan's warrior class. They trained from the early years of childhood in the arts of close combat, strategy, horsemanship, archery, and use of the spear and sword.

sangha   A Sanskrit term meaning "gathering" or "assembly." In Buddhism, it refers to the "spiritual community" of Buddhists. Depending on the sect or country in which the word is being used, *Sangha* can refer to all Buddhist practitioners, to only monks/nuns, exclusively to those who are thought to have achieved nirvana, or to a combination of two or more of these groups.

Santeria   "Way of the Saints," a practice that integrates Catholic icons with Latin superstitions and magic rites that are believed to originate from the Nigerian Yoruba tribe. Today, Santeria is primarily practiced in Cuba, the Caribbean, and in certain parts of the Southern United States (mainly in Florida).

Shaman   One who is thought to be possessed by the spirits. The shaman serves multiple functions in primal religions, including predicting the future and communicating with the spirits on behalf of the tribe.

Shaykh   In Sufism, a mystical offshoot of Islam, a *Shaykh* (often spelled *Sheikh* in the West) is one who has attained the higher paths of wisdom, and therefore possesses a greater understanding of Allah. *Shaykh* are referred to in Persian dialects as *Pir*, meaning "elderly man." An alternative Arabic term is *Mush'a'hid*, meaning "guide" or "director." Before a Sufi *Shaykh* accepts a pupil, the candidate is commonly required to swear a strict oath of allegiance, obedience, and selfless devotion.

Shogun   A Japanese term that originally meant the highest-ranking military lord at any time in ancient Japan. However, the term eventually became the title of a line of Japanese military rulers, beginning with Tokugawa Ieyasu, the first Shogun ruler of a fairly unified Japan.

Shvayambhu   A Sankrit/Hindu term meaning "the creator who was not created," a title for the god Brahman, who existed before existence.

sins   (Specifically, in Judeo-Christianity) must be atoned for according to the *Torah*. Sin means a straying away from what God has declared as good and right. It is a term used in archery to indicate that the arrow has missed its target. According to Hebrew Scripture, sins could be atoned for in the ancient conception by animal sacrifice. Sacrifice was thought to gain the pardon of God. This was not the only means of atonement, however. It was later determined that "repentance," "prayer," and "good deeds" were sufficient means to gain God's forgiveness. On many of the high holy days within Judaism, these means eventually substituted animal sacrifice.

Stathviras   Jain scriptures that were compiled later by Jain monks (but not the *Ganadhars*). These scriptures are included in the text of the *Agamas*.

sudreh   A special shirt worn by Zoroastrians after they have come of age and/or undergone the appropriate rituals of purification.

Suf/Sufi   Means "wool," and is the root word from which Sufism developed. *Sufi* means "clad in wool" and originates from the early Sufi practice of wearing wool garments as a protest against the extravagances of the Caliphs.

Sunya   A Sanskrit term for the Buddhist concept that the Supreme Being (what most Westerners call "God") is so absolutely transcendent that it escapes human understanding, and therefore cannot be properly worshipped (nor does it need to be).

Sunyata   A Sanskrit term meaning "emptiness." In Buddhism, it refers to the concept of nonduality, that two opposites are actually one.

sutras   A Sanskrit term for the narrative sections of Buddhist texts. Often this word is used in Buddhism to refer to the dialogues of the Buddha in sacred texts.

synagogue   In Judaism, a place of prayer, a place of study and education, and a place that does social and charity work. Jewish believers gather at the synagogue on Sabbath for weekly worship.

Tanakh   See *Torah*.

Tao   Pronounced *Dao,* and sometimes spelled that way. Basically, *Tao* means "Path" or "Way" and is the name for an ancient Chinese pseudoreligious philosophy that stresses personal growth through righteous thought and action. It is sometimes called "the way of the universe" or "nature's way." The Taoist term *wu wei,* though somewhat difficult to accurately translate into English, means "non-action" and stresses a nonforced lifestyle that moves in harmonious accord with the forces and impulses of nature. It is the idea that many things happen quietly and effortlessly; for example, plants grow, seasons change, nature reproduces.

Tirthankaras   Literally meaning 24 "bridge builders" or "pathfinders," *Tirthankaras* are "pure" human beings who have shown the way to the liberation of the soul from *samsara* (reincarnation). These have purified their souls of kharmic impurities. Mahavira was the final and greatest *Tirthankara.* Since Jainism is focused on humans gaining release from the endless cycle of reincarnation, it is humans that Jains emulate in their own personal journeys for release. Jains venerate the 24 *Tirhankaras* and have erected 40,000 temples in India to worship these figures. The Jain temple on Mount Abu is considered one of the seven wonders of India.

Torah   The first text, consisting of five books (called the *Pentateuch,* or "five texts"), of the Jewish canon of sacred law, which is called the *Tanakh.*

Torii   A *gateway* found at the front of almost all shrines in Japan that is used to mark the entrance into the sacred. Its distinctive appearance not only identifies the entrance of a shrine but also reminds adherents that they are in a place where a *kami* dwells.

Trimurti   The three-member assembly of primary Hindu gods, making up three natures/roles of the divine—creator, sustainer, and destroyer. These three roles are represented by Brahman (creator), Vishnu (sustainer), and Shiva (destroyer).

tripitaka   A Sanskrit term that means "three baskets," primarily used to refer to the three main sections of the *Pali,* the Canon of Buddhist texts.

triratna   The original Sanskrit name for the Three Jewels of Buddhism.

Varnas   The parts of the Hindu caste structure.

vestments   Liturgical robes worn by the clergy in the performance of ceremonies, such as Mass, blessings, and sacraments.

Voodoo   Voodoo (the correct term is *Vodun*) is primarily practiced today in Haiti and the Southern United States, and integrates Catholic-based icons with the indigenous rites of West and Central Africa.

vrata   A Sanskrit term that roughly translates to "vow."

wu wei   A Chinese/Taoist term that is somewhat difficult to accurately translate into English. While it is often translated as "nonaction," the term refers to the Taoist belief that one should pursue a lifestyle that is "unforced," meaning that your thoughts and actions move in harmonious accord with the forces and impulses of nature and/or the cosmos.

yajnas   In Hinduism, the sacrifices that humans begin making to the gods, beginning in the age called the *Treta Yuga*.

yang and yin   The Chinese yang and yin are simultaneously complementary and opposing principles in nature. These two principles generate all forms of reality. These are not the same as good and evil. One is not expected to win over the other. They are opposed forces providing a dynamic balance to the universe. The emblem of yang and yin provides an improved understanding of the Chinese perspective. It is typically a circle what looks like two intertwined commas that represent two opposing forces. One half is light, representing yang, and the other is dark, representing yin. Inside each division is a small dot that contains the seed of its opposite. The dot indicates that everything contains its opposite and will eventually become its opposite. Yang is the positive force in nature: brightness, warmth, maleness, and so forth. Yin is the negative force in nature darkness, coolness, femaleness, and so forth. From the Chinese view, when these two forces are in harmony life is as it should be.

Yengishiki   The only existing, official record of Shinto rituals. The *Yengishiki* was compiled sometime during the early years of the tenth century C.E., a time period referred to as the Yengi Era, hence the text's title.

yetzer   A Hebrew term for the Judaic concept of the human soul. Humans have been granted free will; therefore, according to Judaism, we have the capacity for both good and evil. Our souls are no different. Judaic theology states that humans have a dualistic soul that is separated into two primary parts—*yetzer ha-tov* (basically, the "good soul") and *yetzer ha-ra* (the "bad soul").

yetzer ha-ra   See *yetzer*.

yetzer ha-tov   See *yetzer*.

Yugas   The ages that make up one cycle of existence in Hindu cosmology.

YHVH   The Hebrew personal name for God that is ineffable. In order to protect this name from "being taken in vain" the Hebrews have only given the consonants without the vowels. It is considered so holy that the Hebrews will always substitute another name for God (*Adonai* or Lord) rather than utter it when reading their sacred text. In traditional Judaism, YHVH is the source of all being and expresses the mercy and condescension of Almighty God.

B

RELIGIOUS ORGANIZATIONS AND RESOURCES

Chapter 2: Judaism

▶ World Jewish Congress—www.worldjewishcongress.org

▶ World Zionist Organization (Israel)—www.wzo.org.il

▶ National Jewish Democratic Council—www.njdc.org

▶ Republican Jewish Coalition—www.rjchq.org

▶ Canadian Jewish Congress—www.cjc.ca

▶ American Council for Judaism—www.acjna.org

▶ Israeli Religious Action Center—www.irac.org

▶ Religious Action Center of Reform Judaism—www.rac.org

▶ Edah (Orthodox Judaism)—www.edah.org

▶ American Jewish Committee—www.ajc.org

Chapter 3: Christianity

▶ Word of Messiah Ministries—www.wordofmessiah.org

▶ Messianic Bureau International—www.messianicbureau.org

▶ Nazarene Israel—www.nazareneisrael.org

▶ Union of Messianic Jewish Congregations (UMJC)—www.umjc.net

Chapter 4: Catholicism

▶ The Vatican's Internet Homepage—www.vatican.va

▶ The Vatican's Online Archives—www.asv.vatican.va

▶ Catholic Internet Directory—www.catholic.net

▶ Catholic World Mission—www.catholicworldmission.org

▶ United States Conference of Catholic Bishops—www.usccb.org

▶ Canadian Conference of Catholic Bishops—www.cccb.ca

▶ Catholic Bishops Conference of England and Wales—www.catholic-ew. org.uk

▶ Eternal Word Television Network—www.ewtn.com

▶ The Pontifical Missions Society—www.worldmissions-catholicchurch.org

▶ Knights of Columbus—www.kofc.org

▶ National Association of Catholic Families (United Kingdom)—www. cfnews.org.uk

▶ The Fraternal Order of Alhambra—www.orderalhambra.org

Chapter 5: Protestantism

An overwhelming number of various Protestant denominations, groups, and/or organizations exist. Therefore, please understand that only a few of the largest are provided here.

- ▶ Lutheran World Federation—www.lutheranworld.org
- ▶ International Lutheran Council—www.ilc-online.org
- ▶ Confessional Evangelical Lutheran Conference—www.celc.info
- ▶ United Methodist Church—www.umc.org
- ▶ Wesleyan Methodist Church—www.wesleyan.org
- ▶ World Council of Churches (WCC)—www.oikoumene.org
- ▶ World Baptist Fellowship—www.wfbi.net
- ▶ National Baptist Convention (USA)—www.nationalbaptist.com
- ▶ Southern Baptist Convention—www.sbc.net
- ▶ Presbyterian Church (USA)—www.pcusa.net
- ▶ Presbyterian Church in America—www.pcanet.org
- ▶ General Council of the Assemblies of God—www.ag.org
- ▶ National Association of Evangelicals—www.nae.net
- ▶ Center for Reformed Theology and Apologetics—www.reformed.org

Chapter 6: Deism

- ▶ Deist Alliance—www.deistalliance.org
- ▶ World Union of Deists—www.deism.com
- ▶ Positive Deism Discussion Group—www.positivedeism.com
- ▶ Modern Deism (part of Deist Alliance)—www.moderndeism.com
- ▶ Deism Information Site—www.deist.info
- ▶ Deism Meet-up Groups Network—www.deism.meetup.com
- ▶ Universist Deism—www.universist.org
- ▶ Deism and Reason—www.sullivan-county.com/deism
- ▶ Panendeism Home Page—www.panendeism.org
- ▶ God's Online Home—www.godonlinehome.com

Chapter 7: Islam

- ▶ Islamic Assembly of North America (IANA)—www.iananet.org

- ▶ Organization of the Islamic Conference—www.oic-oci.org

- ▶ World Assembly of Muslim Youth (WAMY), United Kingdom—www.wamy.co.uk

- ▶ Muslim World League, Canada—www.mwlcanada.org

- ▶ Young Muslim Association—www.ymaonline.org

- ▶ Islamic Culture Foundation—www.funci.org/en

- ▶ Islamic Research Foundation—www.irf.net

- ▶ Islamic Training Foundation—www.islamist.org

- ▶ Muslim American Society—www.masnet.org

- ▶ Islamic Free Market Institute Foundation—www.islamicinstitute.org

- ▶ Islamic Foundation North—www.ifnonline.com

- ▶ Islamic Dawah Foundation (University Texas at Austin)—e-mail islamdf@www.utexas.edu or call 512-299-4532

- ▶ Wisdom Enrichment Foundation (WEFOUND)—www.wefound.org

- ▶ Quilliam Foundation for Counter-Extremism—www.quilliamfoundation.org

Chapter 8: Baha'i

- ▶ The Baha'i International Community—www.bahai.org

- ▶ Baha'i International Community, United Nations Headquarters—www.bic.org

- ▶ Baha'i Institute for Studies in Global Prosperity—www.globalprosperity.org

- ▶ Baha'i Computer and Communication Association (BCCA)—www.bcca.org

- ▶ Canada Baha'i Community—www.ca.bahai.org

- ▶ United Kingdom Baha'i Community—www.bahai.org.uk

- ▶ United States Baha'i Community—www.bahai.us or 1-800-22-UNITE

- ▶ Planet Baha'i—www.planetbahai.org

- ▶ The Baha'i Study Center—www.bahaistudy.org

- ▶ The Baha'i Library—www.bahai-library.org

Chapter 9: Taoism

▶ Universal Tao Center—www.universal-tao.com

▶ Taoist Association of China—www.eng.taoism.org.hk

▶ Center of Traditional Taoist Studies—www.tao.org

▶ Foundation of Tao—www.padrak.com/tao

▶ International Society for Daoist Studies (ISDS)—www.daoiststudies.org

▶ The Daoist Foundation—www.daoistfoundation.org

▶ London Tao Centre—www.healing-tao.co.uk

▶ Wu Dang Tao—www.wudangtao.com

▶ Center for Daoist Studies—www.daoistcenter.org

Chapter 11: Buddhism

▶ Soka Gakkai International, USA—www.sgi-usa.org

▶ Network of Buddhist Organizations (United Kingdom)—www.nbo.org.uk

▶ Buddhist Association of the United States—www.baus.org

▶ American Buddhist Sangha—www.awakeningthedragon.com

▶ Buddha's Light International Association (World Headquarters)—www.blia.org

▶ Dharmakirti College, Tucson, AR—www.dharmakirti.org

▶ The Engaged Zen Foundation—www.engaged-zen.org

▶ Foundation for the Preservation of the Mahayana Tradition (FPMT)—www.fpmt.org

▶ Sakyadhita, International Association for Buddhist Women—www.Sakyadhita.org

▶ UK Association for Buddhist Studies, University of Sunderland—www.sunderland.ac.uk

▶ Buddhist Peace Fellowship—www.bpc.org

▶ European Buddhist Union—www.e-b-u.org

Chapter 12: Shinto

▶ International Shinto Foundation—www.shinto.org

▶ Shinto Online Network Association—www.jinja.jp/english

▶ Jinja-Honcho, The Association of Shinto Shrines—www.jinjahoncho.or.jp/en

▶ The Konko (Konkyo) Churches of North America—www.konkofaith.org

▶ International Shinto Foundation—www.shinto.org (for English page, go to shinto.org/isf/eng/top-e.htm)

▶ Tsubaki Grand Shrine of America (Granite Falls, Washington)—www.tsubakishrine.org or 360-691-6389

▶ Tsubaki Grand Shrine of Japan—www.tsubaki.or.jp

Chapter 13: Hindu Dharma

▶ Hindu Heritage Endowment—www.hheonline.org

▶ Hindu Endowments Board (HEB), Singapore—www.heb.gov.sg

▶ Sreemadbhagbad Gita Sangha—www.gita-sangha.org

▶ Advaita Vedanta Research Center—www.advaita-vedanta.org

▶ The Advaita Fellowship—www.advaita.org

▶ Hindu Academy at the Vivenkananda Centre London (United Kingdom)—www.vivekananda.btinternet.co.uk

▶ The Vedanta Society—This organization has numerous affiliated branches/temples all over the world. Therefore, we suggest doing a simple Internet search if you want to find a Vedanta Society branch near you.

▶ The International Society for Krishna Consciousness (ISKCON)—www.iskcon.com (please note that this organization is exclusively of the Krishna sect)

▶ The Hindu Resource Center—www.hindunet.org

▶ International Sanatana Dharma Society (ISDS)—www.dharmacentral.com

▶ Sri Vaishnava—www.ramanuja.org

Chapter 14: Jainism

▶ International Mahavir Jain Mission—908-362-9793

▶ Jain Center of America (New York)—www.nyjaincenter.org

▶ Young Jains of America—www.yja.org

▶ Jain International Trade Organization (JITO)—www.jito.org

▶ Jain Student Group, University of Michigan—www.umich.edu/~umjains

Chapter 15: Sikhism

- ▶ World Sikh Council—www.worldsikhcouncil.org
- ▶ Sikh Coalition—www.sikhcoalition.org
- ▶ Sikh Net—www.sikhnet.com
- ▶ The Sikh Network Site—www.sikh.net
- ▶ World Sikh Organization—www.worldsikh.org
- ▶ World Sikh News, United Kingdom (WSN)—www.worldsikhnews.com
- ▶ Shiromani Gurdwara Parbandhak Committee—www.sgpc.net
- ▶ The Sikh Wiki—www.sikhiwiki.org

Chapter 16: Zoroastrianism

- ▶ World Zoroastrian Organization (WZO)—www.w-z-o.org
- ▶ The Zarathustrian Assembly—www.zoroastrian.org
- ▶ Federation of Zoroastrian Associations in North America (FEZANA)—www.fezana.org
- ▶ World Alliance of Parsi and Irani Zarthoshtis (WAPIZ)—www.wapiz.com
- ▶ World Zarathushti Chamber of Commerce (WZCC)—www.wzcc.net
- ▶ Parsi Zoroastrian Association of Singapore—www.pza.org.sg
- ▶ Zoroastrian Women's International Network—www.zwin3.net

Chapter 17: Scientology

- ▶ The Church of Scientology—www.scientology.org

Chapter 18: Rastafarianism

- ▶ Church of Haile Selassie I—www.himchurch.org
- ▶ Rasta Speaks—www.rastafarispeaks.com
- ▶ Rasta Order of the Nyabinghi—www.nyahbinghi.org
- ▶ The Rasta Times (online newsletter)—www.rastatimes.com or rastafaritimes.com

Chapter 19: Wicca

- ▶ Covenant of the Goddess—www.cog.org
- ▶ The Aquarian Tabernacle Church of Wicca—www.aquatabch.org

- ▶ Wiccans Against Religious Discrimination (WARD), Michigan—www.ward-mi.fathweb.com

- ▶ WARD, Louisiana—www.ward-la.20m.com

- ▶ WARD, Nebraska—www.geocities.com/wardnebraska

- ▶ The Nine Houses of Gaia Covens—www.9houses.org

- ▶ The Officers of Avalon (for Wiccans in emergency service fields—police, fire dept, EMT, and so on)—www.officersofavalon.com

- ▶ Church of the Celestial Order and Temple of Olympus or Ecclesia Ordonis Caelestis Templum Olympicus (EOCTO)—www.eocto.org

- ▶ Northern Pagan Path or Blyth Wiccan Group (United Kingdom)—www.freewebs.com/northernpath

- ▶ Children of the Circle Covens—www.childrenofthecircle.com

INDEX

K

L

M

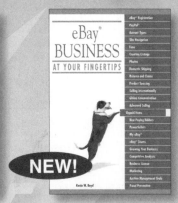

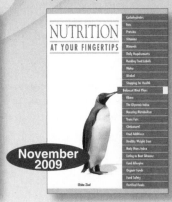